AF478618

Productivity, Efficiency and Economic Growth in China

*Also by Yanrui Wu*

CHINA'S CONSUMER REVOLUTION: the Emerging Patterns of Wealth and Expenditure

CHINA'S ECONOMIC GROWTH: a Miracle with Chinese Characteristics

PRODUCTIVE PERFORMANCE IN CHINESE ENTERPRISES: an Empirical Study

THE MACROECONOMICS OF EAST ASIAN GROWTH

# Productivity, Efficiency and Economic Growth in China

Yanrui Wu
*UWA Business School*
*University of Western Australia*


With contributions from
Chee Kong Wong and Owen Chih-Hung Ho

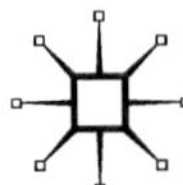

First published 2008 by
PALGRAVE MACMILLAN

Palgrave Macmillan in the UK is an imprint of Macmillan Publishers Limited, registered in England, company number 785998, of Houndmills, Basingstoke, Hampshire RG21 6XS.

Palgrave Macmillan in the US is a division of St Martin's Press LLC, 175 Fifth Avenue, New York, NY 10010.

Palgrave Macmillan is the global academic imprint of the above companies and has companies and representatives throughout the world.

Palgrave® and Macmillan® are registered trademarks in the United States, the United Kingdom, Europe and other countries.

ISBN-13: 978–0–230–20212–2     hardback
ISBN-10: 0–230–20212–8     hardback

This book is printed on paper suitable for recycling and made from fully managed and sustained forest sources. Logging, pulping and manufacturing processes are expected to conform to the environmental regulations of the country of origin.

A catalogue record for this book is available from the British Library.

Library of Congress Cataloging-in-Publication Data
Wu, Yanrui.
  Productivity, efficiency and economic growth in China / by Yanrui Wu.
      p. cm.
   Includes bibliographical references and index.
    ISBN-13: 978–0–230–20212–2 (alk. paper)   1. China—Economic policy—2000–   2. Economic development—China.   3. Industrial productivity—China.   4. Capital productivity—China.   I. Title.
    HC427.95.W825 2008
    338.951—dc22

                                                                2008020587

10   9   8   7   6   5   4   3   2   1
17   16   15   14   13   12   11   10   09   08

Printed and bound in Great Britain by
CPI Antony Rowe, Chippenham and Eastbourne

# Contents

# List of Tables

# List of Figures

# List of Abbreviations

APEC    Asia Pacific Economic Cooperation
BEA     Bureau of Economic Analysis
DEA     data envelopment analysis
FDI      foreign direct investment
GDP    gross domestic product
GRP    gross regional product
ICT      information and communications technology
MII      Ministry of Information Industry
ML      maximum likelihood
MNE    multinational enterprise
MPI     Malmquist productivity index
MPS    material product system
MST    Ministry of Sciences and Technology
NBS    National Bureau of Statistics
NDRC  National Development and Reform Commission
SEZ     special economic zone
SNA    system of national accounts
TE       technical efficiency
TFP     total factor productivity
UN      United Nations
WTO    World Trade Organization

# Preface

This monograph has been prepared for postgraduate students, academics and business analysts who are interested in the Chinese economy and business and who are conducting research in the broader field of development economics. It is also targeted at libraries for acquisition as a useful reference book. Work on this book spans several years. Earlier versions of some chapters have been presented at various conferences and appeared in the form of working papers. They have been recently revised to reflect the latest developments in the Chinese economy and to be consistent with each other as chapters of the book. Several chapters have drawn material from two doctoral dissertations, namely, 'Information and Communications Technology, Productivity and Economic Growth in China' by Chee Kong Wong (PhD dissertation, University of Western Australia, 2007) and 'Foreign Direct Investment in China: Determinants, Effects and Efficiency' by Owen Ho (PhD dissertation, University of Western Australia, 2007). I would also like to thank Routledge (Taylor & Francis Group) for permission to use material from 'The Role of Productivity in China's Growth: New Estimates' (Yanrui Wu, *Journal of Chinese Economic and Business Studies*, 6(2), 141–56, 2008). Unless stated, the materials in the chapters represent original research and are presented here for the first time.

I thank my colleagues, both academic and professional staff, in economics at UWA Business School for their support and input (through their comments, conversations and sometimes jokes) over the years. I would also like to acknowledge Tsun Se Cheong, Callum Jones, Zhao Liang and Clare Yu for their excellent research assistance. Work on the book also benefited from two UWA Research Grants (2004, 2006) and two UWA Business School grants (2005, 2007).

Yanrui Wu
Economics Discipline
UWA Business School

# 1
# Introduction

Fifty years ago economists such as Abramovitz (1956), Kendrick (1956) and Solow (1957) created the concept of 'residual' to account for output growth unexplained by the changes in inputs. This residual is now popularly known as total factor productivity (TFP) growth or the rate of technological progress. It is shown to be responsible for a large proportion of economic growth in developed economies according to empirical studies (Dougherty and Jorgenson, 1996). As the supply of conventional inputs, namely capital and labour, is limited, long-term economic growth relies on the size of the 'residual' which in theory is unlimited. Thus, whether an economy can sustain its growth in the long run depends on productivity changes. This relationship has led to the recent resurgence of interest in productivity and growth analysis in the literature.[1] This book adds to the literature. Its objective is to examine several important issues associated with the relationship between productivity, efficiency and economic growth in the Chinese economy. In this introductory chapter, a brief review of the literature is presented first (Section 1.1). This is then followed by an outline of the core chapters (Section 1.2).

## 1.1 Studies of productivity and economic growth: a review

The Chinese economy has been growing at an average rate of 9.7 per cent per annum since 1978 when an economic reform programme was initiated.[2] This spectacular growth is likened to the economic miracle of the four East Asian Tigers in the 1960s and 1970s.[3] Has productivity growth played a role in China's high, sustained growth over the past decades? The pessimists would probably answer no. For example, researchers such as Krugman (1994), Young (1994) and Kim and Lau (1994) argued that East Asian economic growth has been driven mainly

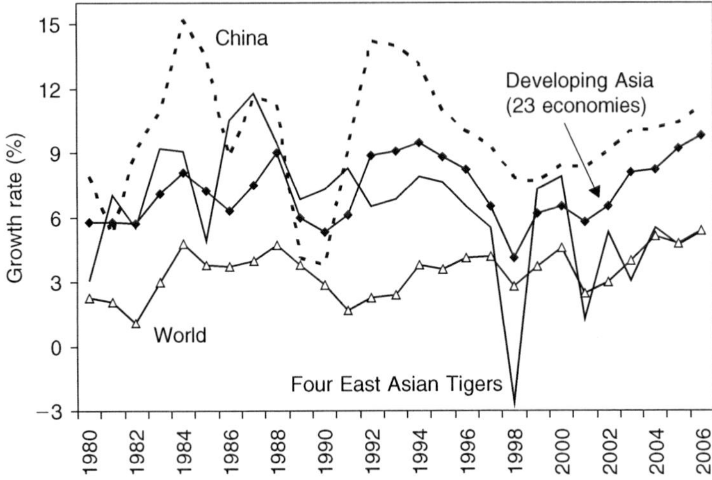


*Figure 1.1*   Asian economic growth, 1980–2006

*Notes*: Four East Asian Tigers refer to South Korea, Taiwan, Singapore and Hong Kong. The raw data are drawn from the *World Economic Outlook 2005* database (International Monetary Fund, 2005) with updates for 2005 and 2006 from the World Economic Outlook 2007 database (International Monetary Fund, 2007). The Chinese data are updated using China's 2004 national survey statistics (National Bureau of Statistics, 2007).

by the expansion of factor inputs with little technological progress and hence could not be sustained in the long run. They were, however, terribly wrong about economic growth in East Asia which, though interrupted by the 1997 Asian financial crisis, has outperformed growth in other regions (Figure 1.1).[4] East Asia led by China is to date still one of the main engines of world economic growth. For instance, China alone contributed to about 14 per cent of the world's real GDP growth in 2006 in terms of market values. This figure is about 30 per cent if real GDP is expressed in purchasing power parity (PPP) terms (International Monetary Fund, 2007).

Whether productivity growth has played a role in China's recent growth can be investigated by examining the sources of economic growth, that is, input changes and the magnitude of the 'residual'. Though the precise estimate is difficult to derive, the majority of the existing studies shows that total factor productivity (TFP) growth has indeed played an important role in economic growth in the last decades, accounting for about one-third to a half of China's growth on an average (Table 1.1).[5] An important factor underlying the wide range of estimates in Table 1.1 is the conceptual difference in defining TFP growth. For

*Table 1.1* Sources of economic growth in China

| Estimated by | Time period | Growth (%) | Contributions (%) | | | |
|---|---|---|---|---|---|---|
| | | | K | L | TFP | Total |
| Maddison (1998) | 1978–95 | 7.5 | 49 | 21 | 30 | 100 |
| Chow and Li (2002) | 1978–98 | 9.3 | 55 | 13 | 32 | 100 |
| Wu (2003) | 1982–97 | 9.5 | 58 | 10 | 32 | 100 |
| Woo (1998) | 1979–94 | 9.3 | 53 | 14 | 33 | 100 |
| Borensztein and Ostry (1996) | 1979–94 | 9.3 | n.a. | n.a. | 41 | 100 |
| Hu and Khan (1997) | 1979–94 | 9.3 | 46 | 13 | 41 | 100 |
| Swamy (2003) | 1980–97 | 10.0 | 39 | 16 | 45 | 100 |
| World Bank (1997a) | 1978–95 | 9.4 | 37 | 17 | 46 | 100 |
| Bosworth and Collins (2003) | 1980–90 | 9.2 | 23 | 31 | 46 | 100 |
| Bosworth and Collins (2003) | 1990–2000 | 10.1 | 32 | 18 | 50 | 100 |

*Note*: *K, L, TFP* are abbreviations for capital, labour and total factor productivity.

example, Woo (1998) isolated labour relocation effects from productivity growth and hence derived a net share of TFP to economic growth of 13 per cent. Another example is Wang and Yao (2003) who separated the impact of human capital from TFP growth and thus obtained a TFP share of about 25 per cent. There are of course exceptions. Young (2003) derived a TFP growth rate of 1.4 per cent for the non-agricultural sectors during the reform period. This would imply a relatively small TFP share over economic growth.

Another strand of the empirical studies has focused on the analysis of efficiency changes. The latter can be dealt with independently or as part of productivity growth.[6] Several earlier studies focused on the agricultural sector where efficiency gains due to the implementation of rural reforms have been substantial.[7] While there is consensus about efficiency improvement in the agricultural sector, a recent study by Brümmer et al. (2006) presented different results. Others were particularly interested in efficiency analysis at the micro level. For example, Lau and Brada (1990), Färe et al. (1996), Kong et al. (1999) and Zheng et al. (2003) considered the state enterprises. Wu (1995) is an exception. He compared three sectors, that is, agriculture, urban industry and rural industry.

At the aggregate level, regional data have been employed for efficiency studies. Wu (2000) found that efficiency changes were mainly responsible for productivity growth in the 1980s while technological progress became more important in the 1990s (Wu, 2003). The latter is supported by Zheng and Hu (2006) and Guillaumont et al. (2006). This book extends the existing literature in several directions. First, it derives capital stock series for Chinese regions and applies the data series to revisit the productivity debate. Second, it investigates the impact of information and communications technology (ICT) on productivity and efficiency and hence economic growth in China. This should be one of the few studies in this field. Finally, as China is one of the largest recipients of foreign direct investment (FDI), two chapters are devoted to explore the role of FDI in the country's growth. An outline of the core chapters is presented in Section 1.2.

## 1.2   Outline of the chapters

This book consists of six core chapters starting with Chapter 2 which presents estimates of regional capital stock series. The lack of capital stock statistics for the Chinese economy has for a long time been one of the major impediments for empirical research. Though many have attempted to derive their own data series, most studies have focused on the national level and their findings are not without controversy. Few studies have provided estimates of capital stock for China's regional economies. Chapter 2 makes several contributions to the literature. First, it presents a critical review of the methods and findings in the existing literature. Second, it proposes an alternative approach to estimate China's regional capital stock values. Third, the derived capital stock series are employed for preliminary analysis of growth, disparity and convergence in China's regional economies. They are also used for empirical work in Chapter 3. Finally, the estimated capital stock data will be available to the public free of charge (see the appendix to Chapter 2), and thus an important resource for economists.

In Chapter 3, the capital stock series derived in Chapter 2 are employed to account for China's economic growth. The chapter aims to revisit the debate about the role of productivity in China's growth, to provide an updated estimate of productivity growth and hence to make a contribution to the understanding of China's economic growth in recent years. Its objective is to propose and apply a growth accounting technique to assess economic performance in China, in particular the role of technological progress in China's recent growth. The findings about the latter may have important policy implications for the sustainability of China's economic growth in the future.

Chapters 4 and 5 explore the impacts of the so-called new economy on productivity, efficiency and economic growth, a topic which is under-documented in the literature. The objective of Chapter 4 is to examine the contribution of ICT capital as a production factor to economic growth in China. This chapter comprises three main parts. First, it describes the relationship between ICT, productivity and economic growth in China by comparing the pattern of growth in ICT capital and labour productivity during the past decades. Second, the chapter attempts to specify an appropriate model to examine the contribution of ICT and other factor inputs to economic growth in China. Finally, the chapter will test the robustness of the model by comparing empirical results based on different estimates of the ICT capital stock. Conclusions will then be drawn about the role of ICT in China's economic growth over the past two decades.

Chapter 5 seeks to estimate the regional ICT capital stock and to analyse the impact of ICT capital on technical efficiency in China's regions. It provides a background review of how the pattern of regional disparity in China has changed as far as ICT investment is concerned. It attempts to investigate the impact of ICT on regional growth and technical efficiency in China. No previous work in this area has been reported.

Chapters 6 and 7 analyse the role of foreign capital in China's growth. Chapter 6 examines the effects of FDI on labour productivity across regions in China. It first briefly surveys the debates and studies in the field. This is followed by modelling discussion and data description with preliminary analysis of labour productivity in China. The chapter then examines the effect of FDI on labour productivity in China. The results show that inward FDI and the presence of foreign-funded enterprises (FFEs) do have spillover effects on labour productivity in China. There is, however, substantial regional variation.

Chapter 7 extends Chapter 6 by evaluating the performance of foreign affiliates relative to that of the state-owned enterprises (SOEs) in China. The data envelopment analysis (DEA) approach combined with Malmquist productivity indexes was employed in the chapter to investigate technical efficiency and its changes at provincial level. It is found that SOEs and FFEs in the municipal cities and the coastal regions performed better than those in the central and western regions. This result is consistent with the major findings of the literature. It is also found that both SOEs and FFEs in the municipal cities have achieved more productivity growth than those in other regions. Finally, in the conclusion, Chapter 8 presents a summary of the findings and discusses possible implications drawn from the results in this book.

# 2
# Measuring China's Capital Stock

China's continuingly high growth for almost three decades has attracted a lot of attention. As a result, a vast literature has emerged.[1] While working on China's economic statistics, researchers have confronted a major problem, i.e. no capital stock data are reported in the Chinese statistical system. Subsequently, researchers have attempted to derive China's capital stock data by themselves. Earlier works include Zhang (1991), He (1992), Chow (1993), Li et al. (1995), Hu and Khan (1997) and the World Bank (1997a). In these studies, the methods involved vary considerably and so do their results.[2] The objective of this chapter is to review previous methods as well as findings, and propose an alternative approach. In particular, the recently released national accounts figures are employed to derive capital stock series for China's 31 regions. A review of the literature is presented in Section 2.1. This is followed by discussion of the existing methods and description of an alternative approach in Section 2.2. New capital stock estimates for China's regional economies together with the preliminary analysis are reported in Section 2.3. The relationship between capital formation and growth in China's regional economies is examined in Section 2.4. Finally summary comments are presented in the concluding section (Section 2.5).

## 2.1  Literature review

Zhang (1991), He (1992) and Chow (1993) are examples of earlier studies on capital stock estimates and economic growth in China. Zhang and He represent two of the pioneering studies conducted by scholars inside China. Their capital stock estimates are based on the statistics of 'accumulation' defined under the traditional Material Product System

(MPS) in China.[3] The latter was replaced by the UN-adopted System of National Accounts (SNA) in the earlier 1990s and subsequently reporting of the 'accumulation' information was discontinued in 1993. Chow (1993) is one of the earlier studies published in English. His study covered the period of 1952–85. He derived capital stock series for five economic sectors, i.e. agriculture, industry, construction, transportation and commerce. Chow's empirical estimations were based on data of national income, accumulation of fixed assets and circulating funds. He also derived an estimate of capital stock in agriculture by using data of the original value of fixed assets. The problem with the data on 'accumulation' or 'original value' of fixed assets is well known (see Chen et al., 1988). Li et al. (1995) derived capital stock series by using the values of fixed and current assets. Their estimates suffer from the same problem as those in Chow (1993). Subsequently, Borensztein and Ostry (1996) and Woo (1998) applied the same database compiled by Li et al. (1995).

Recent works include Hu and Khan (1997), World Bank (1997a) and Maddison (1998). Hu and Khan (1997) derived their own capital stock series following the conventional perpetual inventory approach. They used Chow's estimates of the initial value of capital stock. World Bank (1997a) used the database derived by Nehru and Dhareshwar (1993). The latter also applied the perpetual inventory method. The initial value of capital stock was derived by assuming that the rates of growth of capital and output are equal if the capital–output ratio is constant in a given period. Maddison (1998) derived gross fixed capital stock by 'cumulating the increments in investment' and assuming that capital had a lifespan of 25 years which effectively implies an annual rate of depreciation as high as 17 per cent.[4]

More recent studies include Chow and Li (2002) and Holz (2006a). Chow and Li extended the work by Chow (1993) and derived China's capital stock values up to 1998. They employed regional depreciation values for the 1990s and worked out a rate of depreciation of 5.4 per cent for aggregate capital stock in the nation. This is certainly problematic as there is inconsistency between the national aggregate and the sum of regional values which is discussed in Section 2.3. Holz's work begins with the discussion of conceptual issues associated with 'fixed assets', 'net investment' and 'capital formation'. He questioned the direct use of raw data of these variables in empirical studies and hence, by introducing an alternative approach, reconstructed economy-wide fixed asset values for the period of 1953–2003. His results are, however, not without questions (Chow, 2006; Holz, 2006b).

Those studies surveyed so far mainly focused on capital stock estimates at the national level. There is a lack of investigation at the regional and sector levels.[5] Regional studies have been limited for a long time probably due to the paucity of investment data, rates of depreciation and price deflators at the regional level. Wu (2004) and Zhang et al. (2007) are two exceptions.[6] Wu presented a survey of the main approaches and estimated regional capital stock by assuming a rate of depreciation of 7 per cent for all regions. Zhang et al. also reported their estimates of China's regional capital stock by employing an identical rate of depreciation of 9.6 per cent for all regions. Apparently, the main weakness in the studies by Wu and Zhang et al. is the assumption of the same rate of depreciation for all regions in China. The present study aims to overcome the above-mentioned problems in the existing literature and derive new estimates of capital stock for the Chinese regions. Especially, it employs region-specific rates of depreciation and does not need the estimation of the initial values of capital stock. The estimation technique is documented in Section 2.2.

## 2.2  Capital stock estimation methods

The general technique of estimating capital stock values in this study belongs to the broader category of the conventional perpetual inventory approach according to which the value of capital stock is estimated from gross investment in each year. Symbolically, the estimation technique can be expressed as

$$K_{i,t} = (1 - \delta_i)K_{i,t-1} + \Delta K_{i,t} \tag{2.1}$$

where $K_{i,t}$ is the real value of capital stock for the $i$th region or economy in the $t$th year, $\Delta K_{i,t}$ the real value of incremental capital stock and $\delta_i$ the rate of depreciation for the $i$th region. It is clear in equation (2.1) that the value of capital stock can be computed if the rate of depreciation, $\delta_i$, and the initial value are known. Assume that the initial capital stock was $K_{i,0}$ for the $i$th region or economy, equation (2.1) can then be converted into

$$K_{i,t} = \sum_{0}^{t} (1 - \delta_i)^j \Delta K_{i,t-j} + K_{i,0}(1 - \delta_i)^t \tag{2.2}$$

In the above formula, the only unknown is the initial value of capital stock ($K_{i,0}$), given the rate of depreciation. For the latter, researchers have resorted to various sources such as national accounts, accounting

*Table 2.1*   Selected rates of depreciation and initial values of capital stock

| Authors | Depreciation rates (%) | Initial value in 1952 (billion yuan in 1952 prices) |
|---|---|---|
| Zhang (1991) | n.a. | 200.0[a] |
| He (1992) | n.a. | 50.8[a] |
| Chow (1993) | n.a. | 175.0 |
| Hu and Khan (1997) | 3.6 | 175.0 |
| World Bank (1997a) | 4.0 | n.a. |
| Perkins (1988) | 5.0 | 200.6 |
| Woo (1998) | 5.0 | n.a. |
| Meng and Wang (2000) | 5.0 | 180.0[b] |
| Wang and Yao (2003) | 5.0 | 175.0 |
| Chow and Li (2002) | 5.4[c] | 221.3 |
| Young (2003) | 6.0 | n.a. |
| Maddison (1998) | 17.0 | n.a. |
| Wu (2004)[d] | 7.0 | n.a. |
| Zhang et al. (2007)[d] | 9.6 | n.a. |

[a]These numbers are cited in Zhang et al. (2007).
[b]This is 1953 value in 1980 prices.
[c]This rate was applied for the period of 1978–98 only.
[d]Wu (2004) and Zhang et al. (2007) are regional studies. Wu's approach is similar to what is employed in this chapter. Thus no initial values of capital stock are needed. Zhang et al. assume that the initial value of capital stock in 1952 is equal to the value of fixed investment divided by 10%.
n.a. = not available.

records at the firm level, findings in the existing literature and ad hoc assumptions. As a result, different rates of depreciation have been used, ranging from 3.6 to 17.0 per cent (Table 2.1). Thus, the choice of the rate of depreciation is itself controversial. This chapter proposes an alternative approach to derive the rates of depreciation for the Chinese regions. In particular, this chapter allows a different rate for each of China's regional economies to be obtained with this study. This is the first of its kind in the literature.

As for the derivation of the initial value of capital stock, various approaches have been employed as well. Subsequently, different results have been derived (Table 2.1). While Chow (1993) provided detailed information and conducted sensitivity analysis, Li et al. (1995) and Maddison (1998) did not elaborate on how they estimated the initial value, to cite a few. The main approaches employed in the literature are surveyed in the following section.

### 2.2.1   The conventional approaches

In general, the existing literature has used three approaches in estimating the initial value of capital stock. They are here called the integral, the growth rate and other approaches, respectively, and discussed in detail.

*The integral approach*

The core of this technique is that the capital stock in the initial year is assumed to be the sum of all past investments. Symbolically,

$$K_{i,0} = \int_{-\infty}^{0} \Delta K_{i,t} \, \mathrm{d}t = \frac{\Delta K_{i,0} e^{\theta}}{\theta} \tag{2.3}$$

where $\Delta K_{i,t} = \Delta K_{i,0} e^{\theta(t+1)}$, and $\theta$ and $\Delta K_{i,0}$ are estimated by linear regressions using the investment series available. Among the existing studies, Wu (2000) adopted this approach. Obviously, capital decay is not taken into consideration in the integral approach of estimating the initial value of capital stock. In practice, this approach tends to overestimate the growth of capital stock. For example, Wu (2000) derived an average real rate of growth of 21.5 per cent during the period 1981–95. This figure is twice as big as the estimates derived by other authors. It is 8.9 per cent during 1978–95 according to Maddison (1998) and 7.9 per cent during 1979–95 according to the World Bank (1997a), for instance. Furthermore, in order to apply this approach, one must have investment data which are suitable for regression analysis. This could be difficult in some cases.

*The growth rate approach*

This approach is based on the assumption that the function of investment is to replace depreciation of old capital and create new capital to maintain growth (Harberger, 1978). Thus, the following equations are obtained:

$$\Delta K_{i,1} = (\delta_i + g_i) K_{i,0} \tag{2.4}$$

or

$$K_{i,0} = \frac{\Delta K_{i,1}}{(\delta_i + g_i)} \tag{2.5}$$

Equation (2.4) implies that the incremental capital stock or realized investment in period 1 is the sum of the depreciated capital stock from period 0 and new capital stock created. The latter is assumed to grow at the constant rate of $g_i$ which is often replaced by the average growth rate of the incremental capital stock in the initial period, say, five years.

In practice, authors have also used the rate of growth of investment or GDP when incremental capital stock data are not available. Young (2003) and Islam et al. (2006) followed this approach for their work on China.[7] Other applications include Nadiri and Prucha (1996) on the US and Miyagawa et al. (2004) on Japan. The main advantage of this approach is its simplicity.

*Other approaches*

Apart from the integral and growth rate approaches, several other methods have also been proposed in the literature and are broadly called 'other approaches' here. Examples include Perkins (1988) who assumed that the capital–output ratio was three in the year 1953, and Chow (1993) who relied on the statistics of 'accumulation of fixed assets'. He (1992) and Zhang and Zhang (2003) employed similar raw data as Chow (1993) did.[8] In addition, Holz (2006a) applied official depreciation values and rates of depreciation to generate capital stock series for the period 1978–2003.

Though there are some capital stock estimates for China at the national level, data at the regional level are rare. Thus, this study presents an alternative approach to estimating capital stock series for the Chinese regions. The approach is discussed in the following section.

### 2.2.2  An alternative approach

The main problem associated with the conventional approaches reviewed in the preceding section is the ad hoc nature of dealing with the rate of depreciation and the initial value of capital stock. To overcome these problems, this section proposes an alternative approach which is here called the 'backcasting approach' and which is employed to derive capital stock estimates for China's regions in the rest of the chapter. The results are also compared to those derived following the conventional approaches. In general, the backcasting approach involves three tasks, that is, the choice of deflators, determination of the initial value of capital stock and estimates of region-specific rates of depreciation.

*Choice of deflators*

The first task is to find a time-varying, region-specific price index which is used to convert investment values into real terms. Such an index has not been available in the official statistics until recently.[9] For this purpose, region-specific price indexes since the 1950s are obtained using the following formulae:

$$P_{it}^{\text{constant}} = \frac{Y_{it}^{\text{current}}}{Y_{it}^{\text{constant}}} \tag{2.6}$$

where $P_{it}^{\text{constant}}$, $Y_{it}^{\text{current}}$ and $Y_{it}^{\text{constant}}$ represent price indexes in constant prices, income in current prices and income in constant prices for the $i$th region at period $t$. $Y_{it}^{\text{constant}}$ is defined as

$$Y_{it}^{\text{constant}} = Y_{i0}^{\text{current}} \prod_{0}^{t} (1 + r_i)^k \tag{2.7}$$

where $r_i$ is the real rate of growth in income which is available from 1953 onwards for all regions and $Y_{i0}^{\text{current}}$ the initial income at current prices for the $i$th region. The derived regional price indexes can be used for the estimation of capital stock in each region. As a result, GDP and capital stock data are expressed in 1953 constant prices.[10]

The derived national price indexes are plotted in Figure 2.1. Several observations are worth mentioning. First, because of the price controls under the central planning system, prices fluctuated modestly in China during the pre-reform era (1953–77). The only exception was the hyper-inflation in 1961 due to the severe shortage of food and other goods. Second, the movement of prices has been more volatile during the reform period as the economy has been transformed towards a market-oriented system. This is particularly so during the ten years immediately after urban reforms began in 1985. Finally, the standard deviation of regional price deflators shows the existence of price differentiation among the regions. Thus, empirical analyses applying a single deflator for all regions can be distorted. Over time, however, regional disparity in inflation tends to decline according to Figure 2.1.

*Initial value of capital stock*

The second task deals with the estimation of the initial value of capital stock. For this purpose, the data series for $\Delta K_{i,t}$ available from 1953 onwards are backcasted to the year 1900 and thus the time-series sample has more than 100 observations. Accordingly, equation (2.2) is expanded to

$$K_{i,t} = \sum_{0}^{t-1901} (1 - \delta_i)^k \Delta K_{i,t-k} + (1 - \delta_i)^{t-1900} K_{i,1900} \tag{2.8}$$

Equation (2.8) implies that, given the value of capital stock in 1900, $K_{i,1900}$, and an appropriate rate of depreciation, a capital stock series for each region or economy can be derived. Due to capital decay and the long time horizon, $K_{i,1900}$ can be assumed to be zero. This is reasonable as the lifespan of capital is far shorter than 100 years and, in particular,

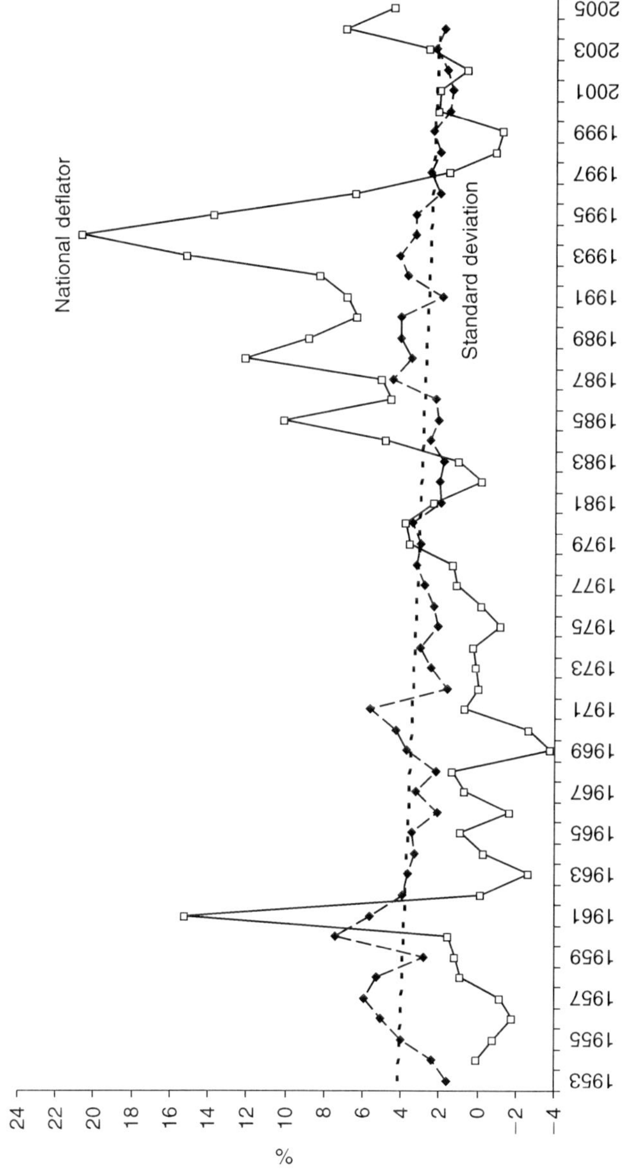


*Figure 2.1* National deflator and standard deviation of regional deflators, 1953–2005
*Source*: Author's own estimates.

as most studies of the Chinese economy only cover the recent decades, i.e. the reform period. Thus, extending the data series avoids the guesstimates of the initial value of capital stock.

*Region-specific rates of depreciation*

The third task is then to derive an appropriate rate of depreciation. The latter has been assumed to be the same for all regions in the existing literature. To remove this assumption, a simulation process is adopted here to generate different rates of depreciation for the regions. This is the first such exercise in the literature. The National Bureau of Statistics (various issues) has released the values of depreciation for each region since 1978. The simulation process begins by assuming a rate of depreciation for each region and then searches for an optimal rate (via repetitive computations) so that the estimated values of depreciation (using the optimal rate) match the actual values of depreciation.[11] The final simulation results are presented in Table 2.2. In general, the rate of depreciation is high in the more developed regions and low in the less developed ones. The three municipal cities also show relatively low rates of depreciation. This may be due to the fact that these cities have relatively large service sectors. It is interesting to note that the mean of the regional rates of depreciation is about 4 per cent which is close to the rate used by Hu and Khan (1997) and the World Bank (1997a). Thus, the application of a rate of depreciation of 7 per cent in Wu (2004), 9.6 per cent in Zhang et al. (2007) and 17 per cent in Maddison (1998) would lead to the underestimation of China's capital stock.

## 2.3  Estimation results

### 2.3.1  Capital stock series

Having completed the three tasks described in the preceding section, regional capital stock data series are obtained. According to the estimates (presented in the appendix to this chapter), China enjoyed rapid capital accumulation immediately after the foundation of the People's Republic in 1949 (with an average rate of growth of 11.9 per cent during 1951–60). But the growth was interrupted due to political campaigns and a major famine in the 1960s (with an average rate of growth of 4.9 per cent during 1961–70). Fortunately, rapid growth has resumed since the early 1970s, maintaining an average rate of growth of 8.3, 9.1 and 10.2 per cent in the 1970s, 1980s and 1990s, respectively. Among the 31 Chinese regions, in terms of the value of capital stock, Shanghai, Jiangsu and Shandong are the top three regions, followed by Zhejiang, Hebei, Guangdong, Beijing

*Table 2.2*   Regional rates of depreciation

| Codes | Regions | Rates of depreciation (%) |
| --- | --- | --- |
| 1 | Beijing | 3.4 |
| 2 | Tianjin | 3.7 |
| 3 | Hebei | 4.3 |
| 4 | Shanxi | 4.0 |
| 5 | Inner Mongolia | 4.3 |
| 6 | Liaoning | 5.8 |
| 7 | Jilin | 5.1 |
| 8 | Heilongjiang | 6.0 |
| 9 | Shanghai | 3.4 |
| 10 | Jiangsu | 4.2 |
| 11 | Zhejiang | 4.0 |
| 12 | Anhui | 5.0 |
| 13 | Fujian | 4.5 |
| 14 | Jiangxi | 3.7 |
| 15 | Shandong | 5.0 |
| 16 | Henan | 4.1 |
| 17 | Hubei | 4.5 |
| 18 | Hunan | 4.5 |
| 19 | Guangdong | 6.9 |
| 20 | Guangxi | 3.3 |
| 21 | Hainan | 2.2 |
| 22 | Chongqing | 5.0 |
| 23 | Sichuan | 4.6 |
| 24 | Guizhou | 2.8 |
| 25 | Yunnan | 2.7 |
| 26 | Tibet | 4.2 |
| 27 | Shaanxi | 3.3 |
| 28 | Gansu | 2.7 |
| 29 | Qinghai | 2.4 |
| 30 | Ningxia | 2.8 |
| 31 | Xinjiang | 2.6 |

*Source*: Author's own estimates.

and Liaoning (see Figure 2.2 for a map of China). Other regions are much smaller. As expected, Guangdong recorded the highest average rate (16.5 per cent) of capital accumulation during 1953–2005. Behind Guangdong are Shanghai (13.3 per cent), Fujian (12.3 per cent), Zhejiang (12.2 per cent) and Jiangsu (12.1 per cent).

### 2.3.2   National vs regional capital stock

Economists specializing in the Chinese economy have for years been puzzled by the discrepancy between national and regional data. Capital

*Figure 2.2*  Map of China
*Source*: Wu (2004).

stock estimates in this study offer some insights into this debate. In general, the sum of regional capital stock values tended to underestimate the national total during 1953–96, while this trend is reversed after 1996 as shown in Figure 2.3. This is consistent with gross capital formation figures, reported by the National Bureau of Statistics (NBS), which show that the sum of regional values underestimated the national total during 1953–93 while the opposite occurred after 1993. One possible explanation is that since the mid 1990s capital has become very mobile in China and a lot of cross-regional investment has taken place. As a result, some investment and hence capital formation have been claimed by both the home and hosting regions. The same reason can be applied to explain the discrepancy between the sum of regional GDP and national GDP reported by the NBS. The former tends to overestimate the latter after 1996 while the opposite is true for data of the period 1953–96. This discrepancy may be a genuine error rather than deliberate data manipulation as argued in

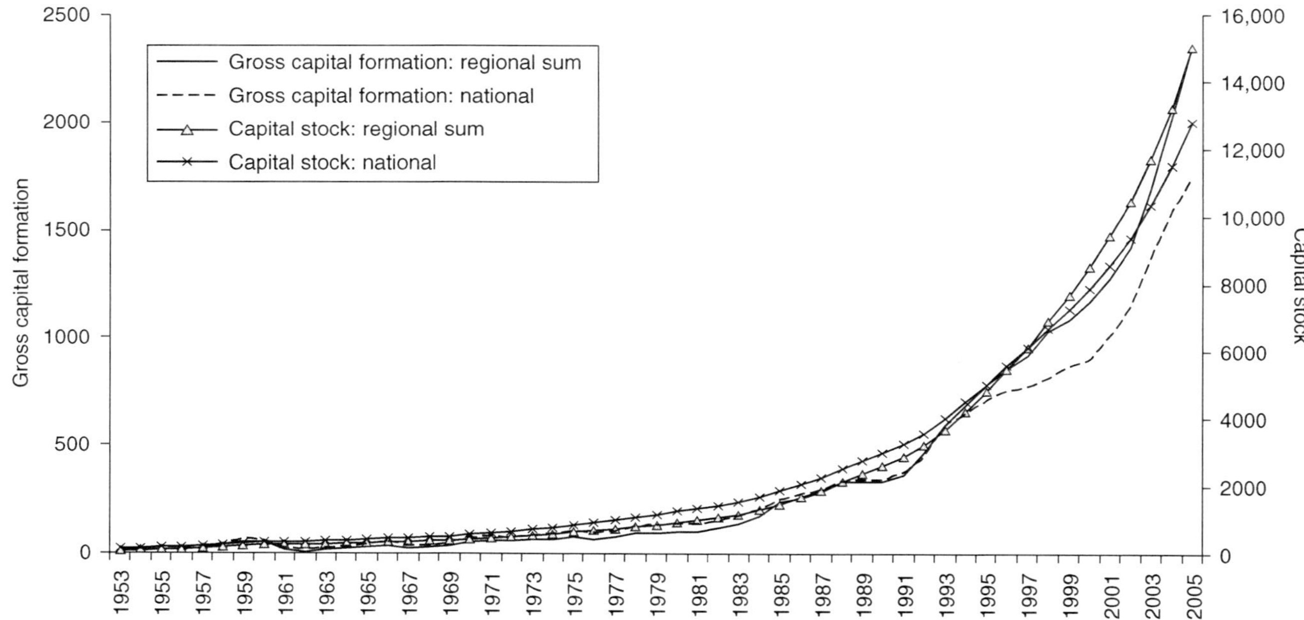


*Figure 2.3*  National aggregate vs regional sum
*Source*: Author's own estimates.

*Table 2.3*  Growth rates of China's capital stock

| Sources | Periods | Growth rate (%) |
|---|---|---|
| Li et al. (1995) | 1979–90 | 9.15 |
| Hu and Khan (1997) | 1979–94 | 7.70 |
| World Bank (1997a) | 1979–95 | 7.90 |
| Maddison (1998) | 1978–95 | 8.86[a] |
| Zhang et al. (2007) | 1979–90 | 10.27 |
|  | 1979–95 | 10.85 |
|  | 1979–2005 | 11.79 |
| This chapter | 1979–90 | 10.08 |
|  | 1979–95 | 10.68 |
|  | 1979–2005 | 11.05 |

[a]Non-residential capital only.

the literature (Rawski, 2001). Overall, the value of capital stock in 1952 was 133.8 billion yuan which is higher than the popularly cited figure (175 billion yuan including land value of 72 billion yuan) derived by Chow (1993).

### 2.3.3  Comparison with other estimates

For a comparison with the estimates by other authors, the growth rates of the derived capital stock in some periods are illustrated in Table 2.3. According to this table, the estimate of capital stock in this study is higher than others cited with the exception of Zhang et al. (2007). It should be pointed out that the numbers in both Zhang et al. and this study are based on the arithmetic means of the estimates of regional capital stock data. However, the estimated rate of growth per annum is still below the rate of 11.5 per cent for Singapore, 13.7 per cent for South Korea and 12.3 per cent for Taiwan during the period 1966–90 (Dougherty and Jorgenson, 1996). The lower estimates derived by other authors are debatable. The explanation may lie in the estimation of the initial capital stock value and the choice of the rate of depreciation. For example, while the World Bank (1997a) used a rate of 4 per cent, Maddison (1998) assumed an average asset life of 25 years, which is equivalent to an annual rate of depreciation of 17 per cent.

In terms of the capital–output ratio which has been popularly used for the estimates of capital stock, it is generally close to three with the exception of a few years during 1952–58 when the ratio was under two. These findings support the argument made by Perkins (1988) who assumed that the ratio should be three. They are, however, higher than those derived by Holz (2006a) and Chow and Li (2002), which may imply that capital stock estimates by the latter authors may be biased downwards due to the use of higher rates of depreciation.

## 2.4   Capital formation and regional growth

Given the estimates of regional capital stock, this section presents some preliminary analysis. A simple growth accounting exercise is conducted first. This is followed by an examination of regional disparity and convergence.

### 2.4.1   Accounting for growth

The role of capital formation in economic growth is a classical topic.[12] The objective here is not to be exhaustive but to present some preliminary analysis of the relationship between capital formation and economic growth in China. Figure 2.4 demonstrates the close movement between the growth rates of China's capital stock and GDP during the past decades. The association between the two indicators is very clear in the 1980s and 1990s. One can thus speculate that capital accumulation has been an important contributor to China's growth in the past two decades.

A more formal investigation is illustrated in Table 2.4 which shows the estimation results of a simple Cobb–Douglas production function using regional data over the period of 1985–2005. The results from similar exercises by Chow and Li (2002) and Chow (2006) using time series data are also presented for the purpose of comparison. While this study derives an average rate of technological progress of 2.33 per cent during 1985–2005, the other two sets of results show an average rate of 2.62 per cent during 1978–98 and 4.86 per cent during 1978–2003. Chow (2006) raised questions about the relatively higher rate of technological progress and the low capital share derived using Holz's data. The capital share estimated in this chapter is slightly higher than that reported by Chow and Li. Overall, technological progress accounts for about 22.1 per cent of the average growth (10.5 per cent) during 1986–2005. The rest is attributed to changes in factor inputs, i.e. growth in capital and labour. Thus, factor inputs, in particular capital, do play the main role in China's growth in the past decades. In the meantime, technological progress has

20

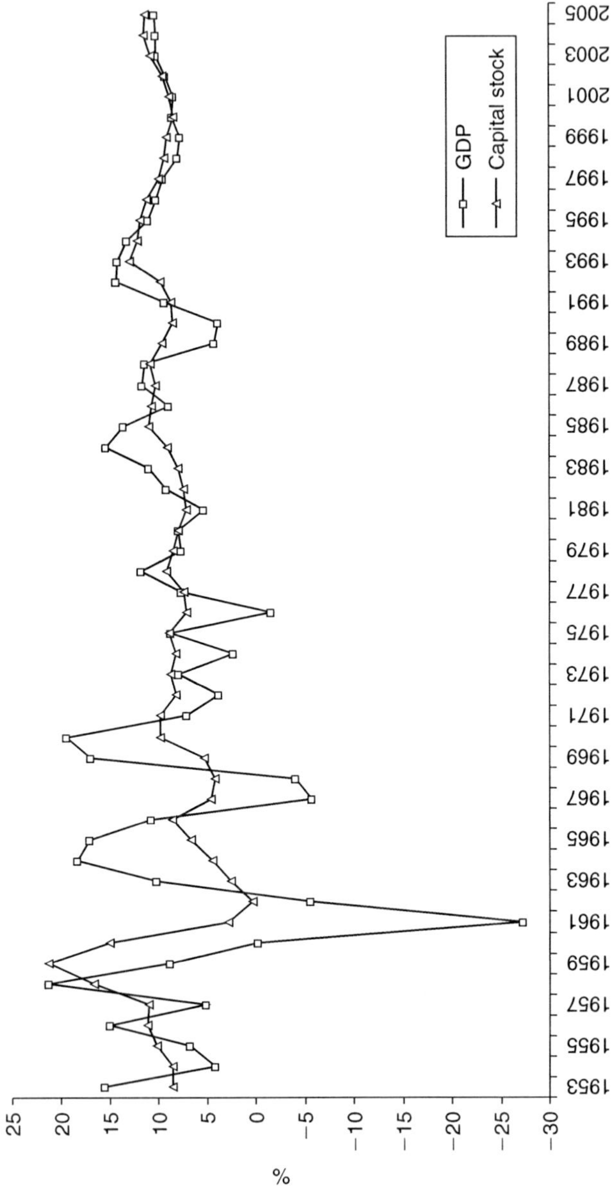


*Figure 2.4* Growth rates of capital stock and gross domestic product (GDP), 1953–2005
*Source*: Author's own estimates.

*Table 2.4*   Results of production function estimation (fixed effect model)

| Variables | This chapter | Chow and Li (2002) | Holz (2006a) |
|---|---|---|---|
| ln (Capital) | 0.6724 (32.212) | 0.6284 (24.357) | 0.3228 (20.050) |
| ln (Labour) | 0.3276 (15.692) | 0.3716 (14.403) | 0.6772 (42.062) |
| Time trend | 0.0233 (11.176) | 0.0262 (10.917) | 0.0486 (25.579) |
| Intercept | | 1.6612 (8.476) | −1.9554 (−53.868) |
| Sample size | 651 (1985–2005) | 47 (1952–98) | 51 (1953–2003) |
| $\bar{R}^2$ | 0.9955 | 0.9946 | 0.9935 |

*Notes*: The numbers in parentheses are $t$-ratios. The results for Holz (2006a) are derived by Chow (2006). The time trend for Chow and Li (2002) and Holz (2006a) covers the period of 1978 and onwards.

also made a substantial contribution which provides the foundation for sustained growth of the Chinese economy.

### 2.4.2   Regional disparity and convergence

Regional disparity and hence convergence have for years been a hotly debated question in China. This question can also be explored in terms of capital stock formation among the regions. Figure 2.5 illustrates the movement of population-weighted coefficients of variation for gross regional product (GRP) per capita, regional capital stock per capita and growth rates of gross regional product during 1953–2005. Several points are worthy of mention. First, disparity in regional income became worse before the initiative of economic reforms, while regional inequality in terms of capital stock per head remained almost the same during the same period. Thus, it might be efficiency that enlarged the regional gap in development as the coefficients of variation in terms of growth rates were high and fluctuated considerably. Second, during the period of economic reforms (from 1978 to 2005), regional income disparity remains high and tends to decline modestly. This is in sharp contrast with the general perception that regional inequality has deteriorated since the beginning of economic reforms. Third, regional disparity in capital formation increased continuously during 1979–98 and then headed in the opposite direction after 1999. One key development since 1999 has been the 'go-west' programme. The latter has boosted investment in the relatively less developed areas and may have contributed to the decline in regional inequality in terms of capital stock per head.[13] Finally, during the reform period of 1978–2005, it seems that all regions enjoyed high economic growth as the coefficients of variations in terms of GRP growth rates were small and showed a declining trend.

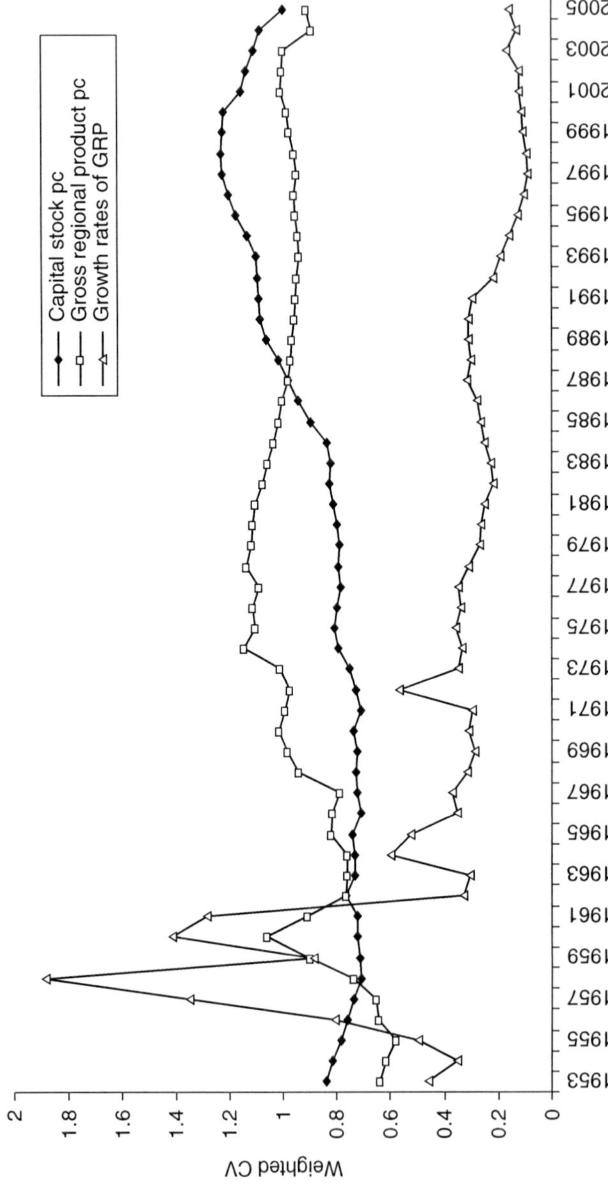


*Figure 2.5* Changing regional disparity, 1953–2005

*Notes*: Growth rates are based on five-year moving average starting in 1953. Annual rates of growth are used for the years 2002–5.

## 2.5  Conclusion

In summary, this chapter presents a review of the literature estimating China's capital stock data and introduces an alternative approach to estimating capital stock series for China's 31 regional economies. This approach overcomes the problems in the existing literature of assuming ad hoc rates of depreciation and initial values of capital stock. In particular, it allows for different depreciation rates for the regions. The derived capital stock data series are important resources for research on the Chinese economy.

Preliminary analyses indicate a close association between capital stock formation and economic growth in China, implying a potentially dominant role of capital stock in boosting economic growth. This is confirmed by the results of production function analysis using regional data. In addition, technological progress is also found to play an important role in China's growth in the past two decades.

Furthermore, the estimated capital stock series can also shed some light on the debate on regional disparity in China. It is found that regional disparity in terms of income per capita became worse well before the initiative of economic reform in 1978. This may be attributed to the variation in regional growth during that period rather than differences in capital formation. In contrast to the popular perception that economic reforms have been responsible for the deterioration of regional disparity, since 1978, regional disparity remains stable with a modest declining trend. However, regional disparity in terms of capital endowment has deteriorated since the mid 1980s. This has, however, been offset by the falling disparity in economic growth rates. In particular, since 1999 when China's 'go-west' programme was initiated, disparity in capital endowment has fallen. Whether this trend is to continue and make a contribution in closing the gap in regional income is yet to be observed in the coming years.

Finally, it should be mentioned that empirical applications of the estimated capital stock series in this study are subject to several qualifications. First, while the use of region-specific rates of depreciation is a major advance in this study, dynamic issues are ignored. Second, due to the non-existence of land markets and hence private land ownership, in particular, rural land market and ownership, land values are not incorporated into the estimates of capital stock. Third, before economic reform began, many Chinese enterprises were located in the interior areas which are often far away from the border regions for strategic reasons during the Cold War era. Since the beginning of economic reforms in 1978, many of those enterprises have been relocated to the coastal regions or closer to the source of raw materials. These relocation activities may affect regional capital stock values and are not reflected in the official statistics.

## Appendix

### China's regional capital stock

Capital stock data reported in this appendix are expressed in billion yuan and in 1953 constant prices and are available in Excel format from the author upon request (the price deflators are also available from the author). The national aggregate figures are presented under the column 'k0' and are not equal to the sum of the regional statistics (refer to the text for an explanation). The regions are coded from 1 to 31 and follow the same order as in Table 2.2 where the rates of depreciation are listed.

| Years | k0 | k1 | k2 | k3 | k4 | k5 | k6 | k7 | k8 | k9 | k10 |
|---|---|---|---|---|---|---|---|---|---|---|---|
| 1952 | 133.8 | 3.0 | 1.3 | 4.9 | 4.2 | 2.6 | 6.8 | 2.9 | 4.0 | 2.5 | 3.4 |
| 1953 | 145.2 | 3.3 | 1.4 | 5.3 | 4.5 | 2.8 | 7.4 | 3.2 | 4.4 | 2.8 | 3.8 |
| 1954 | 157.7 | 3.6 | 1.6 | 5.8 | 4.9 | 3.0 | 8.1 | 3.4 | 4.7 | 3.1 | 4.2 |
| 1955 | 173.6 | 4.2 | 1.8 | 6.9 | 5.3 | 3.1 | 8.7 | 4.0 | 5.4 | 3.7 | 5.2 |
| 1956 | 193.0 | 5.2 | 1.8 | 7.9 | 6.1 | 3.5 | 9.6 | 4.4 | 5.7 | 3.8 | 6.2 |
| 1957 | 214.3 | 6.2 | 2.4 | 9.2 | 7.2 | 4.0 | 11.1 | 4.8 | 6.6 | 5.3 | 7.1 |
| 1958 | 250.1 | 7.8 | 3.3 | 11.8 | 9.2 | 5.5 | 14.5 | 5.6 | 8.5 | 7.5 | 8.3 |
| 1959 | 303.2 | 10.4 | 4.9 | 14.5 | 11.5 | 7.5 | 19.0 | 6.7 | 10.7 | 11.2 | 9.7 |
| 1960 | 348.5 | 12.9 | 5.8 | 17.4 | 13.6 | 9.2 | 23.9 | 7.5 | 13.1 | 14.6 | 11.1 |
| 1961 | 358.3 | 13.4 | 5.7 | 18.2 | 13.8 | 9.5 | 23.3 | 7.8 | 13.1 | 15.3 | 11.6 |
| 1962 | 359.3 | 13.3 | 5.6 | 17.3 | 13.5 | 9.4 | 21.7 | 7.8 | 12.7 | 14.6 | 11.7 |
| 1963 | 368.5 | 13.1 | 5.5 | 17.5 | 13.5 | 9.6 | 22.4 | 8.0 | 13.1 | 15.3 | 12.2 |
| 1964 | 385.1 | 13.4 | 5.7 | 18.0 | 13.6 | 10.0 | 23.6 | 8.3 | 13.4 | 16.4 | 13.2 |
| 1965 | 410.6 | 14.0 | 6.3 | 18.7 | 14.3 | 10.6 | 25.1 | 8.7 | 13.7 | 16.7 | 14.3 |
| 1966 | 445.6 | 14.8 | 7.0 | 19.2 | 15.0 | 11.2 | 26.2 | 9.1 | 13.9 | 18.9 | 15.8 |
| 1967 | 465.8 | 15.2 | 7.4 | 20.1 | 15.2 | 11.2 | 26.9 | 9.4 | 13.8 | 19.2 | 16.5 |
| 1968 | 485.4 | 15.6 | 7.8 | 20.9 | 15.3 | 11.3 | 27.7 | 9.7 | 13.8 | 21.3 | 17.3 |
| 1969 | 510.6 | 16.6 | 8.3 | 22.1 | 15.9 | 11.4 | 28.9 | 10.1 | 14.4 | 21.5 | 18.2 |
| 1970 | 560.5 | 17.5 | 9.1 | 24.0 | 16.9 | 11.9 | 31.0 | 10.8 | 15.3 | 22.9 | 20.1 |
| 1971 | 614.9 | 19.4 | 10.2 | 26.5 | 18.7 | 12.5 | 34.2 | 11.8 | 15.9 | 25.3 | 22.4 |
| 1972 | 664.5 | 20.5 | 11.5 | 28.7 | 20.5 | 13.1 | 36.4 | 12.7 | 16.7 | 28.8 | 24.6 |
| 1973 | 722.5 | 23.0 | 13.2 | 31.0 | 21.8 | 13.8 | 39.3 | 13.8 | 17.7 | 32.5 | 27.2 |
| 1974 | 781.1 | 25.3 | 15.5 | 33.5 | 23.3 | 14.6 | 42.9 | 14.9 | 18.9 | 36.8 | 29.5 |
| 1975 | 850.3 | 27.0 | 17.4 | 36.8 | 24.7 | 15.5 | 47.8 | 16.5 | 20.5 | 40.6 | 32.2 |
| 1976 | 910.1 | 27.8 | 18.9 | 39.9 | 25.8 | 16.6 | 52.4 | 17.2 | 22.0 | 42.9 | 34.9 |
| 1977 | 976.5 | 29.4 | 20.7 | 43.5 | 27.6 | 17.6 | 55.1 | 18.1 | 23.2 | 45.3 | 37.6 |
| 1978 | 1064.9 | 32.1 | 22.5 | 48.1 | 29.6 | 19.1 | 59.2 | 20.1 | 25.6 | 49.6 | 41.8 |
| 1979 | 1154.4 | 35.3 | 24.9 | 52.7 | 31.2 | 20.7 | 63.3 | 21.4 | 28.0 | 53.3 | 46.0 |
| 1980 | 1245.8 | 38.9 | 27.4 | 56.3 | 32.7 | 21.6 | 65.8 | 22.8 | 30.3 | 59.7 | 50.7 |
| 1981 | 1333.1 | 41.8 | 28.8 | 58.5 | 33.9 | 22.5 | 67.7 | 23.9 | 33.2 | 67.2 | 55.3 |
| 1982 | 1430.1 | 44.0 | 31.0 | 62.7 | 35.9 | 24.0 | 70.6 | 25.4 | 37.4 | 76.6 | 62.0 |

*(Continued)*

| Years | k0 | k1 | k2 | k3 | k4 | k5 | k6 | k7 | k8 | k9 | k10 |
|---|---|---|---|---|---|---|---|---|---|---|---|
| 1983 | 1542.8 | 48.1 | 33.8 | 68.1 | 38.8 | 26.3 | 75.1 | 27.1 | 42.6 | 83.6 | 69.1 |
| 1984 | 1681.1 | 54.5 | 37.1 | 75.2 | 43.3 | 29.2 | 83.1 | 30.0 | 48.3 | 94.4 | 79.4 |
| 1985 | 1863.5 | 70.6 | 43.6 | 84.9 | 49.6 | 32.9 | 94.3 | 34.2 | 55.2 | 115.3 | 92.8 |
| 1986 | 2061.1 | 82.6 | 50.4 | 94.1 | 55.7 | 36.1 | 107.4 | 38.1 | 62.8 | 140.3 | 109.4 |
| 1987 | 2271.8 | 98.1 | 56.0 | 103.0 | 62.5 | 39.5 | 122.2 | 42.9 | 70.6 | 165.0 | 127.4 |
| 1988 | 2514.9 | 114.5 | 64.1 | 113.6 | 68.9 | 44.6 | 140.3 | 48.2 | 78.2 | 197.5 | 148.5 |
| 1989 | 2755.3 | 132.6 | 70.8 | 125.3 | 75.1 | 49.5 | 156.3 | 53.4 | 86.0 | 229.0 | 167.1 |
| 1990 | 2986.5 | 149.9 | 76.8 | 138.2 | 81.4 | 54.6 | 172.7 | 59.6 | 94.3 | 254.6 | 187.2 |
| 1991 | 3239.7 | 165.8 | 84.1 | 151.7 | 86.5 | 59.8 | 190.2 | 65.7 | 101.4 | 277.8 | 209.9 |
| 1992 | 3551.7 | 186.2 | 94.0 | 168.5 | 93.4 | 67.6 | 210.3 | 71.8 | 109.5 | 310.6 | 245.5 |
| 1993 | 4007.6 | 215.2 | 106.0 | 191.0 | 102.3 | 77.9 | 240.3 | 79.3 | 118.4 | 354.3 | 291.5 |
| 1994 | 4488.8 | 254.0 | 120.1 | 217.1 | 112.2 | 87.6 | 269.8 | 88.6 | 127.8 | 416.2 | 340.9 |
| 1995 | 5015.5 | 301.4 | 135.4 | 249.3 | 120.8 | 97.0 | 296.1 | 98.0 | 138.7 | 493.1 | 396.6 |
| 1996 | 5564.7 | 337.7 | 152.4 | 287.8 | 130.2 | 107.8 | 320.4 | 111.2 | 150.9 | 584.9 | 454.6 |
| 1997 | 6111.0 | 376.8 | 171.6 | 332.8 | 141.3 | 118.9 | 345.3 | 122.2 | 163.1 | 675.3 | 514.0 |
| 1998 | 6676.8 | 420.7 | 191.7 | 384.9 | 159.6 | 131.2 | 371.5 | 134.6 | 179.7 | 760.9 | 584.3 |
| 1999 | 7273.2 | 469.5 | 211.2 | 439.6 | 175.2 | 144.2 | 397.8 | 148.0 | 193.1 | 841.7 | 661.0 |
| 2000 | 7876.6 | 514.6 | 233.0 | 496.6 | 191.9 | 158.5 | 428.1 | 161.6 | 205.6 | 928.2 | 744.8 |
| 2001 | 8561.9 | 566.7 | 258.0 | 555.1 | 210.1 | 172.3 | 462.8 | 177.2 | 220.6 | 1023.2 | 832.6 |
| 2002 | 9359.1 | 622.7 | 286.7 | 616.3 | 231.0 | 193.2 | 504.3 | 194.9 | 240.3 | 1122.7 | 932.1 |
| 2003 | 10349.2 | 683.6 | 322.0 | 686.9 | 258.4 | 226.5 | 563.2 | 216.9 | 258.0 | 1243.3 | 1060.5 |
| 2004 | 11512.9 | 752.1 | 365.8 | 771.7 | 292.1 | 275.0 | 655.9 | 243.3 | 281.6 | 1384.5 | 1223.0 |
| 2005 | 12790.2 | 846.0 | 415.6 | 864.6 | 337.9 | 346.6 | 761.5 | 279.4 | 308.8 | 1546.1 | 1396.9 |

| Years | k11 | k12 | k13 | k14 | k15 | k16 | k17 | k18 | k19 | k20 | k21 |
|---|---|---|---|---|---|---|---|---|---|---|---|
| 1952 | 2.1 | 2.1 | 1.2 | 2.4 | 4.8 | 4.6 | 3.3 | 2.6 | 0.3 | 3.0 | 0.5 |
| 1953 | 2.4 | 2.3 | 1.3 | 2.6 | 5.3 | 5.0 | 3.5 | 2.8 | 0.3 | 3.2 | 0.6 |
| 1954 | 2.6 | 2.5 | 1.4 | 2.8 | 5.8 | 5.5 | 3.9 | 3.1 | 0.4 | 3.5 | 0.6 |
| 1955 | 3.0 | 3.0 | 1.7 | 2.9 | 7.1 | 6.3 | 4.3 | 3.4 | 0.4 | 3.8 | 0.7 |
| 1956 | 3.4 | 3.5 | 2.5 | 3.1 | 8.5 | 7.3 | 5.0 | 3.8 | 0.5 | 4.3 | 0.8 |
| 1957 | 4.0 | 4.0 | 3.0 | 3.9 | 9.9 | 8.6 | 6.0 | 4.4 | 0.6 | 4.6 | 0.9 |
| 1958 | 5.3 | 5.1 | 4.0 | 4.9 | 11.7 | 11.0 | 7.6 | 5.9 | 0.7 | 5.2 | 1.0 |
| 1959 | 6.9 | 6.2 | 5.3 | 6.2 | 14.0 | 13.9 | 9.3 | 7.9 | 0.8 | 6.1 | 1.1 |
| 1960 | 8.1 | 7.0 | 6.6 | 8.1 | 15.8 | 15.8 | 10.6 | 9.3 | 0.9 | 6.8 | 1.2 |
| 1961 | 8.3 | 7.1 | 6.5 | 8.3 | 16.0 | 15.5 | 10.6 | 9.2 | 1.1 | 7.0 | 1.4 |
| 1962 | 8.5 | 6.9 | 6.2 | 8.4 | 15.9 | 15.1 | 10.5 | 8.9 | 1.3 | 7.1 | 1.5 |
| 1963 | 8.8 | 6.8 | 5.9 | 8.5 | 16.0 | 15.3 | 10.7 | 9.0 | 1.5 | 7.5 | 1.7 |
| 1964 | 9.3 | 7.1 | 6.2 | 8.6 | 16.3 | 15.7 | 10.7 | 9.4 | 1.8 | 7.8 | 1.9 |
| 1965 | 10.0 | 7.5 | 6.5 | 8.9 | 17.4 | 16.3 | 11.2 | 9.9 | 2.1 | 8.2 | 2.1 |
| 1966 | 10.7 | 7.8 | 7.0 | 9.4 | 19.0 | 17.5 | 11.8 | 10.7 | 2.4 | 8.9 | 2.3 |
| 1967 | 11.3 | 7.9 | 6.8 | 9.7 | 20.3 | 18.4 | 12.0 | 11.2 | 2.8 | 9.1 | 2.5 |
| 1968 | 11.8 | 8.0 | 6.7 | 10.1 | 21.3 | 18.9 | 12.1 | 11.6 | 3.3 | 9.5 | 2.8 |
| 1969 | 12.7 | 8.2 | 6.7 | 10.5 | 22.9 | 20.0 | 12.8 | 12.3 | 3.9 | 10.3 | 3.1 |
| 1970 | 13.7 | 8.8 | 7.3 | 11.6 | 24.8 | 22.3 | 14.7 | 13.7 | 4.6 | 11.2 | 3.5 |
| 1971 | 14.8 | 9.5 | 8.3 | 13.0 | 26.8 | 24.1 | 17.0 | 15.6 | 5.4 | 12.3 | 3.9 |
| 1972 | 16.1 | 10.2 | 9.1 | 13.9 | 29.0 | 25.9 | 18.2 | 17.0 | 6.3 | 13.4 | 4.3 |
| 1973 | 17.4 | 11.0 | 9.8 | 14.7 | 31.8 | 27.9 | 19.8 | 18.3 | 7.4 | 14.6 | 4.8 |

(*Continued*)

| Years | k11 | k12 | k13 | k14 | k15 | k16 | k17 | k18 | k19 | k20 | k21 |
|---|---|---|---|---|---|---|---|---|---|---|---|
| 1974 | 18.6 | 11.8 | 10.2 | 15.4 | 33.1 | 30.0 | 21.2 | 19.2 | 8.7 | 15.7 | 5.3 |
| 1975 | 19.6 | 12.5 | 10.7 | 15.9 | 36.8 | 32.3 | 23.6 | 20.3 | 10.1 | 17.2 | 5.9 |
| 1976 | 20.6 | 13.3 | 10.8 | 16.6 | 40.6 | 33.9 | 26.0 | 21.1 | 11.9 | 18.7 | 6.6 |
| 1977 | 22.1 | 14.0 | 11.2 | 17.2 | 44.9 | 36.4 | 28.6 | 22.2 | 13.9 | 20.3 | 7.3 |
| 1978 | 23.9 | 14.7 | 12.6 | 18.7 | 49.2 | 38.8 | 30.3 | 24.4 | 16.9 | 22.1 | 8.2 |
| 1979 | 25.8 | 15.4 | 13.9 | 20.5 | 53.3 | 41.3 | 32.0 | 26.1 | 19.5 | 23.5 | 9.1 |
| 1980 | 28.5 | 16.1 | 15.5 | 22.0 | 58.0 | 44.0 | 33.2 | 27.5 | 22.5 | 25.1 | 10.1 |
| 1981 | 31.2 | 16.6 | 17.1 | 23.3 | 62.1 | 47.1 | 34.8 | 28.9 | 26.7 | 26.6 | 11.2 |
| 1982 | 34.4 | 17.9 | 18.9 | 24.8 | 67.6 | 49.7 | 37.4 | 30.7 | 31.4 | 28.0 | 12.4 |
| 1983 | 37.3 | 19.7 | 20.7 | 26.4 | 73.7 | 54.9 | 40.1 | 32.8 | 35.9 | 29.4 | 13.8 |
| 1984 | 42.8 | 22.4 | 22.9 | 28.6 | 81.9 | 60.7 | 44.1 | 34.9 | 41.3 | 31.0 | 15.4 |
| 1985 | 50.5 | 26.2 | 26.2 | 31.4 | 92.7 | 68.1 | 50.0 | 38.4 | 50.0 | 33.9 | 17.1 |
| 1986 | 59.8 | 30.4 | 30.2 | 34.6 | 104.1 | 75.2 | 55.8 | 42.7 | 58.7 | 37.1 | 19.0 |
| 1987 | 70.7 | 34.5 | 34.5 | 38.2 | 119.0 | 83.5 | 61.9 | 47.6 | 68.4 | 40.3 | 21.1 |
| 1988 | 82.6 | 38.7 | 38.9 | 42.7 | 135.4 | 94.1 | 69.2 | 53.3 | 80.3 | 43.6 | 23.5 |
| 1989 | 92.6 | 42.2 | 43.1 | 46.9 | 152.1 | 104.7 | 74.4 | 57.7 | 92.2 | 46.4 | 26.1 |
| 1990 | 99.9 | 46.0 | 47.3 | 50.1 | 169.7 | 114.9 | 81.0 | 61.7 | 104.4 | 48.6 | 28.3 |
| 1991 | 110.2 | 49.6 | 52.6 | 53.9 | 191.9 | 126.2 | 87.6 | 66.6 | 118.3 | 51.6 | 30.7 |
| 1992 | 127.2 | 54.6 | 60.0 | 59.9 | 220.3 | 141.2 | 96.0 | 73.4 | 141.8 | 57.2 | 35.2 |
| 1993 | 153.7 | 62.2 | 71.7 | 67.6 | 257.4 | 157.0 | 107.3 | 82.0 | 176.9 | 65.3 | 40.5 |
| 1994 | 183.2 | 72.0 | 88.5 | 75.6 | 296.6 | 174.2 | 122.3 | 92.2 | 216.6 | 74.4 | 46.8 |
| 1995 | 223.4 | 83.5 | 108.3 | 84.3 | 339.8 | 195.4 | 140.4 | 104.4 | 258.2 | 85.1 | 52.4 |
| 1996 | 266.2 | 96.8 | 130.8 | 93.5 | 390.0 | 219.2 | 160.6 | 116.8 | 299.4 | 95.3 | 56.9 |
| 1997 | 312.4 | 110.9 | 155.9 | 104.8 | 448.1 | 246.1 | 185.2 | 130.7 | 337.4 | 105.6 | 61.2 |
| 1998 | 364.2 | 125.8 | 184.7 | 117.0 | 512.0 | 276.3 | 213.0 | 146.4 | 380.3 | 117.3 | 66.1 |
| 1999 | 416.2 | 139.7 | 215.6 | 130.1 | 580.2 | 308.4 | 244.4 | 162.4 | 426.6 | 129.3 | 71.5 |
| 2000 | 469.3 | 154.5 | 247.6 | 143.0 | 658.1 | 342.5 | 277.0 | 180.0 | 472.6 | 142.0 | 77.3 |
| 2001 | 525.1 | 170.5 | 281.5 | 157.6 | 739.6 | 378.2 | 308.3 | 200.1 | 523.7 | 156.6 | 82.6 |
| 2002 | 591.0 | 188.5 | 318.2 | 176.0 | 827.8 | 417.4 | 339.1 | 222.4 | 577.9 | 173.3 | 88.2 |
| 2003 | 677.4 | 208.0 | 359.8 | 201.9 | 927.9 | 460.2 | 370.5 | 246.1 | 649.9 | 192.9 | 94.8 |
| 2004 | 780.3 | 234.4 | 407.3 | 232.7 | 1054.4 | 515.5 | 408.6 | 275.5 | 735.6 | 216.9 | 102.1 |
| 2005 | 891.6 | 266.0 | 453.9 | 266.0 | 1198.5 | 582.6 | 448.5 | 307.9 | 849.8 | 247.4 | 110.6 |

| Years | k22 | k23 | k24 | k25 | k26 | k27 | k28 | k29 | k30 | k31 |
|---|---|---|---|---|---|---|---|---|---|---|
| 1952 | 0.4 | 4.0 | 2.0 | 2.8 | 0.0 | 2.9 | 7.7 | 1.0 | 0.8 | 1.8 |
| 1953 | 0.4 | 4.4 | 2.1 | 3.1 | 0.1 | 3.2 | 8.2 | 1.1 | 0.9 | 1.9 |
| 1954 | 0.5 | 4.8 | 2.3 | 3.3 | 0.1 | 3.4 | 8.6 | 1.2 | 0.9 | 2.1 |
| 1955 | 0.5 | 5.6 | 2.4 | 3.6 | 0.1 | 4.0 | 9.5 | 1.4 | 1.0 | 2.4 |
| 1956 | 0.6 | 6.6 | 2.6 | 4.0 | 0.1 | 4.5 | 10.3 | 1.8 | 1.1 | 2.7 |
| 1957 | 0.7 | 7.8 | 3.0 | 4.4 | 0.1 | 4.9 | 11.1 | 2.1 | 1.2 | 3.0 |
| 1958 | 0.8 | 9.6 | 4.0 | 5.2 | 0.1 | 5.7 | 11.7 | 2.2 | 1.4 | 3.5 |
| 1959 | 0.9 | 12.5 | 4.8 | 6.3 | 0.1 | 7.2 | 12.7 | 2.7 | 1.8 | 4.2 |
| 1960 | 1.0 | 14.3 | 5.3 | 7.5 | 0.1 | 8.6 | 13.7 | 3.3 | 2.2 | 5.1 |
| 1961 | 1.1 | 13.5 | 5.2 | 7.7 | 0.1 | 8.7 | 14.3 | 3.2 | 2.3 | 5.6 |
| 1962 | 1.3 | 12.4 | 5.1 | 7.7 | 0.1 | 8.6 | 14.8 | 3.2 | 2.3 | 5.8 |
| 1963 | 1.4 | 12.2 | 5.2 | 7.8 | 0.2 | 8.6 | 15.3 | 3.2 | 2.4 | 6.1 |
| 1964 | 1.6 | 12.5 | 5.5 | 8.2 | 0.2 | 8.9 | 16.0 | 3.2 | 2.5 | 6.6 |

(Continued)

| Years | k22 | k23 | k24 | k25 | k26 | k27 | k28 | k29 | k30 | k31 |
|---|---|---|---|---|---|---|---|---|---|---|
| 1965 | 1.8 | 14.2 | 6.3 | 8.9 | 0.2 | 9.5 | 16.7 | 3.3 | 2.8 | 7.1 |
| 1966 | 2.0 | 17.2 | 7.0 | 9.9 | 0.2 | 10.6 | 17.3 | 3.5 | 3.1 | 7.6 |
| 1967 | 2.3 | 17.9 | 7.3 | 10.4 | 0.3 | 11.0 | 17.9 | 3.6 | 3.4 | 7.9 |
| 1968 | 2.6 | 17.4 | 7.6 | 10.8 | 0.3 | 11.3 | 18.5 | 3.7 | 3.6 | 8.2 |
| 1969 | 2.9 | 18.7 | 8.0 | 11.7 | 0.3 | 12.5 | 19.3 | 3.9 | 3.9 | 8.6 |
| 1970 | 3.3 | 21.8 | 9.2 | 12.8 | 0.4 | 14.4 | 20.2 | 4.1 | 4.4 | 9.2 |
| 1971 | 3.7 | 24.0 | 10.8 | 13.8 | 0.4 | 17.0 | 21.2 | 4.4 | 5.0 | 9.9 |
| 1972 | 4.2 | 26.0 | 11.7 | 14.8 | 0.5 | 19.4 | 22.3 | 5.2 | 5.6 | 10.5 |
| 1973 | 4.7 | 27.8 | 12.6 | 16.0 | 0.5 | 21.0 | 23.5 | 5.5 | 6.2 | 11.3 |
| 1974 | 5.3 | 29.0 | 13.0 | 17.1 | 0.6 | 22.5 | 24.9 | 5.7 | 6.7 | 12.1 |
| 1975 | 6.0 | 31.8 | 13.3 | 18.3 | 0.7 | 24.0 | 26.6 | 6.0 | 7.5 | 13.0 |
| 1976 | 6.8 | 32.5 | 13.6 | 18.9 | 0.7 | 25.1 | 28.1 | 6.3 | 8.1 | 13.8 |
| 1977 | 7.6 | 34.7 | 14.2 | 20.0 | 0.8 | 26.7 | 29.5 | 6.8 | 8.9 | 14.7 |
| 1978 | 8.6 | 37.9 | 15.3 | 21.7 | 0.9 | 28.8 | 31.1 | 7.5 | 9.7 | 16.1 |
| 1979 | 9.7 | 41.2 | 16.3 | 23.4 | 1.1 | 31.0 | 32.6 | 8.3 | 10.5 | 17.6 |
| 1980 | 11.0 | 44.4 | 17.0 | 25.0 | 1.2 | 32.6 | 33.5 | 8.9 | 11.1 | 19.1 |
| 1981 | 12.4 | 46.5 | 17.5 | 26.4 | 1.3 | 34.4 | 34.2 | 9.3 | 11.5 | 20.7 |
| 1982 | 14.0 | 49.0 | 18.2 | 28.3 | 1.5 | 37.0 | 35.2 | 10.0 | 12.0 | 22.7 |
| 1983 | 15.8 | 51.8 | 19.0 | 30.0 | 1.7 | 39.4 | 36.4 | 10.6 | 12.8 | 24.7 |
| 1984 | 17.8 | 55.5 | 20.2 | 32.5 | 1.9 | 42.8 | 37.9 | 11.3 | 13.7 | 27.4 |
| 1985 | 20.1 | 60.4 | 21.8 | 35.5 | 2.1 | 48.8 | 40.0 | 12.5 | 15.2 | 30.9 |
| 1986 | 22.6 | 65.1 | 23.5 | 38.5 | 2.4 | 55.0 | 42.9 | 13.5 | 16.9 | 34.4 |
| 1987 | 25.5 | 70.9 | 25.3 | 41.3 | 2.6 | 61.7 | 45.7 | 14.8 | 18.7 | 38.2 |
| 1988 | 28.8 | 77.4 | 27.3 | 44.9 | 3.0 | 69.6 | 49.0 | 16.0 | 20.6 | 42.7 |
| 1989 | 32.5 | 81.7 | 29.4 | 48.7 | 3.3 | 78.7 | 52.9 | 16.9 | 22.4 | 47.9 |
| 1990 | 36.7 | 85.6 | 31.2 | 52.4 | 3.7 | 85.9 | 57.1 | 17.7 | 24.3 | 53.3 |
| 1991 | 41.3 | 90.3 | 33.1 | 57.6 | 4.2 | 93.4 | 61.4 | 18.6 | 26.3 | 59.3 |
| 1992 | 46.6 | 96.7 | 35.4 | 64.5 | 4.7 | 100.3 | 66.1 | 19.7 | 28.3 | 68.1 |
| 1993 | 52.6 | 107.2 | 38.2 | 73.5 | 5.3 | 112.1 | 71.3 | 20.9 | 30.8 | 79.3 |
| 1994 | 59.4 | 119.0 | 40.7 | 82.8 | 6.0 | 124.5 | 76.9 | 22.1 | 33.0 | 92.1 |
| 1995 | 66.5 | 132.0 | 44.4 | 92.0 | 7.1 | 137.8 | 83.2 | 23.6 | 35.3 | 104.8 |
| 1996 | 74.3 | 153.9 | 48.4 | 102.2 | 7.9 | 151.5 | 90.0 | 25.4 | 37.9 | 114.6 |
| 1997 | 84.8 | 167.1 | 53.2 | 114.1 | 8.7 | 164.2 | 98.1 | 27.7 | 40.6 | 125.7 |
| 1998 | 96.9 | 183.0 | 59.0 | 126.7 | 9.6 | 180.6 | 107.2 | 30.3 | 44.2 | 139.8 |
| 1999 | 108.7 | 199.6 | 65.8 | 139.0 | 10.6 | 198.2 | 117.5 | 33.1 | 48.3 | 151.1 |
| 2000 | 122.8 | 215.3 | 73.8 | 150.8 | 11.7 | 220.7 | 128.8 | 36.3 | 53.3 | 161.4 |
| 2001 | 133.1 | 240.7 | 83.5 | 166.8 | 12.7 | 246.1 | 140.2 | 40.5 | 59.4 | 175.6 |
| 2002 | 145.9 | 270.2 | 93.8 | 181.7 | 14.3 | 274.9 | 154.4 | 45.4 | 66.7 | 191.6 |
| 2003 | 163.8 | 304.3 | 105.4 | 201.4 | 16.8 | 312.8 | 170.1 | 51.2 | 76.0 | 212.0 |
| 2004 | 185.4 | 342.6 | 117.9 | 224.6 | 21.0 | 357.6 | 187.5 | 57.1 | 86.4 | 235.9 |
| 2005 | 210.5 | 389.0 | 131.8 | 256.7 | 25.2 | 407.1 | 209.4 | 63.6 | 98.9 | 262.4 |

# 3
# Revisiting the Productivity Debate

The role of total factor productivity (TFP) in economic growth has been fiercely debated since the emergence of several studies which questioned the sustainability of rapid economic growth in East Asia in the 1980s and 1990s.[1] Though the dispute has never been resolved, it did generate a huge literature investigating the contribution of TFP to economic growth with a particular focus on the emerging Asian economies.[2] Some of the literature has dealt exclusively with the Chinese economy which has achieved impressive growth since the late 1970s when an economic reform programme was implemented throughout the nation.[3] China's growth resembles the patterns of development in other East Asian economies, allowing the literature on productivity studies to be extended to cover the Chinese economy.[4] But China is also different from other high-performing economies in Asia due to the fact that, before economic reforms, the country had had a centrally planned economic system for decades. Studies of China's recent growth may have important policy implications for many other transitional economies as well as for further economic growth in China in the coming decade.

The objective of this chapter is to revisit the debate about the role of productivity in economic growth using China as the setting, to provide the latest assessment with a focus on the past decade and to draw policy implications for sustainable economic growth in China in the near future. Specifically, a stochastic frontier production function is proposed and applied to Chinese regional data over the period of 1992–2004. It is found that TFP growth on average accounted for about 27 per cent of China's growth which is much smaller than the similar estimates for Japan (50 per cent) and Germany (58 per cent).[5] Thus, economic growth in China is still driven by massive injection of factor inputs, in particular capital formation. To achieve the goal of sustainable growth, China has to pursue an alternative model in which productivity is the main driving force for economic growth.

The rest of the chapter first presents some stylized facts about China's recent economic growth. This is followed by a description of the analytical framework. Subsequently, the empirical model and data issues are presented. The chapter then discusses the findings from empirical estimations. Finally, some concluding remarks are reported.

## 3.1   Stylized facts about China's recent growth

Studies of China's rapid economic growth are abundant. A survey of the literature is beyond the scope of this study.[6] Instead, this section highlights some stylized facts about China's economic growth in recent years. These are key characteristics associated with recent developments in the Chinese economy.

### 3.1.1   Managing growth through learning

The recent wave of economic growth began with the famous 'Southern Tour' taken by China's former leader Deng Xiaoping in early 1992. Since then, China has enjoyed robust economic growth with a real rate over 10 per cent per annum (see Figure 3.1). This is a great success given the fact that China's growth had gone through 'boom–bust' cycles in

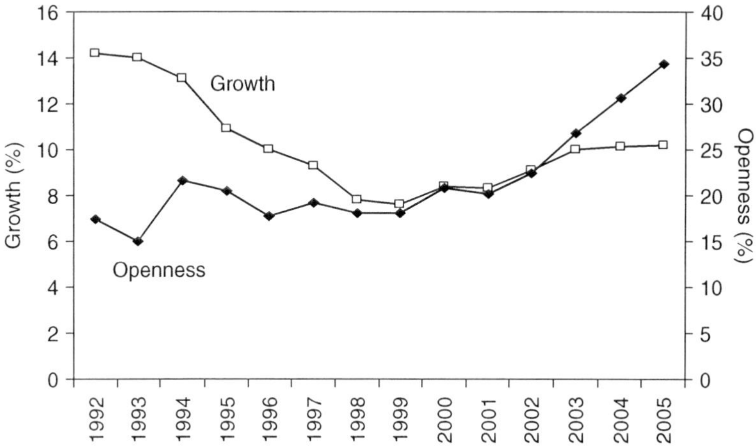


*Figure 3.1*   Rates of growth and openness indicators of China, 1992–2005

Notes: Growth rates are real rates of GDP growth. Openness is defined as the ratio of total value of exports over GDP. All raw data are drawn from the National Bureau of Statistics (2006).

the 1980s and that the world economy suffered from the American economic recession in the early 1990s and the Asian financial crisis in 1997. It is apparent that Chinese policy makers have learnt a lot from their experience in the earlier years of economic reforms and managed well to maintain a viable growth pattern in the 1990s and beyond. Since late 2003, the Chinese economy has shown signs of overheating and hence the central government has acted cautiously to cool it down. As a result of prompt policy responses, the Chinese economy maintained the same trend of growth in 2004 and 2005 according to the National Bureau of Statistics (2006).

### 3.1.2  Growing through opening

It has been argued that economic openness promotes growth (Harrison, 1996; Edwards, 1998). China is no exception. China's recent growth has been associated with increasing economic openness. This is clearly demonstrated in Figure 3.1 which shows the indicator of economic openness over time though the measurement of openness is debatable.[7] In particular, during 2001–5, China has made tremendous efforts to liberalize the economy and to comply with WTO membership requirements.[8] These changes have partly contributed to the rapid increase in exports (and also imports) as shown in Figure 3.1. In addition, China has for years been the world's second largest recipient of foreign direct investment (FDI), behind only the United States, eventually overtaking the US to become the largest FDI hosting country in 2002. With the removal of more barriers to foreign investors under China's WTO agreement, more FDI is expected to flow into the country in the coming decade. It can be anticipated that the Chinese economy will become more integrated with the world economies.

### 3.1.3  Growing through restructuring

Twenty-five years ago, the Chinese economy was very much fully owned and run by the governments at various levels (see Table 3.1).[9] Economic affairs were dominated by the state-owned enterprises (SOEs). Since 1978, China has successfully managed the restructuring of the SOEs. As a result, the state has gradually withdrawn from the corporate sector though the process is not yet fully completed. State ownership has since changed from governments' direct involvement in business management to controls largely through state shareholding. The state ownership now only accounts for a very small share in some sectors such as construction and manufacturing (see Table 3.1). Overall, the state sector now employs less than 10 per cent of China's workforce according to Table 3.1.

*Table 3.1*   Employment shares (%) of the state sector

| Economic sectors | 1978 | 1992 | 2002 |
| --- | --- | --- | --- |
| Agriculture | 2.7 | 1.9 | 1.1 |
| Wholesaling, retailing and catering | 79.6 | 29.0 | 6.4 |
| Construction | 52.3 | 19.5 | 6.7 |
| Manufacturing | 45.9 | 34.8 | 10.2 |
| Transport and telecoms | 62.0 | 37.2 | 20.7 |
| Social services | 59.8 | 37.6 | 24.6 |
| Real estate, etc. | 90.3 | 79.9 | 41.8 |
| Finance and insurance | 55.3 | 60.1 | 46.8 |
| Mining and quarrying | 90.2 | 79.2 | 53.8 |
| Electricity, gas and water | 95.3 | 84.8 | 65.6 |
| R&D services | 98.9 | 75.1 | 70.6 |
| Health, sports and social welfare | 50.4 | 56.6 | 74.9 |
| Education, arts and culture | 61.7 | 69.9 | 80.2 |
| Geological surveying | 99.4 | 88.5 | 83.0 |
| Public services, etc. | 89.3 | 75.8 | 84.7 |
| China | 18.6 | 16.5 | 9.4 |

*Notes*: The share figures are calculated using data from the National Bureau of Statistics (2006). Data from 2003 onwards are not available from the NBS.

### 3.1.4   Growing through efficiency improvement

While the contribution of TFP to economic growth is controversial, the improvement of labour productivity in China is very evident according to Figure 3.2. Labour productivity in constant prices has been rising steadily since 1992. There is, however, variation among the sectors. The fastest growth in labour productivity is recorded in the manufacturing sector. This finding is consistent with the rapid growth of international competitiveness and hence the expansion of China's exports. The agricultural sector has shown the slowest growth. This may be partly due to the existence of millions of surplus labour in the farming sector. It may also be the result of the failure of government policies which have ignored the development of the rural sector in recent years. As a result, the current government in China has initiated some major policy changes in order to boost the development of the rural sector.

In summary, China's economic growth in recent years has been characterized by rapid increases in openness, privatization and efficiency. Chinese policy makers have learnt a lot from their past experience and hence have managed to maintain a stable and sustainable rate of economic growth in the past decade. The following sections aim to

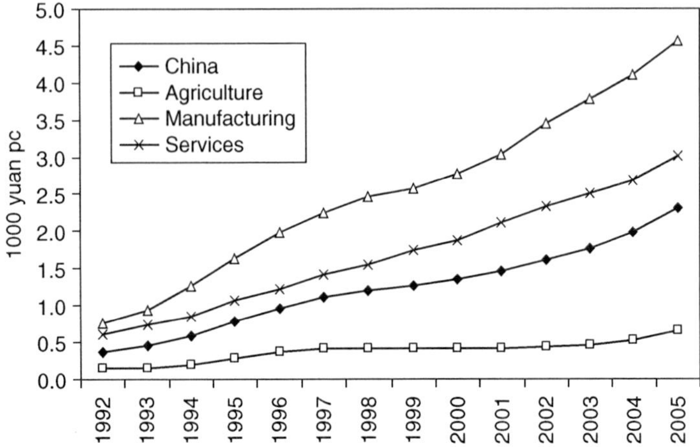


*Figure 3.2*   Labour productivity in the Chinese economy

*Notes*: Labour productivity is measured in thousands of yuan per worker in 1991 constant prices. All numbers are derived using data from the National Bureau of Statistics (2006).

introduce an analytical framework and to examine how those factors discussed have affected China's growth in the past decade.

## 3.2   The analytical framework

To further understand economic growth in China and particularly the role of productivity, a stochastic frontier model is employed in this study.[10] To introduce the technique, assume that several factor inputs, $x$, are used to produce a single output, $y$. Then a standard stochastic frontier production function can be expressed as

$$\ln y = \ln f(x; \alpha) + v - u \tag{3.1}$$

where $\alpha$ is a vector of parameters to be estimated, $v$ is the standard white noise with zero mean and constant variance, $\sigma_v^2$, and $u$ is assumed to capture the inefficiency effect in the production process. The latter is assumed to be non-negative, and independent of $v$. Given equation (3.1), the technical efficiency score (*TE*) can be defined as

$$TE = \exp(-u) \tag{3.2}$$

which can be estimated using its conditional expectation value, i.e. $E(\exp(-u)|v - u)$. The system of equations (3.1) and (3.2) is often employed to decompose output growth into three components, i.e. technological progress, factor input contributions and technical efficiency changes. That is,

$$\mathring{y} = f_t + f_x \mathring{x} + \mathring{TE} \tag{3.3}$$

where $\circ$ denotes percentage changes. $f_t$ and $f_x$ are partial derivatives of $f$ with respect to $t$ and $x$, respectively. Equation (3.3) can be derived by manipulating equations (3.1) and (3.2). According to the conventional definition that productivity growth is the difference between output growth and factor input changes, the following equation can then be obtained:

$$\mathring{TFP} = \left(1 - \frac{1}{\Sigma f_x}\right) \sum f_x \mathring{x} + f_t + \mathring{TE} \tag{3.4}$$

That is, without constant returns to scale assumption, TFP growth is decomposed into three components, i.e. scale efficiency – the first item on the right-hand side of equation (3.4) – technological progress ($f_t$) and efficiency changes ($\mathring{TE}$). Under the assumption of constant returns to scale, equation (3.4) implies that TFP growth is the sum of the rates of technological progress and efficiency changes. Furthermore, if constant returns to scale and zero technical inefficiency are assumed, the system of equations (3.1)–(3.4) becomes the traditional Solow growth accounting framework in which TFP growth and technological progress are identical.

While this study employs a parametric econometric technique, the decomposition in equation (3.4) can also be derived using non-parametric approaches such as data envelopment analysis (DEA).[11] The parametric method employed here has the advantage (over the non-parametric one) of conducting statistical tests. It has been widely applied to analyse economic performance in Yugoslavia (Nishimizu and Page, 1982), Turkey (Taymaz and Saatci, 1997) and China (Wu, 2003), to cite just a few. The key feature of the above-described technique is that performance is measured in terms of output and factor inputs only. However, economic performance is often affected by the environment in which economic activities take place. For this reason, the system of equations (3.1)–(3.4) is extended to incorporate the impact of a vector of exogenous factors, $z$, that influences the production process according to which inputs are converted into output. The elements of $z$ represent features of the environment in which production occurs and they are often called the environmental influences or factors. In this study, economic performance in China is assumed to be affected by factors such as the level of reforms, economic openness and infrastructure development.[12] It should be pointed out that the selection of these three factors is dictated by the availability of data.

In the literature, two approaches have been proposed to assess the impact of environmental factors on economic performance. The first is the so-called two-step approach. In the first step, a stochastic frontier model such as equation (3.1) is estimated and the estimated parameters and fitted residuals are used to derive technical efficiency indexes following equation (3.2), for instance, and other performance indicators. These indexes are then regressed against the exogenous environmental factors considered in the second step. Examples of this type of study include Ali and Flinn (1989), Kalirajan (1990) and Mester (1993, 1997). This approach has, however, been criticized for serious econometric problems (Kumbhakar and Lovell, 2000, p. 264). The second approach can accordingly be called a one-step approach which incorporates the environmental influences directly into the analytical framework. Thus, the tasks can be completed in one step only. The literature applying the one-step method is still growing but also full of controversy. This study falls into the one-step literature.[13]

To begin with a general model, it is assumed that the environmental factors can affect both the structure of production technology and the inefficiency component of the production function. Therefore, the general model incorporating environmental influences in stochastic frontier production functions can be expressed as

$$\ln y = \ln f(x, z; \alpha, \beta) + v - u(x, z; \eta, \delta) \tag{3.5}$$

where $\alpha$, $\beta$, $\eta$ and $\delta$ are parameters to be estimated. Equation (3.5) is clearly a straightforward extension of equation (3.1). The major feature of equation (3.5) is that the environmental variables, $z$, appear in both the main body of the model, $f(\cdot)$, and the inefficiency part, $u(\cdot)$. However, whether $z$ is present in $f(\cdot)$ or $u(\cdot)$ can be statistically tested in empirical analysis.

## 3.3   The empirical model and data issues

### 3.3.1   The empirical model

The empirical analysis is based on a panel database which covers 29 Chinese regions over 13 years.[14] It is assumed that three inputs ($x$'s), human capital, domestic capital and foreign capital, are employed to produce one output $y$, the gross regional product (GRP), and that the production is subjected to the influence of three environmental factors ($z$'s), that is, infrastructure ($z_1$), economic reform ($z_2$) and openness ($z_3$). In logarithmic form, the general model can be specified as follows:

$$\ln y_{it} = \alpha^0 + \sum_j \alpha_j^0 D_j + \alpha_1 t + \alpha_2 t^2 + \sum_j (\beta_j^0 + t\beta_j) \ln x_{ijt}$$

$$+ \sum_{j,k} \beta_{jk} \ln x_{ijt} \ln x_{ikt} + \sum_j (\beta_{0j} + t\beta_j^1) z_{ijt} + v_{it} - u_{it} \qquad (3.6)$$

where $u_{it} = \eta^0 + \sum_h \eta_h^0 t D_h + \sum_k (\eta_k^1 + t\eta_k) z_{ikt} + \sum_j (\delta_j^0 + t\delta_j) \ln x_{ijt} + e_{it}$, $j$ and $k$ take the value of 1, 2 and 3, $h$ ranges from 1 to 4. $e_{it}$ is assumed to be independently distributed, obtained by truncation of a normal distribution with zero mean and constant variance of $\sigma^2$, such as that $u_{it}$ is non-negative and obtained by truncation of the normal distribution with mean $\eta^0 + \sum_h \eta_h^0 t D_h + \sum_k (\eta_k^1 + t\eta_k) z_{ikt} + \sum_j (\delta_j^0 + t\delta_j) \ln x_{ijt}$, and variance of $\sigma^2$. Four dummy variables are introduced to capture the difference between China's four geographically classified regions, i.e. western ($D_1$), central ($D_2$), coastal ($D_3$) and the three large cities ($D_4$).[15]

### 3.3.2 Data issues

The selection of variables included in equation (3.6) is dictated by the availability of China's regional data. The regional data series for the period 1992–2004 are either drawn directly from the Chinese statistical publications or derived using data from the same sources. A brief description of these variables is presented as follows:

- The dependent variable takes the value of GRP expressed in constant prices.
- Domestic capital ($K_d$) is the stock of domestic capital which is also expressed in constant prices. More details about the estimation of regional capital stock are presented in Chapter 2.
- Foreign capital ($K_f$) is the stock of foreign capital estimated following the perpetual inventory method by assuming a rate of depreciation of 4 per cent.[16]
- Human capital ($K_h$) is the product of the number of employed persons and the average years of schooling per head in China (see the appendix to this chapter for more details).
- The first environmental factor ($z_1$) is an indicator of infrastructure development. It is defined as the geometric mean of the length of

highway per square kilometre of land and length of railway per square kilometre of land. The reason for considering both railways and highways is to avoid the bias due to the dominance of one of the facilities in some regions.

- The second environmental factor ($z_2$) is an index of economic reform or marketization. It is defined as the ratio of non-state sector employment over total employment.[17]
- The third environmental factor ($z_3$) is a measure of economic openness defined simply as the ratio of the value of exports over the value of the gross regional product.[18]

## 3.4  Interpretation of the findings

Given the databases described in the preceding section, equation (3.6) can be estimated by the maximum likelihood method.[19] Before reporting the final results, several optional models are considered and tested, depending on how the environmental factors affect the production technology and efficiency performance. That is

- Option I: the environmental variables have no effect on efficiency performance ($\eta_k = \eta_k^1 = 0$ for all $k$).
- Option II: the environmental variables have no effect on the structure of production technology ($\beta_{0j} = \beta_j^1 = 0$ for all $j$).
- Option III: the environmental variables have no effect on either efficiency performance or the structure of production technology ($\eta_k = \eta_k^1 = \beta_{0j} = \beta_j^1 = 0$ for all $k$ and $j$).

The results of statistical tests of the optional models against the general model are reported in Table 3.2. According to this table, the general model cannot be rejected at the level of 5 per cent. Thus, the empirical analysis is based on the general model. The estimation results of the general model or the retained model are reported in Table 3.3. The estimates of most parameters are statistically significant. The inefficiency component contributes to a large part (about 83 per cent) of the variation in the variance of the combined error term. The impacts of the environmental variables on growth and efficiency are, however, not very clear as there are many cross-product terms. The estimated coefficients of the dummy variables imply that the coastal region and three large cities have performed better than the central and western regions, with the latter being the worst performer.

*Table 3.2*   Statistical testing results

| Null hypothesis ($H_0$) | LL | $\chi^2$ | df | CV (5%) | Decision |
|---|---|---|---|---|---|
| I ($\eta_k = \eta_k^1 = 0$) | 527.55 | 140.47 | 6 | 16.81 | Reject $H_0$ |
| II ($\beta_{0j} = \beta_j^1 = 0$) | 470.92 | 253.73 | 15 | 30.58 | Reject $H_0$ |
| III ($\eta_k = \eta_k^1 = \beta_{0j} = \beta_j^1 = 0$) | 402.16 | 391.26 | 21 | 38.93 | Reject $H_0$ |
| General model | 597.78 | | | | |

*Notes*: $j$ and $k$ range from 1 to 3. LL = log-likelihood value. CV (5%) = the critical value at 5%. The $\chi^2$ value is calculated using $-2(LL_r - LL_g)$ which has approximately a $\chi^2$ or mixed $\chi^2$ distribution with the number of restrictions as the degree of freedom. $LL_r$ and $LL_g$ are the values of the restricted and general models, respectively.

Given the empirical specification in equation (3.6) and the estimation results in Table 3.3, each component of productivity growth can be derived using the following equations:

$$\overset{\circ}{TP}_{it} = \alpha_1 + 2\alpha_2 t + \sum_j \beta_j \ln x_{ijt} + \sum_j \beta_j^1 z_{ij}$$
$$- \Omega_{it} \left( \sum_h \eta_h^0 D_h + \sum_k \eta_k z_{ikt} + \sum_j \delta_j \ln x_{ijt} \right) \tag{3.7}$$

$$\overset{\circ}{TE}_{it} = \frac{TE_{it}}{TE_{i,t-1}} - 1 \tag{3.8}$$

$$\overset{\circ}{SE}_{it} = \left( 1 - \frac{1}{\sum_j f_j} \right) \sum_j f_j \overset{\circ}{x}_{ijt} \tag{3.9}$$

where $\Omega_{it} = 1 - (\phi/\Phi_{u_{it}/\sigma - \sigma} - \phi/\Phi_{u_{it}/\sigma})/\sigma$, $\phi$ and $\Phi$ represent the density and distribution functions of a standard normal random variable, respectively, and $f_j = \beta_j^0 + \beta_j t + 2\sum_k \beta_{jk} \ln x_{jkt} - \Omega_{jt}(\delta_j^0 + \delta_j t)$. The results are presented in Figure 3.3. According to this chart, there is considerable fluctuation in the movement of TFP growth rates which seems to be driven mainly by the changes in technical efficiency. The rate of technological progress (TP) and scale efficiency tend to be relatively stable over time. Thus, though the Chinese economy has grown rapidly through the injection of factor inputs, there seems to be little gain from scale efficiency. Figure 3.3 also shows that technical efficiency changes fluctuate over time and they very much determine the movement of TFP growth. Overall, TFP growth has been positive since 1993 with the exception of 1994. Three trough points are observed in technical efficiency changes

*Table 3.3*   Estimation results

| Names | Coefficients | t-values |
| --- | --- | --- |
| Intercept | −3.206 | −5.534 |
| Central | −0.010 | −0.131 |
| Western | −0.160 | −2.041 |
| Coastal | 0.325 | 4.494 |
| Time | −0.170 | −5.512 |
| Time*time | −0.002 | −4.614 |
| Infrastructure | −4.813 | −4.740 |
| Reform | 2.276 | 2.887 |
| Openness | −0.803 | −1.413 |
| $\ln(K_d)$ | 2.970 | 11.709 |
| $\ln(K_f)$ | 0.090 | 1.425 |
| $\ln(K_h)$ | −0.292 | −2.060 |
| $\ln(K_d)*\ln(K_f)$ | 0.012 | 0.776 |
| $\ln(K_d)*\ln(K_h)$ | −0.203 | −4.459 |
| $\ln(K_f)*\ln(K_h)$ | 0.031 | 2.565 |
| $\ln(K_d)*\ln(K_d)$ | −0.137 | −3.392 |
| $\ln(K_f)*\ln(K_f)$ | −0.011 | −3.742 |
| $\ln(K_h)*\ln(K_h)$ | 0.147 | 6.872 |
| Time*$\ln(K_d)$ | 0.048 | 6.547 |
| Time*$\ln(K_f)$ | 0.004 | 2.112 |
| Time*$\ln(K_h)$ | −0.001 | −0.193 |
| Infrastructure*$\ln(K_d)$ | −1.440 | −3.573 |
| Infrastructure*$\ln(K_f)$ | 0.676 | 3.986 |
| Infrastructure*$\ln(K_h)$ | 0.624 | 2.091 |
| Reform*$\ln(K_d)$ | −0.386 | −1.711 |
| Reform*$\ln(K_f)$ | −0.187 | −2.341 |
| Reform*$\ln(K_h)$ | −0.027 | −0.148 |
| Openness*$\ln(K_d)$ | 0.489 | 4.005 |
| Openness*$\ln(K_f)$ | 0.228 | 4.574 |
| Openness*$\ln(K_h)$ | −0.370 | −5.058 |
| Time*infrastructure | 0.095 | 1.702 |
| Time*reform | −0.037 | −1.294 |
| Time*openness | −0.207 | −13.094 |
| *Efficiency components* | | |
| Intercept | 1.662 | 7.415 |
| Time*central | 0.144 | 5.749 |
| Time*western | 0.188 | 7.402 |
| Time*coastal | 0.162 | 6.345 |
| Time*3cities | 0.138 | 5.369 |
| Infrastructure | −2.082 | −3.811 |
| Reform | −1.113 | −4.884 |
| Openness | 2.198 | 15.193 |

(Continued)

*Table 3.3*   (Continued)

| Names | Coefficients | t-values |
|---|---|---|
| $\ln(K_d)$ | −0.242 | −4.285 |
| $\ln(K_f)$ | 0.008 | 0.590 |
| $\ln(K_h)$ | −0.037 | −0.978 |
| Time*$\ln(K_d)$ | 0.008 | 1.401 |
| Time*$\ln(K_f)$ | 0.001 | 0.419 |
| Time*$\ln(K_h)$ | 0.028 | 7.780 |
| Time*infrastructure | 0.219 | 4.327 |
| Time*reform | −0.366 | −12.452 |
| Time*openness | −0.145 | −10.782 |
| $\sigma^2$ | 0.008 | 18.321 |
| $\lambda$ | 0.828 | 32.128 |
| Log-likelihood value | 597.784 | |

*Notes*: 'Western', 'Central', 'Coastal' and '3cities' are four dummy variables representing the four regional groups, i.e. the western, central, coastal and three-city regions. 'ln' means the natural logarithm. $\lambda = \sigma^2/(\sigma_v^2 + \sigma^2)$. $\sigma_v^2$ and $\sigma^2$ are defined in equations (3.1) and (3.6).

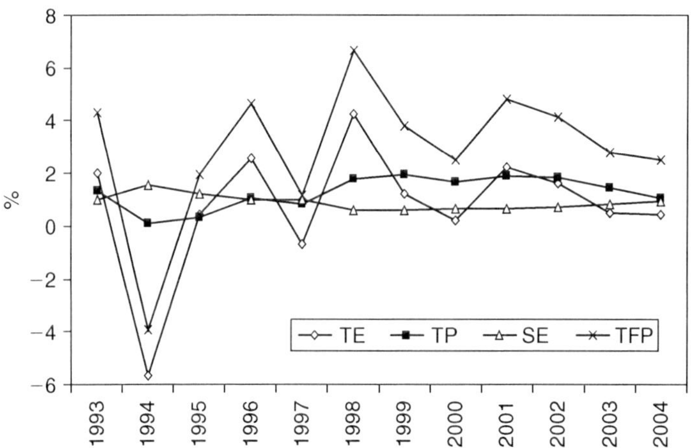


*Figure 3.3*   Rates of TFP growth, technological progress and efficiency change
*Notes*: TP, TE and SE represent the rates of technological progress, technical efficiency change and scale efficiency changes, respectively.

and hence the movement of TFP growth rates. They reflect the one-off negative impacts of China's 1994 currency devaluation (by about 40 per cent), the 1997 Asian financial crisis and the collapse of the information technology sector in 2000.

*Table 3.4*  Sources of growth (%)

| Growth components | 1993–97 | 1998–2000 | 2001–4 | 1993–2004 |
|---|---|---|---|---|
| TFP | 1.64 | 4.30 | 3.56 | 2.94 |
| Technological progress | 0.74 | 1.79 | 1.57 | 1.28 |
| Technical efficiency | −0.26 | 1.89 | 1.19 | 0.76 |
| Scale efficiency | 1.16 | 0.62 | 0.80 | 0.91 |
| Output | 12.40 | 8.99 | 10.95 | 11.06 |
| TFP/output (%) | 13.23 | 47.81 | 32.47 | 26.61 |

*Notes*: TFP/output ratios give the percentage shares of TFP growth over output growth. The numbers are calculated using mean values of each period.

Another way to interpret the results presented in Figure 3.3 is to divide the sample period into sub-periods, i.e. the pre-1997, post-1997 and China WTO accession (2001–4) periods. Table 3.4 reports the results. According to this table, productivity growth has shown a relatively larger contribution to China's growth after the 1997 Asian crisis, and it was mainly driven by gains in technical efficiency and improved technological progress. Since 1998, the Chinese economy has made some adjustment to the post-crisis environment. Economic growth became more balanced in terms of contributions from technological progress, technical efficiency changes and scale efficiency gains. This reflects improvement in economic growth since 1998. Overall, TFP growth accounts for about 27 per cent of total growth in the Chinese economy according to this study. This figure is greater than the 12.9 per cent reported in Woo (1998), 13.5 per cent derived by Wu (2003) and 23 per cent claimed by Young (2003) using pre-1997 data, respectively, but lower than 43 per cent estimated by the World Bank (1997a). The same figure for more developed economies is, however, much higher. For example, according to Dougherty and Jorgenson (1996), productivity growth accounted for 49.8 and 57.6 per cent of output growth during 1960–89 in Japan and Germany, respectively. Thus, there is still scope for the Chinese economy to catch up with the world's best practice in which TFP growth plays a more significant role in economic growth. In order to maintain a sustainable rate of growth in China in the future, policy makers in the country will have to take initiatives to improve productivity performance in the economy.

## 3.5  Conclusion

This chapter applies a stochastic frontier approach to examine China's economic growth in recent years. It is found that growth in China has largely been driven by factor inputs. Total factor productivity growth tends to play a positive role in economic growth, accounting for on average about 27 per cent of economic growth during 1993–2004. Technical efficiency seems to fluctuate considerably over time, reflecting changing internal and external economic conditions. While technological progress tends to be relatively stable over time, scale efficiency has shown hardly any contribution to China's growth during the period considered. The latter may signal the end of a development model in which growth mainly depends on injection of factor inputs.

It is also found in this chapter that, in comparison with advanced economies, China is yet to catch up with the world's best practice in which technological progress is the main driver of economic growth. In order to sustain current growth momentum, China's policy makers will have to address the issue of technological progress though there is still scope to benefit from the deepening of economic reforms. In addition, further growth will have to meet the challenges such as the growing gap between the coastal and interior areas, further restructuring of the state sectors and employment of redundant workers and rural surplus labour.

## Appendix

### Classification of Chinese regions

For economic analysis, China is often divided into three regions, i.e. western (including Ningxia, Xinjiang, Shaanxi, Yunnan, Sichuan, Guizhou, Qinghai, Gansu, Tibet and Chongqing), central (including Shanxi, Hainan, Jilin, Anhui, Heilongjiang, Guangxi, Inner Mongolia, Jiangxi, Hubei, Hunan and Henan) and coastal (including Fujian, Guangdong, Hebei, Jiangsu, Liaoning, Shandong, and Zhejiang). In the literature, the three large cities (Beijing, Tianjin and Shanghai) are generally included in the coastal group. They form a separate group in this study to reflect their distinct economic structure and performance. Tibet and Chongqing are excluded in this study due to missing data.

### Regional human capital stock estimates

Human capital stock is estimated using the average years of schooling which is calculated according to the following formula:

$$YS_{it} = (6PS_{it} + 9JS_{it} + 12SS_{it} + 15SC_{it} + 16HE_{it} + 19PG_{it})/P_{it}$$

where $YS_{it}$ is the average years of schooling. $PS_{it}$, $JS_{it}$, $SS_{it}$, $SC_{it}$, $HE_{it}$ and $PG_{it}$ are, respectively, the numbers of people who are six years old or above and who completed primary school (PS) education, junior high schools (JS), senior high schools or vocational schools (SS), three-year specialized colleges (SC), four-year higher education (HE) and postgraduate studies (PG) in the $i$th region at time $t$. $P_{it}$ is the total population aged six years or older in the $i$th region at time $t$. Statistics for these education groups are available for 1990 and 2000. By interpolation, a human capital stock series is generated for the period 1992–2004 and for all regions covered by the sample.

# 4
# New Economy, Productivity and Growth

The widespread use of computers and the Internet since the early 1990s has affected the world economies on all fronts by improving production methods and changing consumer behaviour. To reflect these changes, the term 'new economy' has emerged and it often refers to an economy that is characterized by increased investment in, and use of, information and communications technology (ICT).[1] While various studies have shown ICT to be instrumental in propelling productivity and economic growth in the developed countries, there has been little research on China, despite the giant developing economy having one of the world's largest ICT markets and a rapidly growing ICT infrastructure (Wong, 2007). Chapters 4 and 5 will add to the literature by focusing on China. This chapter examines the relationship between ICT, productivity and economic growth. Given China's current stage of economic development, it will be interesting to find out how this country is similar to or different from the advanced economies with regard to the contribution of ICT to productivity and economic growth.

The rest of the chapter begins with a preliminary analysis of the relationship between ICT and China's productivity growth using data obtained from Chinese statistical sources (Section 4.1). It then specifies an appropriate model to analyse the contribution of ICT and other factor inputs to economic growth in China (Section 4.2). This is followed by discussion of the empirical findings in Section 4.3. Some sensitivity analysis is presented in Section 4.4 with the final section summarizing the chapter (Section 4.5).

## 4.1  ICT, productivity and the Chinese economy

Current discussions on China's economic development tend to focus on its transition from an agriculture-based to an industrial economy that relies more on the manufacturing sector. A 'new economy' or 'knowledge economy' is normally associated with the tertiary or service sector which relies heavily on the use of communications and computer services. As the tertiary sector has not attained a significant share of total output, it is debated whether it is too early to even discuss the relevance of the new or knowledge economy to China (Lan and Sheehan, 2002). However, the share of tertiary industry output out of total output in China has been gradually increasing since the beginning of economic reforms. The tertiary sector has maintained a share of more than 30 per cent of real GDP since the late 1980s, peaking at 42 per cent in 2002 before dropping to about 40 per cent in 2005 (Figure 4.1). The share of China's primary or agricultural sector, on the other hand, has declined from less than 20 per cent in 1997 to about 12 per cent in 2005, while the secondary industry (comprising mainly manufacturing and construction) made up about 48 per cent of GDP in 2005.[2] At the same time, the Chinese economy is increasingly spurred on through development in the ICT sector. As China is now the world's largest telecommunications (fixed line and mobile phone) market, and achieving rapid growth in its computer industry as well, the implications of the growth in ICT for the rise of the service sector in the Chinese economy cannot be ignored.[3]

Figure 4.2 illustrates the trend of labour productivity growth in China from the beginning of reform in 1979 to 2005. Labour productivity (measured as GDP per worker) declined in 1989 and 1990 when economic sanctions were imposed by the US and other Western countries following the Tiananmen Square incident in June 1989. However, it did not last long, as labour productivity shot up almost immediately soon after, reaching its peak growth rate of 14 per cent in 1992 when Deng Xiaoping went on his southern tour which sparked off an investment boom. From then on, Chinese labour productivity has been rising steadily into the twenty-first century, achieving a peak growth rate of 11.5 per cent in 2004. While there has been much discussion in the literature of a productivity revival in the US and other developed countries after 1995, in China the breaking point appears to be 2000 after which labour productivity has been growing annually at more than 9 per cent (Table 4.1). This point can be reinforced when this chapter examines the growth rate of TFP during that period in a later section.

Productivity gains from ICT investment are controversial as productivity growth was shown to slow down during the 1970s and 1980s when the US invested heavily in ICT equipment. While recent studies have dispelled such controversy by showing that the returns to ICT investments have a positive pay-off for the developed countries, the case has not

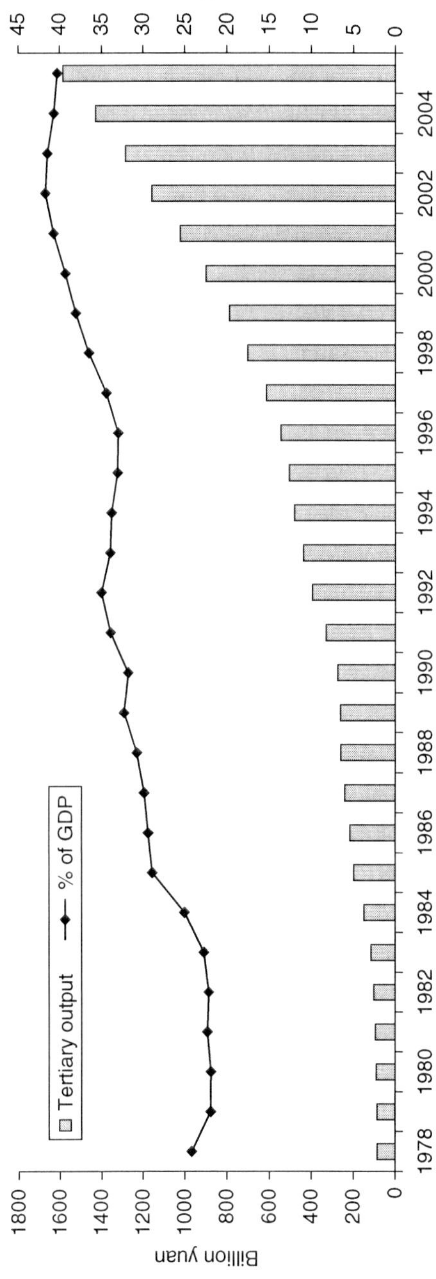

*Figure 4.1* China's tertiary sector output, 1978–2005 (in 1978 constant prices)
*Sources*: National Bureau of Statistics, *China Statistical Yearbook 2005*; *China Statistical Abstract 2006*.

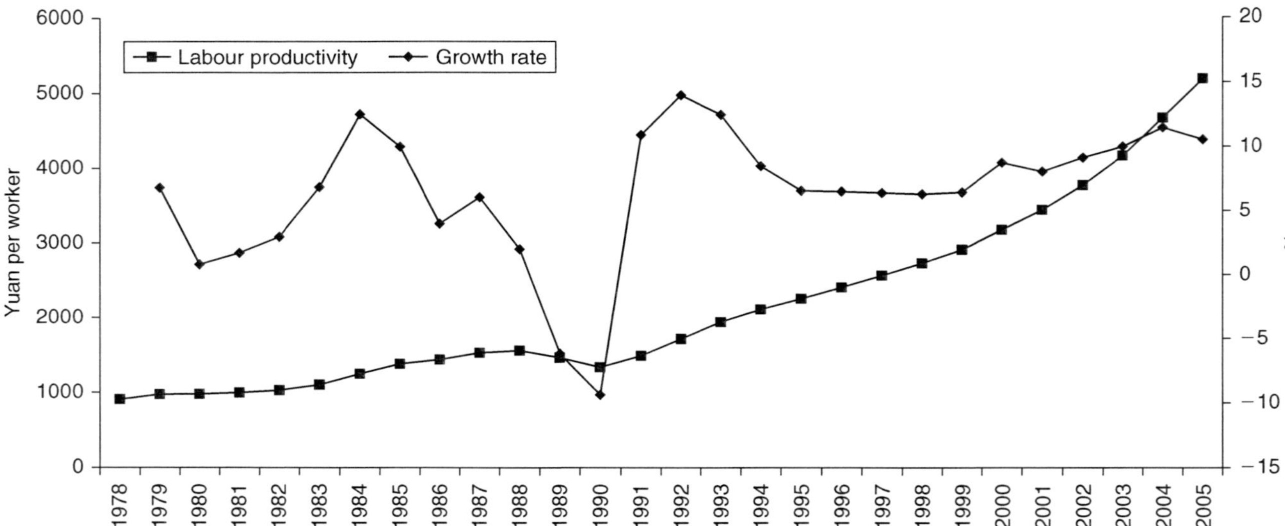


*Figure 4.2*   Labour productivity in China, 1978–2005

*Notes*: The figures in 1990 may be biased during to the revision of employment statistics in that year (when total employment went up by 17 per cent according to the NBS).

*Sources*: National Bureau of Statistics, *China Statistical Yearbook 2005; China Statistical Abstract 2006.*

*Table 4.1*   Growth rate of labour productivity during the Five-Year Plan (FYP) periods (%)

| Five-Year Plan period (FYP) | Labour productivity growth (%) |
| --- | --- |
| 6th (1981–85) | 6.83 |
| 7th (1986–90) | −0.69 |
| 8th (1991–95) | 10.48 |
| 9th (1996–2000) | 6.86 |
| 10th (2001–5) | 9.82 |

*Sources*: National Bureau of Statistics, *China Statistical Yearbook 2005; China Statistical Abstract 2006.*

been the same for developing economies. In a recent study that examined the differences between Asian and non-Asian countries in terms of ICT usage and the resulting productivity gains, it was found that ICT investment was negatively correlated with labour productivity for Asian countries while non-ICT investment was positively correlated with labour productivity (Kraemer and Dedrick, 2002). Kraemer and Dedrick (2002) attributed such a negative correlation to factors such as high prices of computers, a highly regulated telecommunications market with little competition, the problem of coding in the English language, a low level of ICT adoption and usage due to language and trade barriers, industry structure (Asian countries rely more heavily on manufacturing rather than the service sectors, and therefore are more likely to reap gains in productivity from investments in non-ICT capital), and management style of the companies.

By plotting the correlation between the growth rate of ICT investment per worker and real GDP per worker, a different pattern has however been observed for China (Figure 4.3). The trend line is positive, suggesting that the country and its companies are using ICT effectively to improve productivity, in contrast to the findings for Asian countries in general. Some of those factors mentioned above that account for the negative correlation in Asian countries are no longer applicable to China, especially since the 1990s. The rapid expansion of the telecom and computer markets in China, which is followed by the drop in prices of ICT equipment, has benefited residential as well as industrial users of ICT. This was evident in the telecommunications market when the break-up of monopoly since 1993 and bureaucratic reform during the late 1990s initiated pricing competition between different telecommunications

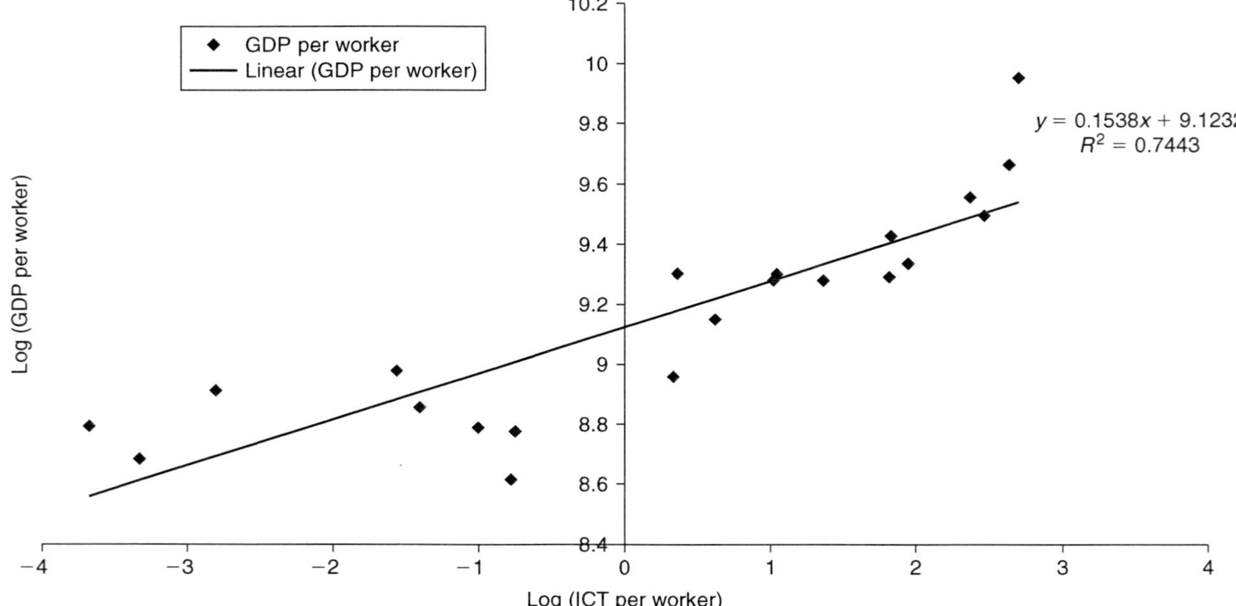


*Figure 4.3*  ICT investment per worker and labour productivity in China, 1985–2004
*Source*: Author's own estimates.

service providers. Furthermore, as discussed earlier, the tertiary or service sectors have become more important contributors to the national output, thus fuelling greater demand for ICT services, such as broadband and wireless Internet access, mobile telephony and other channels of communications. However, as the manufacturing sector still occupies a major share of GDP, the pay-off from investments in non-ICT capital such as factory plant and equipment is expected to be positive as well.

Another way of examining the role of ICT in the national economy is to compare the size and growth rate of ICT capital stock relative to the total capital stock.[4] The share of ICT capital stock out of the total capital stock in China is still miniscule, yet the former has grown at a faster rate than the latter. For instance, ICT capital stock grew by about 22 per cent on average annually from 2000 to 2004, which is almost twice as great as the growth rate (12 per cent) of the total capital stock. The growth rate of China's ICT capital stock is comparable to those of the OECD countries, which fell between 15 and 35 per cent in 1999 (OECD, 2001). The rapid rise in the ratio of ICT capital stock over GDP – almost 3 per cent in 2004 – highlights the role of the new economy as an increasingly significant driver of economic growth in China. An empirical assessment of such a role is presented in the rest of the chapter.

## 4.2   Model specification and data issues

The core objective of this chapter is to examine the sources of economic growth in China that take into consideration the role of ICT capital. To account for the contributions to China's economic growth from various factors including ICT capital, the chapter employs the production function approach which segregates ICT capital from other forms of physical capital inputs employed in the production process. Technological progress, or TFP, is derived as the residual of a production function. The production function in its simplest form appears as

$$Y_t = A \cdot (ICT_t^{\alpha}, KN_t^{\beta}, L_t^{\theta}) \tag{4.1}$$

where $Y_t$ represents real GDP in constant prices, $ICT_t$ and $KN_t$ stand for the stock of ICT and non-ICT capital respectively, and $L_t$ is employment. This method was also applied in the work of Jorgenson et al. (2003, 2005). In terms of growth decomposition, the growth of GDP is the aggregate sum of the share-weighted growth of inputs and changes in TFP, expressed as follows:

$$\dot{Y}_t = \alpha I\dot{C}T_t + \beta K\dot{N}_t + \theta \dot{L}_t + \dot{A}_t \tag{4.2}$$

where $\dot{Y}_t, I\dot{C}T_t, K\dot{N}_t$, and $\dot{L}_t$ are the respective growth rates of real GDP, ICT capital, non-ICT capital and labour, while $\dot{A}_t$ measures TFP growth. The coefficients, that is, $\alpha$, $\beta$ and $\theta$, represent the weighted share of the respective inputs in real GDP, and they determine the elasticity of output with respect to each of the factor inputs. The contribution of an input is therefore dependent on the size of its coefficient, its average growth rate during the entire period of study as well as the growth rate of real GDP. Under the assumption of constant returns to scale, the shares of all inputs add up to one, that is, $\alpha + \beta + \theta = 1$.

Specifically, the variables in the model are defined as follows:

$Y_t = $ real GDP
$ICT_t = $ real value of ICT capital stock
$KN_t = $ real value of non-ICT capital stock
$L_t = $ total employment

Real GDP data are derived from nominal GDP deflated by the constant price index. GDP, consumer price index and total employment data are obtained from *China Statistical Abstract 2006*, and they are available for the period 1978–2005. As for the variable representing labour, unlike in the US and Australian sources, data on the number of hours worked are not available in Chinese statistical sources. As a result, total employment is chosen as the proxy for labour, after some trial and error with various proxies.[5]

ICT capital stock is estimated and available for the period 1983–2004 (see the appendix to this chapter). Non-ICT capital stock is derived from investment in non-ICT capital, which is estimated by first taking the difference between total fixed asset investment and investment in the ICT sector. The real value of non-ICT capital stock is then derived using the same perpetual inventory method. Data for total fixed asset investment is available from 1980 to 2004. As explained in the appendix to this chapter, the ICT capital stock series is based on an assumed depreciation of 15 per cent over the period 1983–2004, with the initial value in 1983 determined by the three approaches of estimation, that is the growth rate, backcasting and integral approaches.

ICT and non-ICT investment statistics are deflated by the fixed asset investment price indexes, which are obtained from the *China Statistical Abstract 2006*. As for the choice of the capital depreciation rate, $\delta$, it is assumed that ICT equipment becomes obsolete faster than other forms of capital. Thus, for non-ICT capital stock, the depreciation rate is 4 per cent for the period from beginning of reform till 1992, and 5 per cent for the period from 1993 onwards. These rates were used by Islam and Dai (2005) and are also close to the regional mean rate derived in Chapter 2.[6]

## 4.3 Estimation results and interpretation

### 4.3.1 Estimation results

To examine the role of ICT in economic growth, the first step is to measure the contribution of ICT capital to economic growth in China. This is accomplished by a regression of output (real GDP) against factor inputs, expressed in the following equation:

$$\ln Y_t = \beta_0 + \beta_1 \ln ICT_t + \beta_2 \ln KN_t + \beta_3 \ln L_t + u_i \qquad (4.3)$$

where total GDP in constant prices, $Y_t$, is a function of ICT capital, non-ICT capital and labour, represented by $ICT_t$, $KN_t$ and $L_t$ respectively. However, the chapter will also apply the translog production function which is an unrestricted form of the Cobb–Douglas production function, that is,

$$\begin{aligned}
\ln Y_{it} = {} & \beta_0 + \beta_1 \ln ICT_t + \beta_2 \ln KN_t + \beta_3 \ln L_t + \gamma_1 (\ln ICT_t)^2 \\
& + \gamma_2 (\ln KN_t)^2 + \gamma_3 (\ln L_t)^2 + \eta_1 (\ln ICT_t \ln KN_t) \\
& + \eta_2 (\ln ICT_t \ln L_t) + \eta_3 (\ln KN_t \ln L_t) + u_t \qquad (4.4)
\end{aligned}$$

where $\beta$, $\gamma$ and $\eta$ are the parameters to be estimated. A test of linear restrictions on the translog function is carried out using the Wald test in the MicroFit program, based on the null hypothesis of $H_0$: $\gamma_1 = \gamma_2 = \gamma_3 = \eta_1 = \eta_2 = \eta_3 = 0$. The test statistic of $\chi^2(6) = 0.0026$ is obtained, and therefore the model specified by the Cobb–Douglas function cannot be rejected at all levels of significance. The sample has 22 observations for the period 1983–2004. The initial estimates of the parameters in equation (4.3) are presented in Table 4.2. All regressions in this chapter are run using MicroFit 4.0.

*Table 4.2*  Regression results: sources of economic growth, 1983–2004

| Explanatory variables | Model specification | | |
|---|---|---|---|
| | *Growth rate* | *Backcasting* | *Integral* |
| Intercept | −4.5390 (−8.330)*** | −4.2741 (−7.802)*** | −4.6831 (−8.593)*** |
| ln *ICT* | 0.1180 (4.652)*** | 0.1210 (4.856)*** | 0.1164 (4.541)*** |
| ln *KN* | 0.5256 (5.635)*** | 0.5146 (5.612)*** | 0.5314 (5.641)*** |
| ln *L* | 0.3850 (1.722)* | 0.3675 (1.717)* | 0.3946 (1.721)* |
| $R^2$ | 0.9955 | 0.9957 | 0.9954 |
| Adjusted $R^2$ | 0.9947 | 0.9950 | 0.9946 |
| Sample size | 22 | 22 | 22 |
| Durbin–Watson statistic | 0.9371 | 0.9574 | 0.9259 |

*Notes*: Figures in parentheses are the *t*-ratios. *, ** and *** indicate significance at 10, 5 and 1%.

All estimates of the parameters have the correct sign. The coefficients of ICT and non-ICT capital are statistically significant at the 1 per cent level, and that of labour at the 10 per cent level. The results show that growth in ICT capital as well as physical capital is positively related to economic growth from the mid-1980s until the beginning of the twenty-first century. The adjusted $R^2$ is shown to be very high, at 0.99. This is not unusual as empirical results for other countries have proven to be similar.[7]

According to the Durbin–Watson statistic obtained from the three estimations, with the values ranging from 0.9259 (integral approach) to 0.9574 (backcasting approach), there is no conclusive evidence of the presence of positive first-order serial correlation as these values lie between the critical values, $d_L = 0.831$ and $d_U = 1.407$. Therefore, another test, the Breusch–Godfrey (BG) test is conducted using EViews 5.0. The test statistic of $\chi^2(1) = 4.2468$ (with *p*-value of 0.039) is obtained, suggesting that the null hypothesis of no serial correlation is rejected at 5%, but not rejected at the 1% level of significance. A sensitivity test (to be discussed later) reveals that a higher Durbin–Watson statistic is obtained at a higher depreciation rate of ICT capital.

As for non-ICT capital stock, this chapter has also attempted to estimate a series using the backcasting and integral approach. However, the regression results based on these estimates show that the labour variable is statistically insignificant at all levels, and therefore the non-ICT capital stock series estimated from the growth rate approach is used here.

*Table 4.3*   Contributions to output growth, 1983–2004 (%)

|  | Period | | | |
| --- | --- | --- | --- | --- |
|  | *1983–2004* | *1983–91* | *1992–2000* | *2001–4* |
| ICT capital | 2.30 | −0.21 | 4.37 | 2.65 |
|  | *(25.1)* | *(−2.5)* | *(46.1)* | *(24.7)* |
| Other capital | 5.51 | 5.58 | 5.23 | 6.01 |
|  | *(60.1)* | *(69.3)* | *(55.1)* | *(56.1)* |
| Labour | 0.84 | 1.58 | 0.39 | 0.39 |
|  | *(9.2)* | *(19.6)* | *(4.1)* | *(3.6)* |
| TFP | 0.52 | 1.10 | −0.51 | 1.66 |
|  | *(5.6)* | *(13.6)* | *(−5.3)* | *(15.5)* |
| Output | 9.17 | 8.05 | 9.49 | 10.70 |
|  | *(100.0)* | *(100.0)* | *(100.0)* | *(100.0)* |

*Note*: Figures in parentheses are the shares of different growth components.

### 4.3.2   Decomposition of output growth

Using the estimates shown in Table 4.2, the sources of economic growth can be derived. The backcasting approach is chosen for computation as it has the largest *t*-ratio for ICT capital and the smallest standard error of the regression among the three estimations. The contributions of the factor accumulations and technical change (or technological progress) to real output growth in China for the period 1983–2004 are shown in Table 4.3, based on the assumed depreciation rate of 15 per cent for ICT capital. The results differ from those of previous studies. For example, Lee and Khatri (2003) show the contribution of ICT capital and TFP in China to be 3 and 43 per cent respectively during the 1990s, while in Wang and Yao (2003), TFP contributed 25 per cent to economic growth and total capital accumulation (ICT and non-ICT capital) contributed to half of economic growth. In another study that includes human capital as a factor input, TFP and human capital contribute to 22 and 13 per cent of total GDP growth, respectively (Qian and Smyth, 2006).

In this study, the contributions from ICT and non-ICT capital sum up to more than 80 per cent of total output growth in China. It is also found that the contribution of ICT capital to growth has fluctuated substantially between the 1980s and more recent years, whereas that of TFP changes takes both negative and positive values during the same period. Finally, Table 4.3 also shows remarkably contrasting results at different periods. During the 1980s, the contribution of ICT capital to economic growth was a negative 2.5 per cent, but the share increased to over 45 per cent in the 1990s. Such a huge jump in the proportional contribution to growth is explained by the sharp increase and the high growth rate of ICT investment during the early 1990s. During the first three years of the twenty-first century, ICT capital contributed about 25 per cent to economic growth. The low share of TFP contribution to economic growth may be attributed to an extremely low share of the ICT-producing industry in GDP, a result that is also found in Europe by Timmer and van Ark (2005).

It is noted that the findings in this study are different from those of other studies that analyse the contribution of ICT capital to Chinese economic growth, namely Lee and Khatri (2003) and Jorgenson and Vu (2005). Lee and Khatri (2003) measure the contribution of ICT capital stock to the growth of GDP and labour productivity in key Asian economies for the period 1990–99, while Jorgenson and Vu (2005) address the impact of ICT investment on the growth of the world economy, 7 regions and 14 major economies during the period 1989–2003. This study shows that the contribution of ICT capital is considerably higher, while that from labour is much lower than the findings of other authors. For instance, the contribution of labour has declined from 20 per cent in the 1980s to about 3 per cent in the most recent years. The contribution of non-ICT capital has also declined from 70 per cent during 1983–91 to 56 per cent during 2001–4. The only finding in this chapter that is close to those of the other authors is the contribution rates from non-ICT capital and TFP during the years of 2001–4.

It is also observed that this chapter has shown a much lower ICT capital–GDP ratio – less than 1 per cent during the 1990s, compared to 2 per cent found in Lee and Khatri (2003). However, it should be noted that the latter measured the ratio of ICT capital stock to non-farm business GDP, whereas this study looks at the ratio to total GDP in China. As for non-ICT capital stock, its ratio over GDP is comparatively higher – 530 per cent in this chapter as opposed to 172 per cent in Lee and Khatri (2003) for the period of 1992–99. This could be attributed to the fact that the non-ICT capital used in this study is derived from investment figures deflated by the fixed asset investment price index, instead of the consumer price index, thus resulting in relatively higher values.

Another difference stems from the definition of ICT investment or spending. Lee and Khatri (2003) used data on total ICT spending which comprises a wide range of components such as spending on hardware, software, IT services (including IT consulting, operations management,

IT training and education, processing and IT support), internal ICT spending (covering IT operating budget, internally customized software, and other expenses related to IT 'that cannot be tied to a vendor'), and other office equipment and telecommunication.[8] However, this study uses only data on investment in communications equipment, computer hardware and software. What can be concluded is that the surge in ICT investment has been a major contributor to TFP growth since the late 1990s.

In another study, Jorgenson and Vu (2005) used the same but a more recent source of data than that of Lee and Khatri (2003). Jorgenson and Vu found a greater contribution of ICT to economic growth in China in recent years, 9 per cent during 1995–2003 vs 25 per cent during 2001–4. The authors attribute the increase in ICT contribution in recent years to the surge in ICT investment, a conclusion supported by this study. Jorgenson and Vu further remarked that the next most important increase in investment in ICT equipment and software after the G7 economies would be in developing Asia, led by China. Thus there is a general consensus that rising ICT investment will lead to further increases in its contribution to China's economic growth.

### 4.3.3  TFP growth in China

One of the indicators of economic performance is total factor productivity (TFP), which is brought about by technological progress and more efficient management practices. Figure 4.4 compares the total output (GDP) index with the input indexes in China, using 1984 as the base year.[9] The output and input indexes illustrate the pace at which each of the variables has grown over the past two decades. The growth rate of TFP, illustrated in Figure 4.5, is derived from the difference between output growth and sum of the share-weighted growth of inputs given in equation (4.5):

$$\Delta \ln A_t = \Delta \ln Y_t - \{\alpha_{ICT} \Delta \ln ICT_t + \beta_{KN} \Delta \ln KN_t + \gamma_L \Delta \ln L_t\} \qquad (4.5)$$

where TFP growth ($\Delta \ln A_t$) is the difference between the growth of real GDP, $Y_t$, and the weighted average growth of factor inputs, that is, ICT capital, non-ICT capital and labour, represented by $ICT_t$, $KN_t$ and $L_t$, respectively; whereas $\alpha$, $\beta$ and $\gamma$ are the corresponding weights of the three factors.

Figure 4.4 shows that ICT capital has been growing much faster than output and all other inputs. This could explain the difference between China and other Asian countries. The latter have been reported to

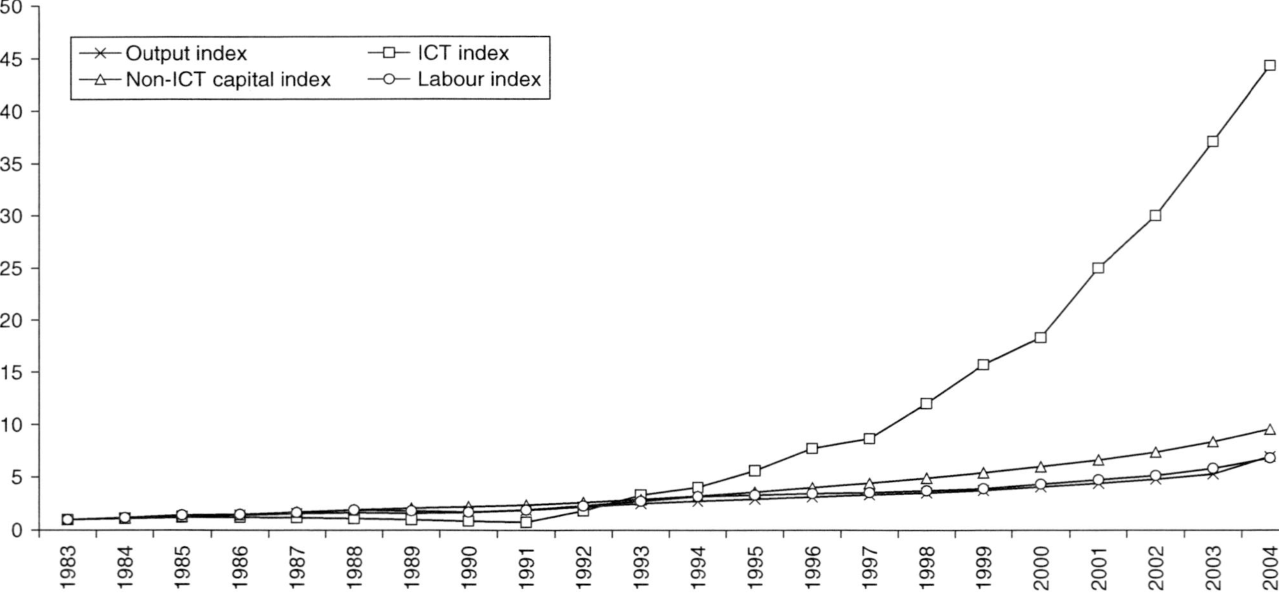


*Figure 4.4*  Output and input indexes in China, 1984–2004
*Sources*: National Bureau of Statistics, *China Statistical Yearbook 2005; China Statistical Abstract 2006. Yearbook of China's Electronics Industry* and *China Statistics Yearbook on High Technology Industry* (various issues).

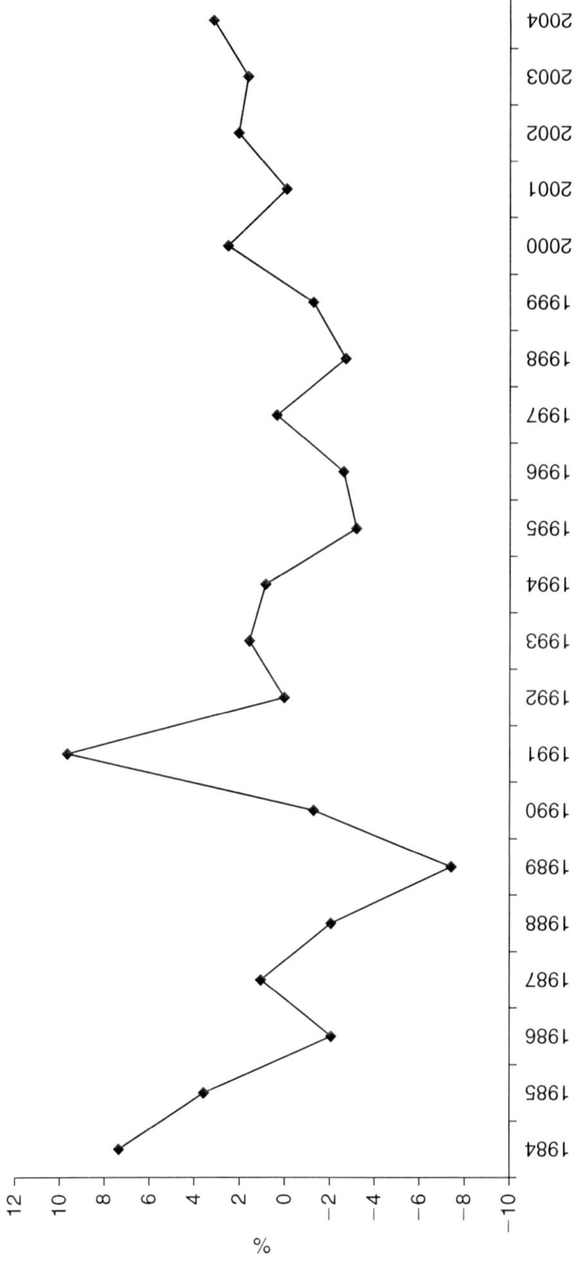



*Figure 4.5* TFP growth in China, 1984–2004

*Sources*: Author's own estimates.

experience a negative correlation between ICT and productivity growth (Kraemer and Dedrick, 2002). China's massive investment in ICT since 1992, made favourable by the building of high-technology industrial parks, has become a major contributor to the rapid growth of ICT capital. By contrast, TFP growth has been shown to be volatile over the last two decades, facing spells of negative growth during the periods 1988–91 and 1996–98. It grew at an annual rate of 0.1 per cent, and negative growths were experienced during 1986–90 and 1995–99 (Figure 4.5). However, it can be observed that since 2001 the growth rate of TFP has shown a positive and increasing trend in China.

## 4.4  Sensitivity analysis

The robustness of the estimation results can be examined with a sensitivity analysis by assuming different rates of depreciation for the ICT capital stock. A series of regressions and tests are run using ICT capital stock determined by depreciation rates that vary from 10 to 30 per cent (Table 4.4). The estimated ICT capital stock has shown a similar trend of contribution to economic growth under different depreciation rates but the elasticity of output with respect to ICT capital falls as $\delta$ increases (Table 4.5). The same is true for the elasticity of output with respect to labour, but the reverse relation holds for the elasticity of output with respect to non-ICT capital. The latter can be explained by the fact that the estimation of non-ICT capital stock is derived from the difference between total fixed asset investment and ICT investment. Therefore, a higher depreciation of ICT capital stock results in an increased share of non-ICT in total capital stock, and thereby a rise in the contribution of non-ICT capital to output growth. In this analysis, the contribution of TFP to output growth is relatively unresponsive to changes in the depreciation rate of ICT capital, although it increased by a miniscule magnitude, as shown in Table 4.5.

As the depreciation rate of ICT capital increases, the regression results become more robust as standard errors are reduced and the $t$-ratios of the coefficients of all variables increase. Using the Breusch–Godfrey test, the null hypothesis of no serial correlation is rejected at 5 per cent but not at the 1 per cent level of significance when the depreciation rate, $\delta = 0.10$, given the test statistic, $\chi^2(1) = 4.8926$ ($p$-value $= 0.027$). However, for depreciation rates of $\delta = 0.20$, 0.25 and 0.30, the corresponding test statistics, $\chi^2(1) = 3.6408$ ($p$-value $= 0.056$), 3.0977 ($p$-value $= 0.078$) and 2.636 ($p$-value $= 0.104$) are produced, which show that the null hypothesis of no serial correlation is rejected at 10 per cent but not at the 5 per cent

*Table 4.4*   Sensitivity tests using various depreciation rates of ICT capital stock

| Indicators | Depreciation rates | | | |
|---|---|---|---|---|
| | *0.10* | *0.20* | *0.25* | *0.30* |
| Intercept | −3.852(−6.427)*** | −4.555 (−8.764)*** | −4.745 (−9.415)*** | −4.875 (−9.845)*** |
| ln *ICT* | 0.143 (4.666)*** | 0.104 (5.023)*** | 0.091 (5.152)*** | 0.080 (5.240)*** |
| ln *KN* | 0.461 (4.359)*** | 0.559 (6.895)*** | 0.595 (8.152)*** | 0.625 (9.332)*** |
| ln *L* | 0.403 (1.785)* | 0.327 (1.609) | 0.286 (1.472) | 0.248 (1.319) |
| Adjusted $R^2$ | 0.9948 | 0.9942 | 0.9953 | 0.9954 |
| Observations | 22 | 22 | 22 | 22 |
| *d*-statistic | 0.9140 | 1.0054 | 1.0561 | 1.1061 |

*Notes*: Figures in parentheses ( ) are the *t*-ratios. *, ** and *** indicate significance at 10, 5 and 1%.

*Table 4.5*   Results of sensitivity analysis

| Depreciation rate of ICT capital (%) | Contribution to output growth (%) | | | |
|---|---|---|---|---|
| | *ICT* | *KN* | *L* | *TFP* |
| 10 | 2.80 *(30.5)* | 4.94 *(53.8)* | 0.92 *(10.1)* | 0.51 *(5.6)* |
| 15 | 2.30 *(25.1)* | 5.51 *(60.1)* | 0.84 *(9.2)* | 0.52 *(5.6)* |
| 20 | 1.92 *(20.9)* | 5.98 *(65.2)* | 0.75 *(8.2)* | 0.52 *(5.7)* |
| 25 | 1.62 *(17.7)* | 6.37 *(69.5)* | 0.66 *(7.2)* | 0.52 *(5.7)* |
| 30 | 1.39 *(15.2)* | 6.70 *(73.0)* | 0.57 *(6.2)* | 0.52 *(5.7)* |

*Note*: Figures in italic parentheses are the shares of various growth components.

level of significance. The results of the sensitivity tests therefore suggest that China may have a depreciation rate of ICT capital stock higher than that of developed countries such as Japan and Korea. The regression results also show that labour becomes statistically insignificant when the assumed depreciation rate of ICT capital stock reaches 20 per cent. Therefore this study assumes 15 per cent as the current depreciation rate of ICT capital stock in China.

In addition, an alternative set of results are also produced using ICT capital stock deflated by the hedonic price index, which showed a much lower initial value of ICT capital stock. The estimation results are presented and discussed in the appendix to this chapter. The findings, which are presented in Tables 4A.6–4A.8 in the appendix, show that the changes in ICT contribution to output growth as $\delta$ changes are lower than that presented in Table 4.4. The contribution of TFP to output growth is also relatively lower – for instance, 1.6 per cent in Table 4A.8 compared with 5.6 per cent in Table 4.5 for $\delta = 0.15$.

## 4.5   Conclusion

The empirical results indicate that China's economic growth has largely been driven by factor accumulation, which shows that the neoclassical approach to growth accounting is still very much relevant today. It is found that the largest share of China's economic growth is due to the expansion of capital formation. Even though ICT capital has only a miniscule share of the total capital stock and GDP, it has grown at a faster rate than other forms of capital. From the fact that ICT investment as a proportion of GDP is much lower than other forms of investment, and yet its contribution to economic growth is almost half of the latter, it can be ascertained that ICT has become an important contributor to the growth of China's economy. The latter will in turn ensure a continued high demand for ICT products and services.

This chapter has shown different findings about the sources of China's economic growth in the late 1990s and the early twenty-first century, even though the actual depreciation rate of China's ICT capital stock is still unknown. Current literature has shown that the contribution of ICT to China's economic growth is less than 10 per cent even during the late 1990s and the early years of this century, much lower than this study's findings of about 25 per cent. The contribution of TFP to economic growth in China is found to be much lower in this study than that from other literature – for instance, about 6 per cent in this chapter vs 35 per cent in Jorgenson and Vu (2005) for the period since 1995.

However, further empirical research on the sources of China's productivity growth is needed. For example, one could investigate whether there has been a capital reallocation between the ICT sector (that is, 'ICT-producing' and 'ICT-using' industries) and the non-ICT sectors. Finally, it should be acknowledged that China's regional disparity in ICT investment should be an issue for examination. It could bring up a debate over whether China should focus its ICT investment in the more developed eastern or coastal regions, or in the inland or western regions. This issue will be partially examined in the next chapter (Chapter 5) which looks at the impact of ICT on technical efficiency in the Chinese regions.

# Appendix

This appendix presents (a) ICT capital stock estimates using several methods and (b) the estimation results based on the hedonic price index.

**ICT capital stock estimates**

In Chapter 2, three methods of capital stock measurement (that is, the integral, growth rate and other approaches) are reviewed and an alternative approach (the backcasting approach) was introduced. To estimate an ICT capital stock series for China, three approaches (the integral, growth rate and backcasting) are attempted here to derive three alternative sets of series for empirical exercises in this chapter and as resources for other authors.

The first approach, the growth rate approach, assumes that the only unknown variable is the initial value of capital stock which can be estimated as follows:

$$K_0 = \frac{I_1}{\delta + \gamma} \tag{4A.1}$$

where $K_0$ is the value of ICT capital stock in the initial year, which is determined by $I_1$, the level of ICT investment in the first year of the series that is available from the statistical source; $\delta$, the depreciation rate for ICT capital, and $\gamma$, the average growth rate of real GDP. This method has been applied for calculating the initial value of ICT capital stock in the US (Shinjo and Zhang, 2003), Japan (Miyagawa et al., 2004) and the Central American countries (Reinsdorf and Cover, 2005). Nadiri and Prucha (1996) also applied the same formula for calculating the initial value of the US R&D capital stock by using the growth rate of total capital stock reported in Musgrave (1992) and an arbitrary depreciation rate of 10 per cent.

Owing to the time series data available for this exercise, the initial year is taken to be 1983. In the absence of data on the price of acquisition of capital goods, the choice of the depreciation rate for China's ICT capital is based on those used by other authors. The depreciation rate used for the period after 1983 is based on Kim (2002) who assumed a rate of 14 per cent for Korean ICT capital for the period of 1977–2000. The study

*Table 4A.1*   Real ICT investment in China, 1984–2004 (using CPI)

| Year | Telecommunications | Computer | Total |
| --- | --- | --- | --- |
| 1984 | 122.86 | 97.95 | 220.81 |
| 1985 | 130.39 | 104.88 | 235.27 |
| 1986 | 102.05 | 85.75 | 187.81 |
| 1987 | 100.50 | 26.46 | 129.96 |
| 1988 | 57.46 | 56.70 | 114.15 |
| 1989 | 13.17 | 20.38 | 33.55 |
| 1990 | 10.87 | 12.34 | 23.21 |
| 1991 | 8.60 | 8.00 | 16.60 |
| 1992 | 712.30 | 215.22 | 927.52 |
| 1993 | 523.87 | 723.52 | 1,247.40 |
| 1994 | 615.46 | 356.23 | 971.69 |
| 1995 | 1,441.08 | 495.64 | 1,936.72 |
| 1996 | 2,227.73 | 475.76 | 2,703.49 |
| 1997 | 956.76 | 983.92 | 1,940.69 |
| 1998 | 2,591.67 | 761.67 | 4,353.33 |
| 1999 | 2,813.16 | 2,199.11 | 5,012.27 |
| 2000 | 3,053.50 | 1,443.46 | 4,496.97 |
| 2001 | 6,230.77 | 2,378.57 | 8,609.34 |
| 2002 | 4,303.18 | 3,605.26 | 7,908.44 |
| 2003 | 4,503.22 | 5,880.36 | 10,383.58 |
| 2004 | 4,611.79 | 6,596.04 | 11,207.83 |

Unit: million yuan.

thus adopts a depreciation rate of 15 per cent for China's ICT capital stock from 1983 to 2004. To determine the value of $\gamma$, the growth rate of real GDP during the three years before the initial year, that is, 1981–83, is taken from Wu (2004), which is equivalent to about 10 per cent. Thus, to calculate the initial value of ICT capital stock in 1983, it is assumed that $\delta = 0.15$ and $\gamma = 0.10$.

As no data on an ICT price index are available in Chinese statistical sources, unlike that of the US in which the hedonic price index is available from the website of the Bureau of Economic Analysis (BEA) of the US Department of Commerce, ICT investment is deflated by the fixed asset investment price index at constant prices (1991 = 1) obtained from *China Statistical Yearbook*. The real ICT investment and capital stock data derived using this approach are presented in Tables 4A.1 and 4A.2. Using the formula in equation (4A.1), the initial value of ICT capital stock in 1983 is estimated to be about 887 million yuan.

*Table 4A.2*   ICT capital stock series in China, 1983–2004 (using CPI)

| Year | Rates of depreciation | | | | |
|---|---|---|---|---|---|
| | *0.10* | *0.15* | *0.20* | *0.25* | *0.30* |
| *Growth rate approach* | | | | | |
| 1983 | 886.80 | 886.80 | 886.80 | 886.80 | 886.80 |
| 1984 | 1,018.93 | 974.59 | 930.25 | 885.91 | 841.57 |
| 1985 | 1,152.31 | 1,063.68 | 979.48 | 899.71 | 824.37 |
| 1986 | 1,224.89 | 1,091.93 | 971.39 | 862.59 | 764.87 |
| 1987 | 1,232.35 | 1,058.10 | 907.06 | 776.90 | 665.36 |
| 1988 | 1,223.27 | 1,013.54 | 839.81 | 696.83 | 579.91 |
| 1989 | 1,134.50 | 895.06 | 705.40 | 556.17 | 439.49 |
| 1990 | 1,004.26 | 784.01 | 587.53 | 440.34 | 330.85 |
| 1991 | 956.43 | 683.01 | 486.62 | 346.86 | 248.20 |
| 1992 | 1,788.31 | 1,508.08 | 1,316.82 | 1,187.66 | 1,101.26 |
| 1993 | 2,856.88 | 2,529.26 | 2,300.85 | 2,138.14 | 2,018.28 |
| 1994 | 3,542.88 | 3,121.56 | 2,812.37 | 2,575.29 | 2,384.48 |
| 1995 | 5,125.31 | 4,590.04 | 4,186.61 | 3,868.19 | 3,605.86 |
| 1996 | 7,316.27 | 6,605.03 | 6,052.79 | 5,604.64 | 5,227.59 |
| 1997 | 8,525.33 | 7,554.97 | 6,782.92 | 6,144.16 | 5,600.00 |
| 1998 | 12,026.13 | 10,775.05 | 9,779.67 | 8,961.46 | 8,273.34 |
| 1999 | 15,835.79 | 14,171.07 | 12,836.00 | 11,733.36 | 10,803.60 |
| 2000 | 18,749.18 | 16,542.37 | 14,765.77 | 13,296.99 | 12,059.49 |
| 2001 | 25,483.60 | 22,670.36 | 20,421.96 | 18,582.08 | 17,050.98 |
| 2002 | 30,843.68 | 27,178.25 | 24,246.01 | 21,845.00 | 19,844.13 |
| 2003 | 38,142.90 | 33,485.09 | 29,780.39 | 26,767.34 | 24,274.48 |
| 2004 | 45,536.43 | 39,670.15 | 35,032.14 | 31,283.33 | 28,199.96 |
| *Backcasting approach* | | | | | |
| 1983 | 734.42 | 734.42 | 734.42 | 734.42 | 734.42 |
| 1984 | 881.80 | 845.07 | 808.35 | 771.63 | 734.91 |
| 1985 | 1,028.89 | 953.59 | 881.95 | 814.00 | 749.71 |
| 1986 | 1,113.81 | 998.35 | 893.37 | 798.30 | 712.60 |
| 1987 | 1,132.38 | 978.56 | 844.65 | 728.68 | 628.78 |
| 1988 | 1,133.30 | 945.93 | 789.88 | 660.67 | 554.30 |
| 1989 | 1,053.52 | 837.59 | 665.45 | 529.05 | 421.56 |
| 1990 | 971.38 | 735.16 | 555.57 | 420.00 | 318.31 |
| 1991 | 890.84 | 641.49 | 461.06 | 331.60 | 239.41 |
| 1992 | 1,729.28 | 1,472.79 | 1,296.37 | 1,176.22 | 1,095.11 |
| 1993 | 2,803.75 | 2,499.26 | 2,284.49 | 2,129.56 | 2,013.97 |
| 1994 | 3,495.06 | 3,096.06 | 2,799.28 | 2,568.86 | 2,381.47 |
| 1995 | 5,082.27 | 4,568.37 | 4,176.14 | 3,863.36 | 3,603.75 |
| 1996 | 7,277.54 | 6,586.61 | 6,044.41 | 5,601.02 | 5,226.12 |
| 1997 | 8,490.47 | 7,539.31 | 6,776.21 | 6,141.45 | 5,598.97 |
| 1998 | 11,994.76 | 10,761.74 | 9,774.30 | 8,959.42 | 8,272.61 |

(*Continued*)

*Table 4A.2   (Continued)*

| Year | Rates of depreciation | | | | |
|---|---|---|---|---|---|
| | 0.10 | 0.15 | 0.20 | 0.25 | 0.30 |
| 1999 | 15,807.55 | 14,159.75 | 12,831.71 | 11,731.84 | 10,803.10 |
| 2000 | 18,723.76 | 16,532.76 | 14,762.34 | 13,295.84 | 12,059.14 |
| 2001 | 25,460.73 | 22,662.18 | 20,419.21 | 18,581.22 | 17,050.74 |
| 2002 | 30,823.10 | 27,171.30 | 24,243.81 | 21,844.36 | 19,843.96 |
| 2003 | 38,124.37 | 33,479.19 | 29,778.63 | 26,766.85 | 24,274.35 |
| 2004 | 45,519.76 | 39,665.13 | 35,030.73 | 31,282.97 | 28,199.87 |
| *Integral approach* | | | | | |
| 1983 | 984.47 | 984.47 | 984.47 | 984.47 | 984.47 |
| 1984 | 1,106.84 | 1,057.61 | 1,008.39 | 959.17 | 909.94 |
| 1985 | 1,231.42 | 1,134.24 | 1,041.98 | 954.65 | 872.23 |
| 1986 | 1,296.09 | 1,151.91 | 1,021.39 | 903.79 | 798.37 |
| 1987 | 1,296.43 | 1,109.08 | 947.07 | 807.80 | 688.81 |
| 1988 | 1,280.95 | 1,056.87 | 871.81 | 720.00 | 596.32 |
| 1989 | 1,186.40 | 931.89 | 731.00 | 573.55 | 450.98 |
| 1990 | 1,090.98 | 815.32 | 608.01 | 453.38 | 338.90 |
| 1991 | 998.48 | 709.62 | 503.01 | 356.63 | 253.83 |
| 1992 | 1,826.15 | 1,530.70 | 1,329.93 | 1,195.00 | 1,105.20 |
| 1993 | 2,890.93 | 2,548.49 | 2,311.34 | 2,143.64 | 2,021.04 |
| 1994 | 3,573.53 | 3,137.91 | 2,820.76 | 2,579.42 | 2,386.41 |
| 1995 | 5,152.89 | 4,603.94 | 4,193.32 | 3,871.28 | 3,607.21 |
| 1996 | 7,341.10 | 6,616.84 | 6,058.15 | 5,606.96 | 5,228.54 |
| 1997 | 8,547.67 | 7,565.00 | 6,787.21 | 6,145.91 | 5,600.67 |
| 1998 | 12,046.24 | 10,783.59 | 9,783.10 | 8,962.76 | 8,273.80 |
| 1999 | 15,853.89 | 14,178.32 | 12,838.75 | 11,734.34 | 10,803.93 |
| 2000 | 18,765.46 | 16,548.54 | 14,767.97 | 13,297.72 | 12,059.72 |
| 2001 | 25,498.26 | 22,675.60 | 20,423.71 | 18,582.63 | 17,051.14 |
| 2002 | 30,856.88 | 27,182.70 | 24,247.41 | 21,845.42 | 19,844.24 |
| 2003 | 38,154.77 | 33,488.88 | 29,781.52 | 26,767.65 | 24,274.55 |
| 2004 | 45,547.12 | 39,673.37 | 35,033.04 | 31,283.56 | 28,200.01 |

Unit: million yuan.

The second approach attempts to estimate the data series for incremental value of capital stock by backcasting to a much earlier period, 1950, assuming ICT investment increases at a constant rate. The equation (5.1) is then expanded to the following form, used in Wu (2004):

$$K_{i,t} = \sum_{0}^{t-1951} (1 - r)^k I_{t-k} + (1 - \delta)^{t-1950} K_{i,1950} \qquad (4A.2)$$

where a capital stock series can be derived given the value of capital stock in 1950 and a given depreciation rate. ICT investment is first backcast to 1951, assuming that it had been growing at a constant rate ($r$) of 19 per cent since that year till the early 1980s. Next, in order to derive the value of ICT capital stock in 1950, a few assumptions are made. It is assumed that the ICT equipment used in the 1980s is similar to those of the US and Japan in the 1970s. It was also noted that in 1987, China was still 'ten to fifteen years behind the world leaders in almost all aspects of the computer spectrum except for the area of Chinese I/O' (Witzell and Smith, 1989). By comparing the depreciation rates for office, computing and accounting machinery in the US and Japan corresponding to the period before and after 1978, used by Fraumeni (1997) and Miyagawa et al. (2004), it can be assumed that the depreciation rate before the 1980s is lower than that of the period after. Therefore, since the depreciation rate for the period after 1983 is already assumed to be $\delta = 0.15$, it is assumed that the depreciation rate for the period of 1950–83 is lower, at $\delta = 0.10$. Using this approach, the initial value of capital is estimated to be 5 million yuan in 1950, and 734 million yuan in 1983 (see Table 4A.2).

The third approach, that is the integral approach, assumes capital stock in the first period to be the sum of all past investments, as used in Wu (2004). By using the investment data of 1951, and assuming a constant growth rate of $r$, the value of ICT capital stock in the initial year (1983) can be expressed as follows:

$$K_{1983} = I_{1951} \cdot \sum_{t=0}^{31} (1 + r)^t \tag{4A.3}$$

where the value of ICT investment in 1951 was estimated to be 0.75 million yuan, and $r$ is assumed to be 19 per cent. This approach yields the highest initial value of ICT capital stock at 984 million yuan in 1983 (see Table 4A.2).

### Estimation results using hedonic price index

An alternative set of ICT investment and capital stock series is also derived using the ICT hedonic price index reported by the Bureau of Economic Analysis (BEA http://bea.gov/bea/dn/nipaweb/index.asp), as no data are available for an ICT price index in Chinese statistical sources (see Tables 4A.3 and 4A.4). The hedonic price index for ICT is used in US and Japanese statistical sources (Shinjo and Zhang, 2003). The use of the US hedonic price index for ICT as an appropriate proxy measure of price changes of ICT assets in other countries is supported by Timmer

*Table 4A.3*   Real ICT investment in China, 1984–2004 (using hedonic price indexes)

|  | Telecommunications | Computer | Total |
|---|---|---|---|
| 1984 | 2.80 | 2.23 | 5.03 |
| 1985 | 3.71 | 2.98 | 6.69 |
| 1986 | 3.58 | 3.01 | 6.58 |
| 1987 | 4.41 | 1.29 | 5.70 |
| 1988 | 3.28 | 3.23 | 6.51 |
| 1989 | 0.96 | 1.49 | 2.45 |
| 1990 | 0.93 | 1.06 | 2.00 |
| 1991 | 0.92 | 0.85 | 1.77 |
| 1992 | 105.13 | 31.77 | 136.90 |
| 1993 | 119.52 | 165.07 | 284.59 |
| 1994 | 177.56 | 102.77 | 280.33 |
| 1995 | 552.34 | 189.97 | 742.31 |
| 1996 | 1,239.26 | 264.66 | 1,503.92 |
| 1997 | 746.54 | 767.73 | 1,514.27 |
| 1998 | 2,811.93 | 1,911.39 | 4,723.33 |
| 1999 | 4,151.44 | 3,245.27 | 7,396.71 |
| 2000 | 5,536.00 | 2,617.00 | 8,153.00 |
| 2001 | 14,372.62 | 5,486.69 | 19,859.32 |
| 2002 | 12,302.51 | 10,307.21 | 22,609.72 |
| 2003 | 15,544.44 | 20,298.15 | 35,842.59 |
| 2004 | 18,298.39 | 26,171.37 | 44,469.76 |

Unit: million yuan.

and van Ark (2005). As the ICT hedonic price index uses 2000 as the base year, all other variables, that is, GDP and non-ICT investment, are deflated by the consumer price index and fixed asset investment price index, respectively, and converted to the same base year (see Table 4A.5). In this case, since investment in the initial years was deflated by a higher price index, considerably lower initial values of ICT capital stock in 1983 are obtained, that is, 9, 12 and 22 million yuan respectively, according to the three approaches (see Table 4A.4).

The initial estimates of the parameters in equation (4.3) are presented in Table 4A.6. All estimated coefficients are statistically significant with the correct sign given the levels of significance. The Durbin–Watson statistics obtained from the three different model specifications, with the values ranging from 0.9282 to 0.9305, show that there is no conclusive evidence of the presence of positive first-order serial correlation as

*Table 4A.4*　Alternative ICT capital stock series in China, 1983–2004

| Year | Rates of depreciation | | | | |
|---|---|---|---|---|---|
| | *0.10* | *0.15* | *0.20* | *0.25* | *0.30* |
| *Growth rate approach* | | | | | |
| 1983 | 9.08 | 9.08 | 9.08 | 9.08 | 9.08 |
| 1984 | 13.21 | 12.75 | 12.30 | 11.84 | 11.39 |
| 1985 | 18.58 | 17.53 | 16.53 | 15.58 | 14.67 |
| 1986 | 23.30 | 21.49 | 19.81 | 18.27 | 16.85 |
| 1987 | 26.68 | 23.97 | 21.55 | 19.40 | 17.50 |
| 1988 | 30.52 | 26.88 | 23.75 | 21.06 | 18.76 |
| 1989 | 29.92 | 25.30 | 21.45 | 18.25 | 15.58 |
| 1990 | 28.92 | 23.50 | 19.16 | 15.68 | 12.90 |
| 1991 | 27.80 | 21.74 | 17.09 | 13.53 | 10.80 |
| 1992 | 161.91 | 155.38 | 150.57 | 147.04 | 144.46 |
| 1993 | 430.31 | 416.66 | 405.05 | 394.87 | 385.71 |
| 1994 | 667.62 | 634.50 | 604.37 | 576.49 | 550.33 |
| 1995 | 1,343.17 | 1,281.64 | 1,225.81 | 1,174.68 | 1,127.55 |
| 1996 | 2,712.77 | 2,593.31 | 2,484.57 | 2,384.93 | 2,293.20 |
| 1997 | 3,955.77 | 3,718.59 | 3,501.93 | 3,302.97 | 3,119.52 |
| 1998 | 8,283.52 | 7,884.13 | 7,524.87 | 7,200.56 | 6,906.99 |
| 1999 | 14,851.87 | 14,098.22 | 13,416.60 | 12,797.12 | 12,231.60 |
| 2000 | 21,519.69 | 20,136.48 | 18,886.28 | 17,750.84 | 16,715.12 |
| 2001 | 39,227.03 | 36,975.33 | 34,968.34 | 33,172.45 | 31,559.90 |
| 2002 | 57,914.05 | 54,038.74 | 50,584.39 | 47,489.05 | 44,701.65 |
| 2003 | 87,965.24 | 81,775.53 | 76,310.11 | 71,459.38 | 67,133.75 |
| 2004 | 123,638.50 | 113,979.00 | 105,517.80 | 98,064.30 | 91,463.38 |
| *Backcasting approach* | | | | | |
| 1983 | 12.10 | 12.10 | 12.10 | 12.10 | 12.10 |
| 1984 | 15.93 | 15.32 | 14.72 | 14.11 | 13.51 |
| 1985 | 21.03 | 19.71 | 18.46 | 17.28 | 16.15 |
| 1986 | 25.51 | 23.34 | 21.36 | 19.54 | 17.89 |
| 1987 | 28.66 | 25.55 | 22.79 | 20.36 | 18.23 |
| 1988 | 32.30 | 28.22 | 24.74 | 21.78 | 19.27 |
| 1989 | 31.52 | 26.44 | 22.24 | 18.78 | 15.94 |
| 1990 | 30.37 | 24.47 | 19.79 | 16.08 | 13.15 |
| 1991 | 29.10 | 22.57 | 17.60 | 13.83 | 10.97 |
| 1992 | 163.08 | 156.08 | 150.98 | 147.27 | 144.58 |
| 1993 | 431.37 | 417.26 | 405.37 | 395.04 | 385.79 |
| 1994 | 668.56 | 635.00 | 604.63 | 576.62 | 550.39 |
| 1995 | 1,344.02 | 1,282.07 | 1,226.02 | 1,174.78 | 1,127.59 |
| 1996 | 2,713.54 | 2,593.68 | 2,484.74 | 2,385.00 | 2,293.23 |
| 1997 | 3,956.46 | 3,718.90 | 3,502.06 | 3,303.03 | 3,119.54 |
| 1998 | 8,284.14 | 7,884.39 | 7,524.98 | 7,200.60 | 6,907.00 |

*(Continued)*

*Table 4A.4*   (Continued)

| Year | Rates of depreciation | | | | |
|---|---|---|---|---|---|
| | *0.10* | *0.15* | *0.20* | *0.25* | *0.30* |
| 1999 | 14,852.43 | 14,098.44 | 13,416.69 | 12,797.15 | 12,231.61 |
| 2000 | 21,520.19 | 20,136.67 | 18,886.35 | 17,750.87 | 16,715.13 |
| 2001 | 39,227.49 | 36,975.49 | 34,968.40 | 33,172.47 | 31,559.90 |
| 2002 | 57,914.46 | 54,038.88 | 50,584.44 | 47,489.07 | 44,701.65 |
| 2003 | 87,965.60 | 81,775.64 | 76,310.14 | 71,459.39 | 67,133.75 |
| 2004 | 123,638.80 | 113,979.10 | 105,517.90 | 98,064.30 | 91,463.38 |
| *Integral approach* | | | | | |
| 1983 | 22.45 | 22.45 | 22.45 | 22.45 | 22.45 |
| 1984 | 25.24 | 24.11 | 22.99 | 21.87 | 20.75 |
| 1985 | 29.40 | 27.19 | 25.09 | 23.09 | 21.21 |
| 1986 | 33.05 | 29.69 | 26.65 | 23.90 | 21.43 |
| 1987 | 35.45 | 30.95 | 27.03 | 23.63 | 20.71 |
| 1988 | 38.41 | 32.81 | 28.13 | 24.23 | 21.00 |
| 1989 | 37.02 | 30.34 | 24.95 | 20.63 | 17.15 |
| 1990 | 35.31 | 27.78 | 21.96 | 17.46 | 14.00 |
| 1991 | 33.55 | 25.39 | 19.34 | 14.87 | 11.57 |
| 1992 | 167.09 | 158.47 | 152.36 | 148.05 | 145.00 |
| 1993 | 434.97 | 419.29 | 406.48 | 395.62 | 386.09 |
| 1994 | 671.81 | 636.73 | 605.52 | 577.05 | 550.60 |
| 1995 | 1,346.94 | 1,283.54 | 1,226.73 | 1,175.10 | 1,127.73 |
| 1996 | 2,716.17 | 2,594.93 | 2,485.30 | 2,385.25 | 2,293.33 |
| 1997 | 3,958.83 | 3,719.96 | 3,502.52 | 3,303.21 | 3,119.61 |
| 1998 | 8,286.27 | 7,885.29 | 7,525.34 | 7,200.73 | 6,907.05 |
| 1999 | 14,854.35 | 14,099.21 | 13,416.98 | 12,797.26 | 12,231.64 |
| 2000 | 21,521.92 | 20,137.33 | 18,886.58 | 17,750.94 | 16,715.15 |
| 2001 | 39,229.04 | 36,976.04 | 34,968.58 | 33,172.52 | 31,559.92 |
| 2002 | 57,915.85 | 54,039.35 | 50,584.58 | 47,489.11 | 44,701.66 |
| 2003 | 87,966.86 | 81,776.04 | 76,310.26 | 71,459.43 | 67,133.76 |
| 2004 | 123,639.90 | 113,979.40 | 105,518.00 | 98,064.33 | 91,463.39 |

Unit: million yuan.

these values lie between $d_L = 0.831$ and $d_U = 1.407$. The Breusch–Godfrey (BG) test suggests that the null hypothesis of no serial correlation is rejected at the 5 per cent, but not rejected at the 1 per cent, level of significance.

Using the estimates shown in Table 4A.6, the sources of economic growth can be derived. The results derived using the backcasting approach are chosen for computation as they show the largest $t$-ratio for

*Table 4A.5*   Price deflators

| Year | Consumer price indexes (2000 = 1) | Fixed asset investment price indexes (2000 = 1) | ICT hedonic price indexes (2000 = 1) |
|---|---|---|---|
| 1983 | 0.265 | 0.306 | 27.884 |
| 1984 | 0.270 | 0.284 | 22.603 |
| 1985 | 0.277 | 0.298 | 19.021 |
| 1986 | 0.303 | 0.314 | 16.255 |
| 1987 | 0.323 | 0.339 | 14.011 |
| 1988 | 0.346 | 0.407 | 12.945 |
| 1989 | 0.412 | 0.484 | 12.006 |
| 1990 | 0.486 | 0.497 | 10.485 |
| 1991 | 0.501 | 0.552 | 9.387 |
| 1992 | 0.518 | 0.636 | 7.812 |
| 1993 | 0.551 | 0.805 | 6.395 |
| 1994 | 0.632 | 0.889 | 5.584 |
| 1995 | 0.784 | 0.941 | 4.451 |
| 1996 | 0.918 | 0.978 | 3.189 |
| 1997 | 0.994 | 0.995 | 2.312 |
| 1998 | 1.022 | 0.993 | 1.659 |
| 1999 | 1.014 | 0.989 | 1.215 |
| 2000 | 1.000 | 1.000 | 1.000 |
| 2001 | 1.004 | 1.004 | 0.789 |
| 2002 | 1.011 | 1.006 | 0.638 |
| 2003 | 1.003 | 1.028 | 0.540 |
| 2004 | 1.015 | 1.085 | 0.496 |

*Table 4A.6*   Regression results of China's sources of economic growth, 1983–2004

| Explanatory variables | Model specification | | |
|---|---|---|---|
| | Growth rate | Backcasting | Integral |
| Intercept | −3.0330 (−3.110)*** | −2.4662 (−2.414)*** | −3.1539 (−3.253)*** |
| ln $ICT$ | 0.1337 (2.860)*** | 0.1342 (2.895)*** | 0.1340 (2.855)*** |
| ln $KN$ | 0.4513 (5.712)*** | 0.4299 (5.051)*** | 0.4554 (5.856)*** |
| ln $L$ | 0.4541 (2.207)*** | 0.4077 (2.102)*** | 0.4647 (2.229)*** |
| $R^2$ | 0.9764 | 0.9765 | 0.9763 |
| Adjusted $R^2$ | 0.9724 | 0.9726 | 0.9724 |
| Standard error | 0.0855 | 0.0851 | 0.0855 |
| Observations | 22 | 22 | 22 |
| Durbin–Watson statistic | 0.9283 | 0.9305 | 0.9282 |

*Note*: Figures in parentheses are the *t*-ratios. *, ** and *** indicate significance at 10, 5 and 1%.

*Table 4A.7*   Contributions to output growth in China, 1983–2004 (%)

|  | Period | | | |
|---|---|---|---|---|
|  | *1983–2004* | *1983–91* | *1992–2000* | *2000–4* |
| ICT capital | 2.79 | 0.29 | 5.01 | 2.97 |
|  | (30.1) | (2.6) | (61.8) | (21.0) |
| Other capital | 5.41 | 6.26 | 4.76 | 5.16 |
|  | (58.2) | (76.5) | (58.8) | (36.5) |
| Labour | 0.94 | 1.75 | 0.43 | 0.43 |
|  | (10.1) | (21.4) | (5.4) | (3.1) |
| TFP | 0.15 | −0.04 | −2.10 | 5.58 |
|  | (1.6) | (−0.4) | (−26.0) | (39.5) |
| Output | 9.28 | 8.19 | 8.10 | 14.14 |
|  | (100.0) | (100.0) | (100.0) | (100.0) |

*Note*: Figures in parentheses are the shares of each factor growth.

ICT capital. The contributions of the factor accumulations and technical change (or technological progress) to real output growth in China for the period 1983–2004 are shown in Table 4A.7. The estimation results do not differ much from those reported in Table 4.2. The contributions of ICT and non-ICT capital sum up to more than 80 per cent. Similarly, this study also finds that the contribution of ICT capital to growth has largely fluctuated between the 1980s and the recent years, whereas that of TFP has increased to more than 40 per cent during the most recent years. Finally, Table 4A.7 also shows remarkably contrasting results at different periods. During the 1980s, ICT capital had a contribution of only 3 per cent to economic growth, but its share increased to more than 60 per cent in the 1990s. During the first three years of the twenty-first century, ICT capital contributed 21 per cent to economic growth.

The robustness of the estimation results can be examined using a sensitivity analysis by assuming different rates of depreciation for the ICT capital stock. The estimated ICT capital stock shows a similar trend of contribution under different depreciation rates (Table 4A.8). Similar to the results shown in Table 4.5, the contribution of ICT capital becomes lower as $\delta$ increases, whereas that of TFP gets higher. As the depreciation rate of ICT capital increases, the regression results become more robust as standard errors are reduced and the *t*-ratios of all variables increase.

*Table 4A.8*   Results of sensitivity analysis

| Depreciation rate of ICT capital stock (%) | Contribution to output growth (%) | | | |
|---|---|---|---|---|
| | *ICT* | *KN* | *L* | *TFP* |
| 10 | 2.88 | 5.41 | 0.94 | 0.06 |
| | *(31.0)* | *(58.2)* | *(10.1)* | *(0.7)* |
| 15 | 2.79 | 5.41 | 0.94 | 0.15 |
| | *(30.1)* | *(58.2)* | *(10.1)* | *(1.6)* |
| 20 | 2.71 | 5.41 | 0.94 | 0.23 |
| | *(29.2)* | *(58.2)* | *(10.1)* | *(2.5)* |
| 25 | 2.64 | 5.41 | 0.94 | 0.30 |
| | *(28.5)* | *(58.2)* | *(10.1)* | *(3.2)* |
| 30 | 2.58 | 5.41 | 0.94 | 0.36 |
| | *(27.8)* | *(58.2)* | *(10.1)* | *(3.9)* |

*Note*: Figures in italic parentheses are the shares of each factor growth.

# 5
# New Economy and Efficiency among the Regions

In Chapter 4, the impact of the new economy on China's economic growth using data at the national level was examined. This chapter extends the discussion to regional growth and disparities in China, using data at the provincial level. The role of ICT in propelling China's regional growth is, however, very rarely discussed despite the country's emergence as one of the world's largest ICT markets. This chapter hence has two main objectives: (a) to estimate China's regional ICT capital stock and (b) to examine the impact of ICT investment on technical efficiency in China's regions.

The chapter begins with an account of the pattern of ICT investment in different regions over the past decade (from 1996 to 2004). This is followed by discussion of the literature concerned with the concept of technical efficiency and its relationship with ICT investment. The next section deals with the method applied in this study to assess the impact of ICT capital stock as well as other inputs on technical efficiency using regional data. Data for ICT and other forms of capital stock are derived from investment figures. Finally, based on the estimation results, the pattern of changes in the effect of ICT on technical efficiency among Chinese regions is illustrated.

## 5.1  ICT investment in Chinese regions

Testifying the increasing importance of ICT to China's economy, the ICT sector has been placed among the ten categories for high priority development by the National Development and Reform Commission (NDRC) and the Ministry of Science and Technology (MST).[1] According to the former Chinese Premier Zhu Rongji's 'Report on National Economic and Social Development during the Tenth Five-Year Plan', among the eight most important tasks to be achieved during the Tenth Five-Year Plan (2001–5) are 'changing the structure of industry towards more high-technology industry', 'developing the western region in a strategy of regionally balanced economic development' and 'investing in human capital in a strategy of promoting science, technology and education for the betterment of the nation' (Chow, 2002). The report thus marked a gradual shift of attention from 'focusing on the rapid development of the coastal (eastern) region' to one of 'promoting development of the interior' (Lai, 2002).[2] As China seeks to develop its inland (central and western) regions, a key question is whether investment in ICT will help reduce the country's regional disparity.

To further boost the development of the ICT industry, and to develop China into an internationally competitive ICT powerhouse instead of being merely a manufacturing centre, the Ministry of Information Industry (MII) set up several information industry bases in 2004.[3] In addition, the MII has also outlined development schemes for 23 special ICT sectors, such as digital television, mobile telecommunications and automobile electronics, a part of the Eleventh Five-Year Plan (2006–10) programme.[4]

The ICT industry has shown robust growth in different regions in the country, supported by preferential policies for regional development.[5] For instance, the ICT industries in north-eastern Jilin province and south-western Guizhou province grew by almost 30 per cent and more than 50 per cent, respectively.[6] To illustrate the relationship between ICT investment and labour productivity in China, a scatter diagram plotting the correlation between ICT investment per worker and GDP per worker among China's regions is drawn in Figure 5.1. Although most regions are shown to cluster close to the point of origin in the graph, it can be seen that ICT investment and labour productivity are in general correlated positively.

In 2004, the majority of the regions had a GDP per worker below 5000 yuan, and ICT investment per worker below 50 yuan.[7] The municipal city of Shanghai is an outlier which has GDP per worker and ICT investment per worker of almost 98,000 yuan and 254 yuan in 2004, respectively. In descending order of the level of ICT investment per worker, Shanghai is followed by Jiangsu (having less than half of Shanghai's investment and the second-highest GDP per worker among the regions after Guangdong), Tianjin, Guangdong (the province with the highest GDP per worker) and Beijing. Interestingly, in 2004, Jiangsu and Guangdong and the three municipal cities are the only areas with an ICT investment per worker at above 50 yuan, which is considerably higher than the national average of about 24 yuan per worker, and they account for three-quarters

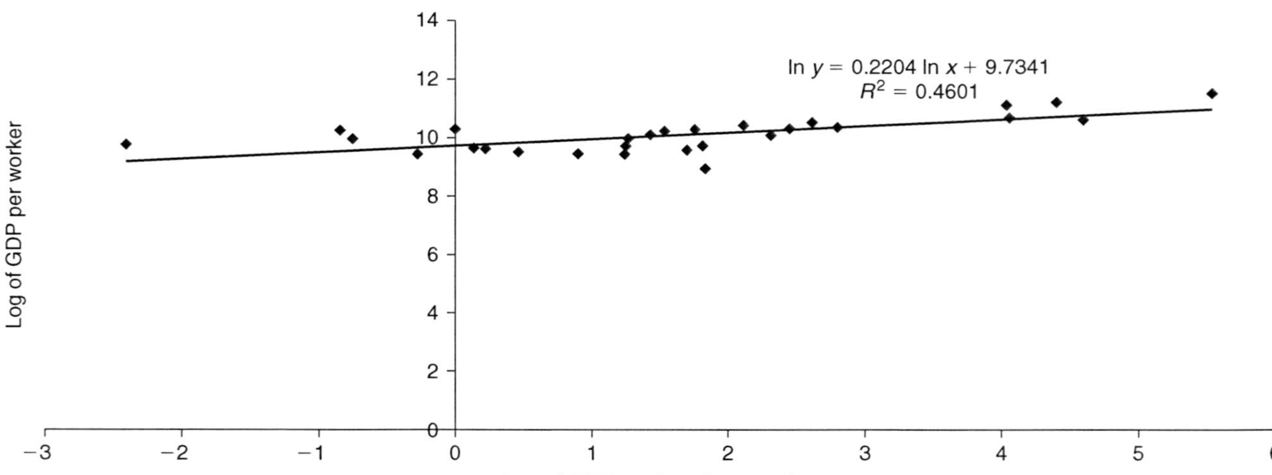


*Figure 5.1* Correlation between GDP per worker and ICT investment per worker in China's provinces, 2004
*Source*: National Bureau of Statistics, *Yearbook of China's Electronics Industry* and *China Statistics Yearbook on High Technology Industry* (various issues).

of total ICT investment in the whole of China (for ICT investment in individual province/municipal city, see the appendix to this chapter).

ICT investment (in real terms) in China had increased ninefold in a decade between 1993 and 2004, from 1.25 billion to 11.21 billion yuan (see Table 4A.1). In terms of aggregate ICT investment, the highest is found in the eastern region which had two-thirds of the national ICT investment in 2004 (Figure 5.2). The three municipal cities of Beijing, Tianjin and Shanghai made up the bulk of ICT investment during the 1990s, but their shares gradually fell behind those of the eastern region since 1999. However, it should be noted that investment in the eastern region was mainly concentrated in a few provinces such as Guangdong, Fujian, Jiangsu and Zhejiang. Between 1996 and 2004, it appears that the share of ICT investment had risen only in the eastern region, from 43 to 65 per cent. The shares of the municipal cities, central and western regions had dropped from 33 to 24 per cent, 16 to 5 per cent, and 8 to 5 per cent respectively. Yet, China, on average, still has a proportionately low ratio of ICT investment to GDP – 0.2 per cent in 2000 compared with Japan's 4.5 per cent, and 0.34 per cent in 2004.[8] The shares of ICT investment to GDP in the regions are much lower. For instance, in 2004, the respective shares for the municipal cities, eastern, central and western regions are 0.08, 0.22, 0.019 and 0.017 per cent (Figure 5.3).

## 5.2   ICT and technical efficiency: a review

The concepts of productivity and efficiency are among the most commonly used measures of firm or economic performance in economics literature. Productivity generally refers to the ratio of output to inputs, that is, the amount of output produced by the weighted total amount of inputs such as capital and labour. Efficiency, on the other hand, usually means the difference or gap between the actual and potential output produced given inputs (see Section 7.1 for more detailed discussion). Any variation in productivity can be attributed to differences in production technology or differences in the *efficiency* of the production process (Lovell, 1993, p. 3). The term 'efficiency' is used interchangeably with 'productive efficiency', which is made up of two components: technical efficiency and allocative efficiency. The former is concerned with 'maximising output for given inputs, or minimising inputs for a given output', while the latter is concerned with the allocation of resources that produces a given quantity of output at minimum cost given the input prices (Coelli et al., 2005). This chapter focuses on examining the effects of ICT on *technical* efficiency in the Chinese regions.

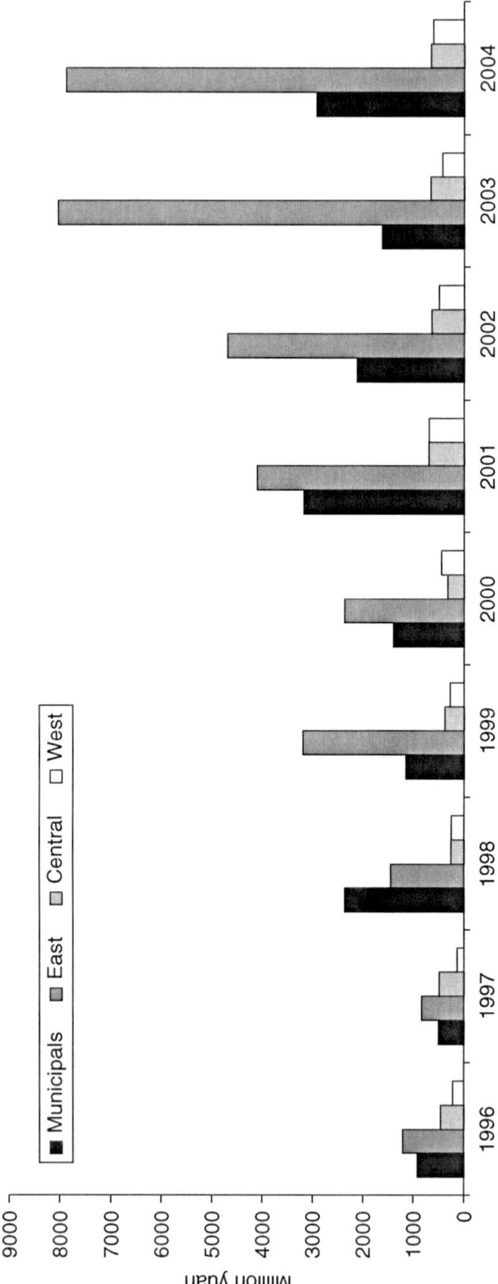


*Figure 5.2*  Total ICT investment in China's regions, 1996–2004
*Source*: National Bureau of Statistics, *Yearbook of China's Electronics Industry* and *China Statistics Yearbook on High Technology Industry* (various issues).

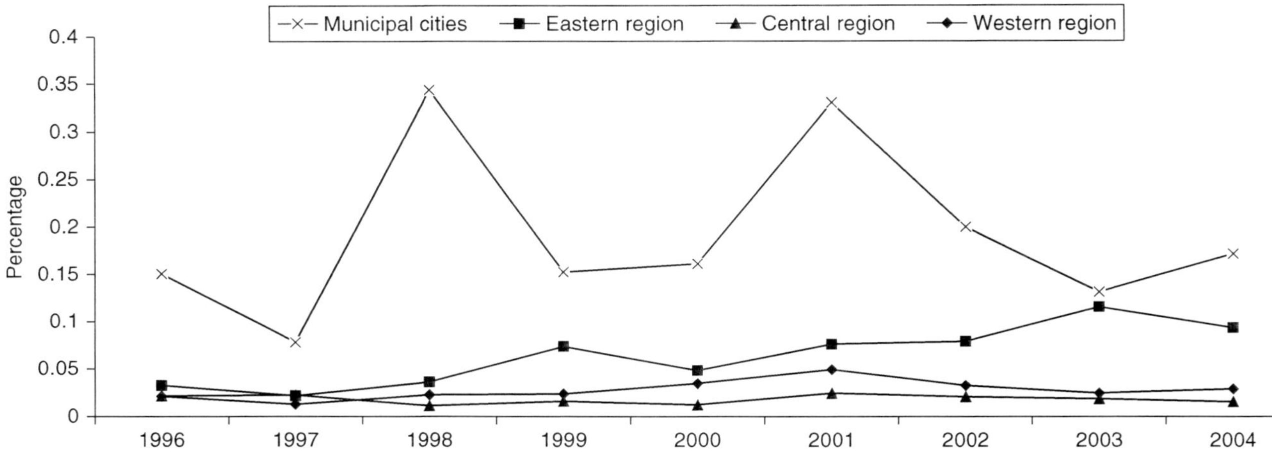


*Figure 5.3*   Ratio of ICT investment to GDP in China's regions, 1996–2004

*Source*: National Bureau of Statistics, *Yearbook of China's Electronics Industry* and *China Statistics Yearbook on High Technology Industry* (various issues).

### 5.2.1   Efficiency measurement

Many studies have provided definitions and measures of technical efficiency. For instance, in Koopmans (1951), 'a producer is technically efficient if an increase in any output requires a reduction in at least one other output or an increase in at least one input, and if a reduction in any input requires an increase in at least one other input or a reduction in at least one output'. The key emphasis is on efficient production relative to the 'production possibility frontier'. The earliest study that calculates efficiency measures is found in Farrell (1957) who analysed technical efficiency 'in terms of realized deviations from an idealized frontier isoquant' (Greene, 1993). Since then, several approaches have been developed to measure efficiency. One of the approaches is the econometric method which is employed in this chapter. This approach bears two main characteristics, that is, (i) stochastic which distinguishes the effects of noise from the effects of inefficiency and (ii) parametric which compounds the effects arising from misspecification of a functional form with inefficiency (Lovell, 1993, p. 19). The advantages and disadvantages of this technique are discussed in more detail in Section 7.2.

A typical stochastic frontier production function can be expressed as

$$y_i = f(x_i; \beta) \exp\{v_i - u_i\} \tag{5.1}$$

where output $y_i$ is the dependent variable, the inputs $x_i$ represent a set of explanatory variables, and $\beta$ is a vector of production technology parameters to be estimated. The random disturbance term given by $v_i$ captures statistical noise and is assumed to be independently and identically distributed as $N(0, \sigma_v^2)$. The disturbance term $u_i$ is a measure of technical inefficiency, a positive error component which is assumed to be independently distributed of $v_i$. Technical efficiency is given by the ratio of actual output, $y_i$, to the maximum potential output which is given by the stochastic production frontier, represented by $f(x_i; \beta)\exp\{v_i\}$ (see Chapter 7 for a more detailed discussion). The stochastic production frontier is in turn determined by the structure of production technology, that is the deterministic production frontier (Lovell, 1993, p. 20). Therefore, technical efficiency (*TE*) can be measured as

$$TE_i = \frac{y_i}{f(x_i; \beta)\exp\{v_i\}} = \exp\{-u_i\} \tag{5.2}$$

Having devised a technique for measuring technical efficiency, the outcome is normally generated as 'efficiency scores'. The distribution of efficiency scores can be evaluated using a one-stage analysis, where the efficiency scores are obtained from a regression of the dependent variable against a vector of explanatory variables. Efficiency scores are bounded by zero and one or below one. Some studies have attempted to transform efficiency scores for use as a dependent variable in a two-stage analysis (Kalirajan and Shand, 1988). Lovell (1993), however, advised caution on the use of explanatory variables in the second stage, which are those that the decision maker has no control over during the period under consideration, including quasi-fixed variables, socio-economic and demographic characteristics, the weather and so on.

The relationship between technical efficiency and other explanatory variables can be given as follows:

$$\exp\{-u_i\} = g(z_i; \gamma)\exp\{e_i\} \tag{5.3}$$

where $\exp\{-u_i\} = TE_i$, as given in equation (5.2). The application of this model for empirical analysis of the relationship between ICT and technical efficiency in the Chinese regions will be further discussed in Section 5.3.

### 5.2.2   ICT and technical efficiency

How does ICT affect economic performance and technical efficiency (TE)? From an organizational perspective, communication effectiveness is enhanced with computer networks transferring information at a reduced time and transaction costs required for task accomplishment (Shao and Lin, 2001). This in turn enables management to make sound decisions and better utilize resources, which would enhance a firm's capability to produce more output with the same amount of inputs (Shao and Lin, 2002).

There is extensive research documenting the positive correlation between ICT investments and productivity growth. However, literature that examines the impact of ICT on technical efficiency is limited. Shao and Lin (2001) found that 'the increase in technical efficiency incurred by ICT is one source for the productivity growth witnessed in previous studies'. In theory, technical inefficiency occurs when a country or firm produces output below its production possibility frontier curve, given inputs. Measuring the impact of ICT on firm performance by using the stochastic production frontier method, Shao and Lin (2001) found that ICT indeed has a positive impact on a firm's technical efficiency.

The same conclusion is also found in Becchetti et al. (2003) who used a stochastic frontier approach to estimate the impact of ICT investment on efficiency for small and medium-sized firms in Italy. The authors found that ICT investment affects firm efficiency by increasing the demand for skilled labour as well as average labour productivity, introducing new products or processes of communications, and increasing the average capacity utilization of telecommunications networks.

One empirical work that investigates the impact of ICT on regional economies is Susiluoto (2003) who defined regional efficiency as 'a region's ability to use its basic productive resources in an economic way to produce well being. In recognising the difference in the resource base of regions, a region with a good knowledge base, for instance, must produce more than its poorer neighbour in order to be equally efficient.' By applying the data development analysis (DEA) method to examine the effects of the ICT sector on economic efficiency among the regions of Finland, Susiluoto showed that 'raising ICT investment in the regional economy increases the performance level or efficiency of the regions'.[9]

### 5.2.3 China-related studies

Regional studies tend to look at the 'catch up' hypothesis of Abramovitz (1986) which postulates that technologically backward countries or regions (followers) have the potential for catching up with the more advanced (leaders) through faster growth in productivity. The narrowing of such a technological gap between the leaders and followers, or in other words, convergence, rests on the condition that 'improvement of social capabilities in backward regions attracts advanced technology and other production factors into these regions' (Jia, 1998).

Evidence of convergence in China's regional economies on the basis of technical efficiency performance is found in Wu (1999), who applied a stochastic frontier model to examine productivity growth among China's regions for the period of 1981–95. In an earlier study of China's state enterprises, Kalirajan and Zhao (1997) showed improvement in technical efficiency from 1986 to 1989 due to economic reform. They found an increasing trend in technical efficiency in all provinces during the four-year period, the highest being in Shanghai with an average TE score of 0.98. Recent studies that investigated convergence among China's regions included Yao and Zhang (2001) and Bhalla et al. (2003). The latter found evidence of convergence within 'pre-defined geo-economic sub-regions' such as the 'east', 'central' and 'west', but not between the sub-regions.

Other authors have focused on studies of industrial efficiency. For example, Kong et al. (1998) estimated a stochastic frontier production function for four Chinese industries (that is, building materials, chemicals, machinery and textiles) for the period 1990–94. Using regional dummies to capture the efficiency differences between the state-owned enterprises in three provinces, Sichuan, Shanxi and Jilin and those in Jiangsu province, they found that firms in the latter province which is more developed are more efficient. In a study on China's iron and steel industry using data from the 1995 industrial census, Zhang and Zhang (2001) measured technical efficiency of all large and medium-sized enterprises with a stochastic frontier production function. They found that location has not much impact on technical efficiency, although enterprises in the eastern region tend to be more efficient than those in other regions. One of their most important findings is that technical efficiency is closely related to the vintage of an enterprise's fixed capital assets, as efficient enterprises are those that use relatively new capital equipment. This could suggest that investment in new ICT equipment is crucial to improving firm efficiency.

Finally, in another study on China's iron and steel industry, Movshuk (2004) examined technological progress and changes in productive efficiency for about 100 large and medium enterprises during 1988–2000 using a stochastic frontier model. This chapter will extend the existing literature by including ICT capital in the production function, and provide new empirical findings of technical efficiency scores for the period 1995–2004.

## 5.3  Modelling framework

This section proposes a stochastic frontier model and applies it to test for the effect of ICT on technical efficiency in China's regions. The stochastic frontier model takes into account the differences between the ideal and actual output, thereby seeking to maximize technical efficiency theoretically (that is, minimizing the differences). These differences are attributed to factors 'that might not be under the control of the agent being studied', such as bad weather, breakdown of equipment, or any other random factors that might be construed as inefficiency (Greene, 1993, p. 76).

The model proposed by Battese and Coelli (1995) postulates the existence of technical inefficiency in the production process. The stochastic frontier model (referred to as the BC model) is conventionally expressed as follows:

$$\ln Y_{it} = \ln f(X_{it}, \beta) + \varepsilon_{it}$$

$$\varepsilon_{it} = v_{it} - u_{it} \tag{5.4}$$

where $X$ and $\beta$ are the vectors of the independent variables and unknown parameters to be estimated. The disturbance term, $\varepsilon_{it}$, is defined as the difference between $v_{it}$, a random measurement error assumed to be i.i.d. $N(0, \sigma_v^2)$ and independently distributed of $u_{it}$; and $u_{it}$, a non-negative random variable associated with technical inefficiency in production which is assumed to be independently distributed such that $u_{it}$ is truncated at zero of the normal distribution with mean, $\mu$, and variance, $\sigma^2$ (Battese and Coelli, 1995).

The BC model was further extended to analyse the influence of 'firm-specific environmental conditions' on economic performance in Wu (2001). By developing a model which examines the effect of environmental variables on technical inefficiency, equation (5.4) is rewritten as (adapted from Wu, 2001)

$$\ln Y_{it} = \ln f(x_{it}, z_{it}, t) + v_{it} - u_{it}(x_{it}, z_{it}, t) \tag{5.5}$$

where $z_{it}$ represents the 'environmental variables', such as ICT capital stock in this model, $x_{it}$ represents all other explanatory variables and $t$ is a time-trend variable. This model can be used to test the influence of the environmental variable on technical efficiency in the form of $u_{it} = u_{it}(z_{it}, t)$, as proposed by Battese and Coelli (1995). In this model, the estimates of the unknown parameters of the frontier production function can be obtained using the maximum likelihood (ML) method (O'Donnell et al., 2005).

In this chapter, a one-stage method is used to capture the effect of ICT on technical efficiency. The hypothesis is that ICT investment has a positive effect on regional technical efficiency in the production process among China's regions. The stochastic frontier model is designed to capture the effects of efficiency change resulting from factor inputs which incorporate the ICT capital stock. Following the model of Kumbhakar and Wang (2005), the efficiency effect of ICT in a specific region is determined by its endowment of ICT capital per worker, given by the ratio of ICT to labour in logarithmic form ($ICT_{it} - L_{it}$). By applying the KW model to equation (5.4), the Cobb–Douglas production function is specified as follows:

$$\ln Y_{it} = \beta_1 + \beta_2 \ln ICT_{it} + \beta_3 \ln KN_{it} + \beta_4 \ln L_{it} + v_{it} - u_{it} \tag{5.6}$$

$$u_{it} = \delta_0 + \delta_1(ICT_{it} - L_{it})$$

$$i = 1, 2, \ldots, 28 \text{ (provinces)}$$

$$t = 1, 2, \ldots, 10 \text{ (time: 1995, \ldots, 2004)}$$

where $Y$, $ICT$, $KN$ and $L$ stand for real output, ICT capital stock, non-ICT capital stock and employment, respectively.

This chapter will also apply the more flexible translog production function specified as follows:

$$\ln Y_{it} = \beta_0 + \beta_1 \ln ICT_{it} + \beta_2 \ln KN_{it} + \beta_3 \ln L_{it} + \gamma_1 (\ln ICT_{it})^2$$
$$+ \gamma_2 (\ln KN_{it})^2 + \gamma_3 (\ln L_{it})^2 + \eta_1 (\ln ICT_{it} \ln KN_{it})$$
$$+ \eta_2 (\ln ICT_{it} \ln L_{it}) + \eta_3 (\ln KN_{it} \ln L_{it}) + v_{it} - u_{it} \qquad (5.7)$$
$$u_{it} = \delta_0 + \delta_1 \ln (ICT_{it} - L_{it})$$
$$i = 1, 2, \ldots, 28 \text{ (provinces)}$$
$$t = 1, 2, \ldots, 10 \text{ (time: 1995, } \ldots, 2004)$$

where $\beta$, $\gamma$ and $\eta$ are the parameters to be estimated.

## 5.4   Description of data

### 5.4.1   Output and labour

Output is defined as real GDP, which is derived from nominal GDP deflated by the consumer price index (CPI) in 1978 constant prices. The data for GDP and employment for the period 1995–2004 is obtained from *China Statistical Yearbook*. In order to take into account the inter-regional differences in price level, the regional CPI at constant prices for each municipal city, province and autonomous region is derived by dividing the national CPI in constant prices by the individual region's CPI in current prices.

### 5.4.2   ICT capital stock

The ICT capital stock is estimated based on real ICT investment data that are derived from 'investment in capital construction' and 'investment in innovation' from the communications equipment, and computer (hardware and software) industries, obtained from *China Statistical Yearbook on High Technology Industry*, deflated by the regional fixed asset price index which is obtained from *China Statistical Yearbook*. As data for investment in the ICT industry by region are only available for the period 1995–2004, the empirical analysis only covers this period. It should be noted that data for Qinghai province and Tibet are not available, and therefore the analysis will not cover these two regions. To calculate the regional CPI in constant prices, the fixed asset price index for each province/municipal city is derived from dividing the national fixed asset price index by the individual region's fixed asset investment price index.

The initial ICT capital stock is estimated using the following formula, that is, the growth rate approach discussed in Chapter 2, which has also been used by Shinjo and Zhang (2003) and Miyagawa et al. (2004) for the estimation of Japanese ICT capital stock:

$$K_t = \frac{I_{t+1}}{\gamma + \delta} \tag{5.8}$$

where $\gamma$ is the average annual growth rate of ICT capital investment ($I$) and $\delta$ is the weighted average rate of depreciation. The real ICT capital stock is then derived as follows:

$$K_t = I_t + (1 - \delta)K_{t-1} \tag{5.9}$$

where the capital stock, $K$, at year $t$ is dependent on the level of ICT investment, $I_t$ in the same year and capital stock level in the preceding year which is deflated by the rate of depreciation, $\delta$. The *non-ICT* capital stock series is derived from non-ICT investment figures, which is the difference between total fixed asset investment and real ICT investment.

Figures for ICT capital investment are deflated by the fixed asset price index, to be consistent with the method of estimation used in Chapter 4. Similar to Chapter 4, the choice of the capital depreciation rate, $\delta$, for ICT capital stock is based on empirical studies of Kim (2002) and Miyagawa et al. (2004), while that of non-ICT capital stock is based on Islam and Dai (2005). The rate of depreciation for non-ICT capital stock is assumed to be 5 per cent, based on the rate for total capital stock used in Islam and Dai (2005). Since ICT equipment becomes obsolete faster than other forms of capital, this study adopts 15 per cent as the proxy depreciation rate for China's ICT capital stock in 1995–2004, that is, $\delta = 0.15$, used in the preceding chapter.

The ICT capital stock is estimated for the municipal cities, eastern, central and western regions (Figure 5.4). The share of ICT capital stock has changed remarkably over the past ten years. In 1995, the municipal cities and eastern region took up one-third of ICT capital stock respectively, with the central region having another one-fifth of the total. However, by 2004, while the share of the eastern region has increased to 64 per cent, those of the municipal cities and central region have dropped to 24 and 7 per cent, respectively. The share of the western region has declined slightly during the same period, from 8 per cent in 1995 to about 5 per cent in 2004.

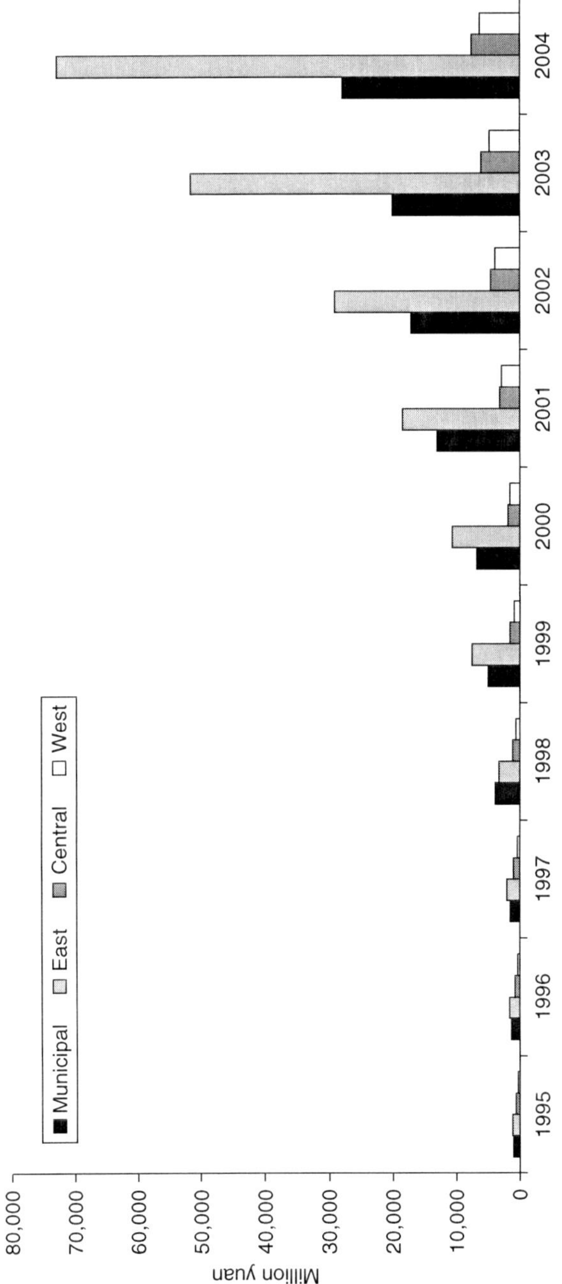



*Figure 5.4*  ICT capital stock in China's regions, 1995–2004
*Source*: State Statistical Bureau, *Yearbook of China's Electronics Industry* and *China Statistics Yearbook on High Technology Industry* (various issues).

## 5.5  Estimation results and interpretation

### 5.5.1  Estimation results

The empirical work begins with a regression of output (real GDP) against factor inputs, that is, ICT capital, non-ICT capital and labour, expressed in equations (5.6) and (5.7), respectively. The sample has 280 observations for the period 1995–2004. The initial estimates of the parameters are presented in Table 5.1. All coefficients of the parameters are statistically significant with the correct sign. The results show that the growth of ICT capital as well as physical capital and labour is positively related to China's economic growth in the 1990s and the beginning of the twenty-first century. The likelihood ratio test ($\chi^2(6) = 57.677$) shows that the production is better described by the translog function as the null hypothesis of $\gamma_1 = \gamma_2 = \gamma_3 = \eta_1 = \eta_2 = \eta_3 = 0$ is rejected.[10]

### 5.5.2  ICT and technical efficiency in China

The next objective of this chapter is to examine the effect of ICT on technical efficiency. The estimation results obtained from the translog

*Table 5.1*  Estimation results of the stochastic frontier models

| | Cobb–Douglas | | Translog | |
|---|---|---|---|---|
| | *Parameter* | *t-statistic* | *Parameter* | *t-statistic* |
| *Production frontier* | | | | |
| Intercept | 2.5827 | 9.394 | 11.4319 | 3.090 |
| ln *ICT* | 0.0446 | 3.383 | 0.0999 | 0.521 |
| ln *KN* | 0.5894 | 22.834 | −1.0772 | −1.542 |
| ln *L* | 0.3868 | 20.723 | 1.7736 | 5.394 |
| $(\ln ICT)^2$ | | | 0.0375 | 5.976 |
| $(\ln KN)^2$ | | | 0.0809 | 2.397 |
| $(\ln L)^2$ | | | −0.0163 | −0.637 |
| ln *ICT* ln *KN* | | | −0.0379 | −2.055 |
| ln *ICT* ln *L* | | | −0.0372 | −2.211 |
| ln *KN* ln *L* | | | −0.0747 | −2.148 |
| *Efficiency effects* | | | | |
| Intercept | 0.2081 | 1.329 | 0.9624 | 6.156 |
| $\ln(ICT - L)$ | −0.0364 | −1.847 | −0.2673 | −5.183 |
| $\sigma_u^2$ | 0.0634 | 2.943 | 0.0453 | 9.010 |
| $\gamma$ | 0.7834 | 8.143 | 0.8392 | 17.254 |
| Log likelihood value | 61.5448 | | 90.3834 | |

*Notes*: Dependent variable $=$ ln *GDP*; observations $=$ 280.

model in equation (5.7) are used. The technical efficiency scores are estimated by using the computer program FRONTIER 4.1.[11] A region that is efficient in production will have a TE score of one, or technical inefficiency ($U$) score of zero (Tong and Chan, 2003). In the empirical results, $\delta_1$ is found to be negative, therefore implying that ICT has a negative impact on technical inefficiency; in other words, it has a positive impact on technical efficiency. Based on the unrestricted frontier model specified by equation (5.7), $\delta_1$ is found to be statistically significant at all levels, thus proving that ICT has had an important impact on technical efficiency across the country during the past decade.

Performance of individual regions is shown in Table 5.2 which also includes the results by Kalirajan and Zhao (1997). By plotting the average TE scores in each region over the years 1995–2004, it can be seen that all regions have experienced a gradually increasing trend in technical efficiency over the past decade (Figure 5.5). However, there was a slight decline in technical efficiency in 1995–97, which suggests that the Asian financial crisis had a negative impact on technical efficiency. This can also be attributed to a fall in ICT investment occurring in many regions in 1997, except for Liaoning, Guangxi, Hainan, Shanxi, Heilongjiang and Ningxia (see Table 5A.1 in the appendix to this chapter). It can also be noticed that only the municipal cities and eastern regions have average TE scores which are consistently above the national average since the mid-1990s. The central region has a TE score that approximated the national average in 2004, however.

Among the regions, the municipal cities have the highest average TE score of 0.92 over the period 1995–2004. The highest average TE for an individual area is found in Tianjin and Shanghai, followed by Fujian, Guangdong, Heilongjiang, Jiangsu and Beijing, which are the only areas with TE scores of 0.9 and above (Table 5.2). As of 2004, the highest TE scores were found in Tianjin (0.98), Beijing, Shanghai and Guangdong (0.97 each), followed by Jiangsu (0.96), Fujian (0.95) and Shandong (0.94). The lowest TE scores, in ascending order, were found in Xinjiang (0.29), Yunnan (0.41) and Guizhou (0.47) of the western region. The north-eastern provinces of Liaoning, Jilin and Heilongjiang have performed comparatively well, having TE scores over 0.91 in 2004, while Liaoning and Heilongjiang have consistently scored over 0.9 since 2001. These provinces could be further boosted with the implementation of the 'North-east revitalization' programme which has produced positive effects for economic growth in the region.[12] As a matter of fact, the North-East Revitalization Office of the State Council approved over 260 ICT projects amounting to 4 billion yuan (US$481 million) in an overall

*Table 5.2*  Average technical efficiency (TE) in China's regions

| Region/province | Average TE, 1986–89 (Kalirajan and Zhao, 1997) | Average TE, 1995–2004 (this study) |
|---|---|---|
| Beijing | 0.9207 | 0.9014 |
| Tianjin | 0.9098 | 0.9610 |
| Shanghai | 0.9802 | 0.9468 |
| *Municipal cities* | *0.9369* | *0.9364* |
| Hebei | 0.8444 | 0.7163 |
| Liaoning | 0.8759 | 0.8699 |
| Jiangsu | 0.8999 | 0.9048 |
| Zhejiang | 0.9599 | 0.7832 |
| Fujian | 0.9241 | 0.9265 |
| Shandong | 0.9514 | 0.8832 |
| Guangdong | 0.8967 | 0.9196 |
| Guangxi | 0.8615 | 0.4695 |
| Hainan | 0.8085 | 0.5651 |
| *Eastern region* | *0.8914* | *0.7820* |
| Shanxi | 0.7235 | 0.5239 |
| Inner Mongolia | 0.6324 | 0.6004 |
| Jilin | 0.7810 | 0.7724 |
| Heilongjiang | 0.8971 | 0.9121 |
| Anhui | 0.9121 | 0.5131 |
| Jiangxi | 0.7330 | 0.6094 |
| Henan | 0.7711 | 0.6395 |
| Hubei | 0.8393 | 0.6949 |
| Hunan | 0.8516 | 0.6517 |
| *Central region* | *0.7934* | *0.6575* |
| Sichuan | 0.6716 | 0.6465 |
| Guizhou | 0.7464 | 0.3407 |
| Yunnan | 0.9668 | 0.2323 |
| Shaanxi | 0.6170 | 0.5787 |
| Gansu | 0.7282 | 0.4400 |
| Ningxia | 0.6846 | 0.4331 |
| Xinjiang | 0.7539 | 0.2894 |
| *Western region* | *0.7384* | *0.4230* |
| National | 0.8265 | 0.6997 |

*Note*: The TE scores from Kalirajan and Zhao (1997) are for state enterprises only.

plan for the development of the ICT sector as part of the economic revitalization of the north-eastern region.[13] In the western region, the effect of ICT on technical efficiency is lifted by the higher scores achieved by Sichuan and Shaanxi provinces.

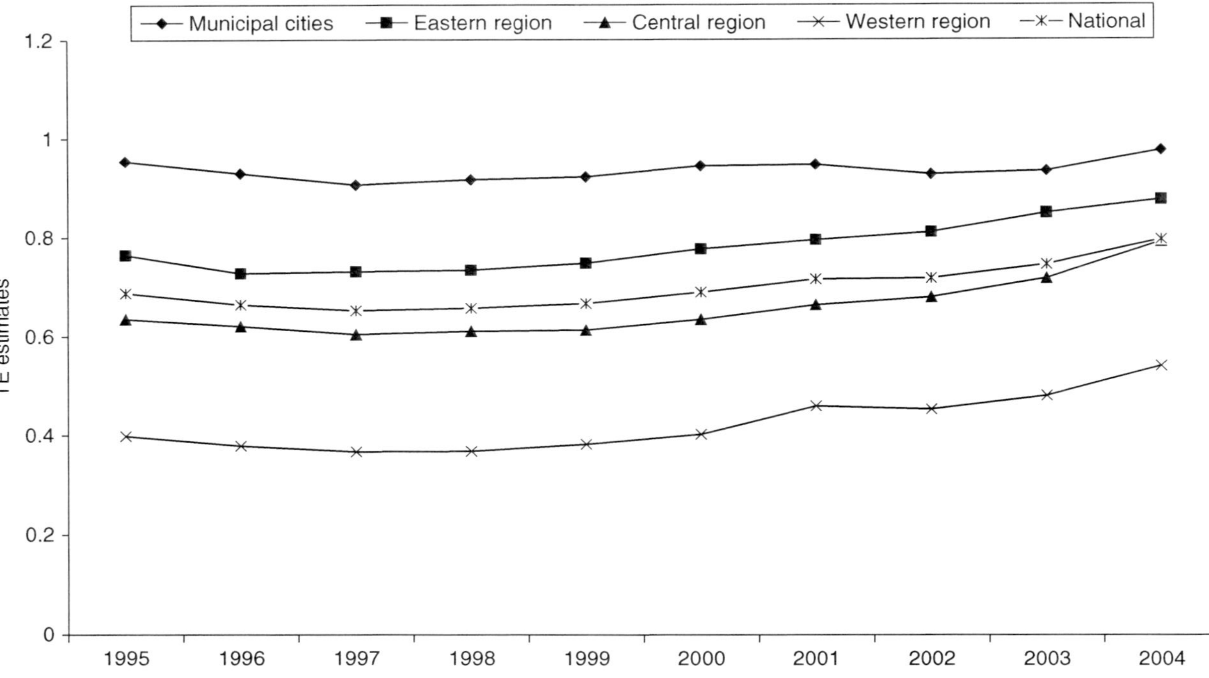


*Figure 5.5*   The effect of ICT on technical efficiency, 1995–2004

## 5.6   Conclusion

This chapter has shown that ICT investment has had a significantly positive effect on regional technical efficiency in China during the 1990s and the early years of the twenty-first century. As such, ICT investment is expected to be an important driver of China's economic growth. Although most of the investment is pumped into the coastal region and municipal cities, the rising technical efficiency of the central and western regions suggests a rapid catch-up of the latter with the more developed regions within the next decade. The exceptional performance of the three north-eastern provinces indicates the strong priority given to development in these areas.

There is thus a case for supporting greater investment in infrastructure and ICT equipment, especially in the central and western regions. While the Japanese experience has shown the rate of return on ICT capital stock to be higher than that on other forms of capital, thereby encouraging policies which stimulate ICT investment (Miyagawa et al., 2004), there is no reason why China, having the potential for training of a much larger base of skilled labour to better utilize its ICT resources, could not do the same.

There are areas for further research in this field of study. China's economic efficiency could be better evaluated using industrial or firm-level data. Chapter 7 will attempt to present an industry-level study examining the effect of foreign capital on efficiency performance. The issue of factor reallocation between ICT and non-ICT capital, as has been studied for developed economies, has so far been unaccounted for. It is not known whether there is any substitution of ICT capital for non-ICT capital, as data on the price of ICT capital are unavailable. Thus it still remains to be seen whether the same substitution has taken place as shown in the developed countries.

# Appendix

*Table 5A.1*   Real ICT investment in China's regions, 1996–2004 (million yuan)

| Region/province | 1996 | 1997 | 1998 | 1999 | 2000 | 2001 | 2002 | 2003 | 2004 |
| --- | --- | --- | --- | --- | --- | --- | --- | --- | --- |
| Beijing | 212.91 | 130.39 | 213.60 | 189.27 | 244.27 | 156.20 | 131.61 | 121.03 | 506.43 |
| Tianjin | 334.79 | 210.27 | 1388.91 | 485.92 | 476.47 | 1019.56 | 324.59 | 274.28 | 343.54 |
| Shanghai | 374.14 | 162.74 | 761.11 | 474.82 | 675.86 | 1993.04 | 1653.83 | 1221.36 | 2063.06 |
| Hebei | 135.86 | 46.42 | 96.83 | 81.75 | 38.38 | 136.30 | 118.79 | 259.01 | 142.40 |
| Liaoning | 34.75 | 36.24 | 97.05 | 105.94 | 144.21 | 188.98 | 186.35 | 213.00 | 161.77 |
| Jiangsu | 229.20 | 138.12 | 129.34 | 138.84 | 184.76 | 359.24 | 661.19 | 3381.34 | 3682.07 |
| Zhejiang | 39.18 | 23.07 | 47.74 | 198.67 | 115.36 | 336.56 | 374.88 | 484.77 | 421.60 |
| Fujian | 76.79 | 51.51 | 120.20 | 89.08 | 158.79 | 302.67 | 224.43 | 424.48 | 298.47 |
| Shandong | 175.62 | 126.26 | 89.70 | 126.27 | 178.90 | 370.50 | 403.67 | 622.30 | 571.43 |
| Guangdong | 509.84 | 386.62 | 843.91 | 2429.24 | 1526.41 | 2360.05 | 2701.66 | 2478.10 | 2499.45 |
| Guangxi | 5.76 | 17.25 | 16.16 | 9.00 | 8.57 | 24.05 | 3.96 | 121.15 | 65.04 |
| Hainan | 0.26 | 7.75 | 4.04 | 6.39 | 6.82 | 16.34 | 6.59 | 19.22 | 1.72 |
| Shanxi | 3.00 | 6.50 | 13.52 | 6.22 | 11.01 | 14.92 | 10.12 | 5.31 | 148.97 |
| Inner Mongolia | 10.27 | 1.21 | 0.94 | 8.20 | 0.00 | 0.30 | 2.32 | 14.37 | 59.09 |
| Jilin | 24.09 | 12.69 | 8.38 | 158.98 | 43.66 | 66.64 | 100.14 | 16.46 | 51.67 |
| Heilongjiang | 172.35 | 376.90 | 51.91 | 54.64 | 24.45 | 23.15 | 1.29 | 7.82 | 6.96 |
| Anhui | 9.23 | 9.23 | 15.72 | 14.31 | 16.92 | 82.87 | 78.13 | 182.85 | 54.86 |
| Jiangxi | 21.62 | 8.93 | 21.10 | 6.50 | 3.78 | 19.91 | 49.34 | 78.90 | 125.27 |
| Henan | 128.34 | 20.68 | 54.85 | 9.84 | 43.95 | 141.64 | 76.49 | 95.11 | 69.72 |
| Hubei | 28.38 | 15.35 | 56.78 | 55.10 | 37.49 | 225.54 | 203.06 | 236.83 | 91.73 |
| Hunan | 60.34 | 37.88 | 34.82 | 68.91 | 143.46 | 122.64 | 119.98 | 17.84 | 41.20 |
| Sichuan | 142.74 | 108.03 | 164.74 | 179.38 | 250.71 | 392.16 | 349.60 | 185.85 | 338.48 |
| Guizhou | 5.73 | 2.46 | 8.78 | 9.44 | 18.93 | 39.06 | 30.14 | 124.84 | 135.96 |
| Yunnan | 0.27 | 1.07 | 2.52 | 2.58 | 2.12 | 1.78 | 1.56 | 12.34 | 18.22 |
| Shaanxi | 61.21 | 22.71 | 65.39 | 73.97 | 151.84 | 203.59 | 96.85 | 50.37 | 65.58 |
| Gansu | 6.78 | 2.86 | 8.81 | 7.73 | 16.34 | 28.75 | 14.29 | 50.60 | 45.64 |
| Ningxia | 0.00 | 0.41 | 0.24 | 1.84 | 2.94 | 20.26 | 2.13 | 1.10 | 0.27 |
| Xinjiang | 0.55 | 0.10 | 0.24 | 0.26 | 0.00 | 2.56 | 0.09 | 0.00 | 0.00 |

*Source: China Statistical Yearbook on High Technology Industry 2002–2004.*

*Table 5A.2*  ICT capital stock in China's regions, 1995–2004 (million yuan)

| Region/province | 1995 | 1996 | 1997 | 1998 | 1999 | 2000 | 2001 | 2002 | 2003 | 2004 |
|---|---|---|---|---|---|---|---|---|---|---|
| Beijing | 566.85 | 694.73 | 720.91 | 826.37 | 891.68 | 1002.20 | 1008.07 | 988.47 | 961.23 | 1323.47 |
| Tianjin | 799.80 | 1014.63 | 1072.70 | 2300.70 | 2441.52 | 2551.76 | 3188.56 | 3034.86 | 2853.91 | 2769.36 |
| Shanghai | 902.69 | 1141.43 | 1132.96 | 1724.13 | 1940.32 | 2325.14 | 3969.41 | 5027.83 | 5495.02 | 6733.82 |
| Hebei | 325.74 | 412.74 | 397.25 | 434.50 | 451.07 | 421.79 | 494.82 | 539.39 | 717.49 | 752.27 |
| Liaoning | 95.65 | 116.05 | 134.88 | 211.69 | 285.88 | 387.20 | 518.10 | 626.73 | 745.71 | 795.63 |
| Jiangsu | 516.59 | 668.30 | 706.18 | 729.59 | 758.99 | 829.90 | 1064.66 | 1566.15 | 4712.57 | 7687.76 |
| Zhejiang | 84.04 | 110.62 | 117.10 | 147.28 | 323.85 | 390.63 | 668.60 | 943.19 | 1286.48 | 1515.11 |
| Fujian | 157.91 | 211.01 | 230.86 | 316.43 | 358.05 | 463.13 | 696.33 | 816.31 | 1118.34 | 1249.06 |
| Shandong | 413.95 | 527.47 | 574.61 | 578.12 | 617.67 | 703.92 | 968.84 | 1227.18 | 1665.40 | 1987.02 |
| Guangdong | 1174.06 | 1507.79 | 1668.24 | 2261.92 | 4351.87 | 5225.50 | 6801.72 | 8483.12 | 9688.75 | 10734.89 |
| Guangxi | 12.72 | 16.57 | 31.33 | 42.79 | 45.37 | 47.14 | 64.12 | 58.46 | 170.85 | 210.26 |
| Hainan | 0.68 | 0.84 | 8.46 | 11.23 | 15.94 | 20.37 | 33.66 | 35.20 | 49.14 | 43.49 |
| Shanxi | 8.17 | 9.93 | 14.94 | 26.22 | 28.50 | 35.23 | 44.87 | 48.25 | 46.33 | 188.34 |
| Inner Mongolia | 27.27 | 33.46 | 29.65 | 26.14 | 30.42 | 25.86 | 22.28 | 21.26 | 32.44 | 86.67 |
| Jilin | 62.58 | 77.29 | 78.38 | 75.01 | 222.74 | 232.99 | 264.68 | 325.12 | 292.81 | 300.55 |
| Heilongjiang | 435.50 | 542.53 | 838.05 | 764.25 | 704.26 | 623.07 | 552.76 | 471.14 | 408.28 | 329.35 |
| Anhui | 20.25 | 26.44 | 31.71 | 42.67 | 50.58 | 59.92 | 133.80 | 191.85 | 345.92 | 348.89 |
| Jiangxi | 53.33 | 66.95 | 65.83 | 77.06 | 72.00 | 49.61 | 75.14 | 113.21 | 175.13 | 274.13 |
| Henan | 295.53 | 379.54 | 343.29 | 346.65 | 304.49 | 302.77 | 399.00 | 415.63 | 448.40 | 450.86 |
| Hubei | 68.82 | 86.88 | 89.20 | 132.60 | 167.81 | 180.13 | 378.65 | 524.91 | 683.01 | 672.29 |
| Hunan | 146.14 | 184.55 | 194.75 | 200.36 | 239.22 | 346.79 | 417.41 | 474.78 | 421.40 | 399.39 |
| Sichuan | 349.02 | 439.41 | 481.53 | 574.04 | 667.31 | 817.92 | 1087.39 | 1273.88 | 1268.65 | 1416.84 |
| Guizhou | 16.10 | 19.41 | 18.96 | 24.90 | 30.61 | 44.95 | 77.26 | 95.81 | 206.28 | 311.29 |
| Yunnan | 0.72 | 0.89 | 1.82 | 4.07 | 6.04 | 7.26 | 7.95 | 8.32 | 19.41 | 34.72 |
| Shaanxi | 171.63 | 207.09 | 198.74 | 234.32 | 273.15 | 384.01 | 530.00 | 547.35 | 515.61 | 503.85 |
| Gansu | 20.28 | 24.03 | 23.28 | 28.60 | 32.04 | 43.57 | 65.78 | 70.20 | 110.26 | 139.36 |
| Ningxia | 1.06 | 0.90 | 1.18 | 1.24 | 2.90 | 5.41 | 24.86 | 23.26 | 20.87 | 18.01 |
| Xinjiang | 1.40 | 1.74 | 1.58 | 1.58 | 1.60 | 1.36 | 3.72 | 3.25 | 2.76 | 2.35 |

# 6
# Foreign Direct Investment and Productivity Growth

China's phenomenal growth has coincided with substantial inflows of foreign direct investment (FDI) over the past decades. Researchers thus argue that increased inflows of FDI into China might have played an important role in the country's economic development (Zhang, 1999). The objective of this chapter is to examine whether the growth of inward FDI in the Chinese economy has generated significant productivity spillover effects on domestic firms. In addition, this study also investigates regional variation in spillover effects with the aim of comparing the western, central and coastal regions in China. Furthermore, this chapter also sheds some light on the possible variation in spillover effects before and after the Asian financial crisis in 1997.

The rest of the chapter is organized as follows. Section 6.1 briefly summarizes the general theories and debates regarding spillover effects of FDI. Section 6.2 reviews studies of spillover effects resulting from FDI in China. Section 6.3 discusses the modelling framework and data issues. Section 6.4 presents empirical results and interpretation and Section 6.5 concludes the chapter.

## 6.1   FDI and its spillover effects: a brief review

### 6.1.1   The debates

Ruane and Ugur (2004) pointed out that the existing literature distinguishes between the direct and indirect effects of FDI on host countries. Direct effects are reflected in capital formation, employment and trade associated with inflows of FDI, while the indirect effects manifest themselves in improved technology and management practices in local companies as a result of contact with multinational enterprises (MNEs).

Further to direct and indirect effect classification, Lenger and Taymaz (2006) specifically identified three types of FDI spillover, that is, horizontal, vertical and labour spillovers. Horizontal spillovers are those that affect firms operating in the same industry or in the same region. Vertical spillovers are those that affect firms operating in vertically related industries, such as from foreign suppliers to domestic users or from foreign users to domestic suppliers. Labour spillovers are those that result from labour turnover, for instance employment by domestic firms of workers who previously worked for foreign firms.

There are various channels through which inward FDI can benefit local firms in the host country (Fosfuri et al., 2001; Cheung and Lin, 2004):

- There may exist backward and forward linkages between foreign affiliates and local firms. That is, domestic firms can learn about the products and technologies brought in by foreign investors.
- Foreign affiliates may increase local firms' productivity through 'demonstration effects'. By the presence of MNEs in the domestic markets, foreign products/technologies can inspire and stimulate local innovators to develop new products and processes.
- Spillovers arise when subsidiaries of foreign firms train local employees who later join local firms or set up their own companies, thereby equipping the local firm with the technological, marketing and managerial knowledge of MNEs.

Evidence of the effects of FDI and multinational presence on recipient economies is varied. The study by Castellani and Zanfei (2003) concluded that the existing literature identified both positive and negative effects of FDI on host country economic performance. A benefit arising from FDI is that MNEs may affect local productivity by training workers and managers who then move on to work in domestic enterprises. Furthermore, the presence of MNEs creates demand for local inputs, increases the specialization and efficiency of upstream and downstream activities and generates positive externalities for local industries. MNEs also exert competitive pressures to improve the static and dynamic efficiency of domestic firms. However, a foreign presence may negatively affect productivity of local firms, particularly in the short term, to the extent that MNEs can monopolize markets and draw demand from domestic firms, causing them to cut production and reduce their efficiency. MNEs can also substitute local suppliers with foreign ones, and thus disrupt existing linkages (Castellani and Zanfei, 2003).

## 6.1.2  Empirical studies

Numerous empirical work on FDI and its spillover effects on productivity in countries other than China has been undertaken. Examples include Bende-Nabende et al. (2003), Castellani and Zanfei (2003), Chung et al. (2003), Damijan et al. (2003), Lorentzen et al. (2003), Mcvicar (2002), Sanna-Randaccio (2002), Sjoholm (1999) and Todo and Miyamoto (2002), to cite a few. Among these studies, Chung et al. (2003) focused on the US car parts industry; Bende-Nabende et al. (2003) looked at some Asia Pacific Economic Cooperation (APEC) economies (Hong Kong, Taiwan, Japan, Philippines and Thailand); Feinberg and Majumdar (2001) examined the pharmaceutical industry in India; Sjoholm (1999) and Todo and Miyamoto (2002) both investigated Indonesian firms; Castellani and Zanfei (2003) and Sadik and Bolbol (2001) considered Arab countries; Liu et al. (2000) and Mcvicar (2002) probed European countries (UK, Belgium, France, Italy and Spain); and Damijan et al. (2003) and Lorentzen et al. (2003) included several Eastern European countries in their studies. The existing studies have explored the spillover effects of FDI on productivity using either cross-section or panel data (Table 6.1). The most common measure of productivity in the reviewed literature is real GDP or gross output per unit of labour.

Current studies of different countries have resulted in contrasting findings. The studies of Indonesian industry by Sjoholm (1999) and Todo and Miyamoto (2002) provided evidence to support the argument that FDI and the presence of MNEs result in technology transfer. The results show that increased competition increases the degree of spillovers from FDI. Using panel data from 1995 to 1997, Todo and Miyamoto (2002) found that R&D activities and human resource development conducted by MNEs stimulate knowledge diffusion from MNEs to domestic firms.[1] Furthermore, R&D activities by a domestic firm may also promote knowledge diffusion from MNEs to the firm in the host country.

In the US and some other APEC economies, however, the spillover effects seem to be less significant. Chung et al. (2003) examined the US car parts industry with Japanese assemblers between 1979 and 1991 and found that the productivity of local suppliers who sold components to the Japanese transplants did not grow faster than the productivity of unaffiliated suppliers, and therefore there was no evidence of direct technology transfer affecting US suppliers' productivity. The study by Bende-Nabende et al. (2003) used panel data of some APEC countries (Hong Kong, Taiwan, Japan, Philippines and Thailand) from the period 1965–99. Their study indicates that the direct long-run impact of FDI on

*Table 6.1* Literature on spillover effects

| Author(s) | Types of spillover | Variables | Data type |
| --- | --- | --- | --- |
| Bende-Nabende et al. (2003) | Spillover on productivity | *Output* (log), *GDP value*; *CF* (log), capital stock; *EMP* (log), number employed; *FDI* (log), values of FDI; *HC* (log), total mean years of education (human capital); *M* (log), import value of machinery; and *X* (log), exports | Panel data |
| Castellani and Zanfei (2003) | Spillover on productivity | *Y* (log), real output; *L* (log), number of employees; *K* (log), stock of capital; *M* (log), use of raw materials and energy; *F* (log), sum of workers employed by all foreign-owned firms; and *D* (log), sum of employment in domestic firms | Panel data (firm level) |
| Damijan et al. (2003) | Technology spillover on productivity | *Y*, gross output; *K*, capital stocks; *L*, number of employees; *N*, materials used in production; *F*, foreign ownership; *RD*, R&D expenditures of the firm measured as ratio to total sales; *HS*, share of foreign-owned firms; *X*, export propensity, exports to sales ratio; and *I*, imports propensity, ratio of imports to the material costs (all variables are first-differentiated) | Panel data (firm level) |
| Feinberg and Majumdar (2001) | Spillover on productivity | *Y*, deflate value of production using wholesale price index (WPI); *C*, physical capital, deflated net fixed assets; *L*, labour input, dividing firm's total wage by a measure of unit labour costs; *R*, raw material; *KO*, total R&D stock, deflated R&D expenditure; *KF*, foreign R&D stock; and *KD*, foreign R&D stock | Panel data (firm level) |
| Liu et al. (2000) | Spillover on productivity | *VAD*, value added per worker; *CID*, physical capital intensity, measured by capital–labour ratio; *HCD*, human capital; *IAD*, intangible asset per worker; *SID*, average size of firms in the particular industry; *CR*, industry concentration ratio; *FP*, the presence of MNEs; and *GAP*, the technology gap | Panel data (industrial level) |

| Study | Focus | Variables | Data |
|---|---|---|---|
| Mcvicar (2002) | Spillover on productivity | $TFP$ (log), TFP for industry; $LRD$ (log), log FDI-weighted R&D stock; $RDdj$ (log), domestic own-sector foreign R&D stocks; $RDfj$ (log), import-weighted own-sector foreign R&D stocks; $RDdi$ (log), domestic input–output weighted outside sector R&D stocks; and $RDfi$, import-use weighted foreign R&D stocks | Panel data (industrial level) |
| Sadik and Bolbol (2001) | Spillover on productivity | $dY/Y$, growth rate of GDP; $FDI/Y$, ratio of FDI to GDP; $dL/L$, growth rate of labour; and $I/Y$, ratio of investment to GDP (growth-accounting equation) | Panel data |
| Sjoholm (1999) | Spillover on labour productivity | Effect on the level of labour productivity: $VA/L$ (log), value added per employee; $I/L$, total investment per employee (capital intensity); $FDI$ (log), share of foreign gross output; and $SCALE$ (log), ratio between an establishment's production and the average production in the same sector<br>Effect on growth in productivity: $\Delta Y$, value added; or $Y/L$; $\Delta L$, number of employees; $\Delta I/Q$, share of gross output (investment level); or $\Delta I/L$, as for investment level; and $\Delta FDI$, average foreign share of a sector's gross output | Cross-section data (industrial-level) |
| Todo and Miyamoto (2002) | Spillover on productivity | $Y$ (log), value added per efficiency unit of labour for each domestic firm. Value added is deflated by the wholesale price index; $KE$, expenditure on R&D by domestic firm; $KE \times FDI$, the product of R&D expenditures and industry-wide FDI; $MNEke$, FDI with R&D; and $MNEnoKe$, FDI without R&D (fixed effect model applied) | Cross-section data |

output was significant and positive for the comparatively less developed economies, that is, the Philippines and Thailand. However, the impact was negative in the advanced economies such as Japan and Taiwan. Moreover, it is found that the characteristics of the FDI spillover process in the developed economies were similar to those in the less developed economies. But, overall, the positive spillovers were more evident in the less developed economies.

The spillover effects varied among the European countries examined in the literature. Lorentzen et al. (2003) examined the issue using cross-section data from the automotive supply sector in Eastern Europe and found that the car component suppliers in Eastern European countries did absorb foreign technology. Affiliation with networks centred on MNEs greatly increases the rate of technology transfer. The authors also argued that ownership structure is a significant issue because technology transfer is dependent on the degree of control that MNEs exercise over the use of assets. Similar results are also found in a study by Liu et al. (2000) which examined the productivity spillovers of FDI on UK manufacturing industries. Damijan et al. (2003), however, showed contrasting results to Lorentzen et al. (2003). Using firm-level data from eight transitional economies in Central and Eastern Europe (Bulgaria, the Czech Republic, Estonia, Hungary, Poland, Romania, Slovakia and Slovenia) for the period 1994–98, Damijan et al. (2003) found no or even negative horizontal knowledge spillover from foreign-owned firms to domestic firms. Their study further clarified that technology is being transferred to local firms primarily through direct foreign linkages. The spillovers through arm's-length trade are only occasionally present, while the spillovers from foreign to domestic firms are negative or insignificant.

To sum up, the main findings of the literature surveyed are that inward FDI is an important source for economic development and that it often leads to greater productivity in the host country. This chapter is motivated by these findings as well as the fact that inflows of FDI in China have grown rapidly in recent history.


## 6.2   Studies of FDI in China

There are a number of studies on FDI in China (see Table 6.2). Most of these have examined the determinants of FDI and the important role it plays in promoting exports and growth. However, literature on productivity spillover effects of FDI is rare. A typical framework pertaining to the relationship  between FDI and spillover effects in the Chinese economy

*Table 6.2* Literature on spillover effects in the Chinese economy

| Studies | Types of spillover | Independent variables | Data type |
| --- | --- | --- | --- |
| Cheung and Lin (2004) | Spillover on innovation (R&D technology) | *Patent Applications* (log), measure of R&D output; *FDI* (log), the values lagged one period; *S&Tper* (log), number of personnel for science and technical development; *S&Texp* (log), expenditures on science and technical development; *Fexport* (log), share of foreign-funded enterprises export to its gross output; and *PGDP* (log), per capita GDP | Panel data (provincial level) |
| Hu and Jefferson (2002) | Spillover on productivity | $Y$, value added; $K$ (log), net value of fixed asset; $L$ (log), number of workers; *Firm-level FDI*, foreign share of a firm's equity; *Industry-level FDI*, sales-weighted average of firm-level FDI; and *FirmFDI* × *IndustryFDI* | Cross-section data |
| Liu (2002a) | Spillover on productivity | $Q$, value added; $L$, labour; $K$, capital; $H$, percentage of registered capital owned by foreign investors; and $\overline{H}$, share of foreign equity participation in industry | Panel data (industrial level) |

can be found in Cheung and Lin (2004), Hu and Jefferson (2002) and Liu (2002a). These studies followed a production function approach.

Cheung and Lin (2004) argued that FDI can boost innovation activity and hence productivity growth in the host country via spillover channels such as skilled labour turnovers, demonstration effects and supplier–customer relationships. They examined the extent to which FDI into China has affected innovation activities in Chinese firms. Their analysis is based on provincial-level data from 1995 to 2000 and the number of patent applications is used as a measure of R&D output. They found that there is some positive spillover effect from FDI on the number of domestic patent applications according to panel data analysis.[2] FDI has the strongest spillover effect on minor innovations (especially for external design patents). Spatially, the spillover effects of FDI are stronger in the western region where FDI inflow is spatially more concentrated. In addition, the estimation results by Cheung and Lin (2004) reveal that science and technical personnel and R&D expenditure are the most important determinants of innovation.

Another study of spillover effects in China is Hu and Jefferson (2002) who showed similar results to Cheung and Lin (2004). The authors used data from large and medium-size enterprises in China's electronic and textile industries to examine the spillover effects on the productivity and sales of domestic firms. They found that the spillover effects of FDI on domestic firms in the electronics industry are negative and statistically significant, but for the textile industry the results are negative and statistically insignificant. In the short run, FDI is found to enhance the productivity of FDI receiving firms, but depress that of non-FDI domestic firms. However, in the long run, for both electronic and textile industries, the productivity gap between domestic and FDI receiving firms narrows. It is clear that domestic firms are able to absorb technology and know-how that are introduced to the industry from abroad.

The positive spillover effects of FDI on productivity were also found by Liu (2002a) in a study of 29 manufacturing industries in the Shenzhen special economic zone (SEZ) for the period from 1993 to 1998. Liu showed that FDI had significant spillover effects on both the level and growth rate of productivity of manufacturing industries. Specifically, the productivity of the state-owned and joint-owned sectors is more responsive than that of other domestic sectors to increases in FDI in the industry.

The limited evidence cited above indicates that FDI or the presence of MNEs has positive spillover effects on productivity in domestic firms. However, due to the limited number of studies, the issue remains unclear, particularly with regard to regional variations in China. This chapter is complementary to the above literature. It examines the spillover effects of FDI on productivity using the provincial data. The geographical aspects of FDI spillovers are also investigated for the Chinese economy in this chapter.

## 6.3   Modelling framework and data issues

As indicated earlier in the literature review, empirical evidence shows that FDI can have a positive effect on productivity in host countries. To present an empirical exercise using the Chinese data, the following model is considered:

$$\ln(PRO_{it}) = \alpha_0 + \alpha_1 \ln(FDI_{it}) + \alpha_2 \ln(K_{it}) + \alpha_3 \ln(TRADE_{it})$$

$$+ \alpha_4 \ln(LF_{it}) + \varepsilon_{it} \tag{6.1}$$

where the left-hand side variable, *PRO*, is the 'spillover' indicator, that is, labour productivity, and the explanatory variables, *FDI*, *K*, *TRADE* and *LF* represent the intensities of FDI, capital and trade, and employment in foreign-funded firms, respectively.[3] The basic theory underlying the above model is that knowledge and/or technology can be transferred to host countries either through foreign participation or through international trade.

The empirical estimation of equation (6.1) is based on panel data of 28 regions for the period 1993–2002.[4] All data used in this chapter were obtained from various issues of *China Statistical Yearbook*, and explained in detail as follows:

- *Labour productivity (PRO)* is defined as the ratio of real GDP to the number of staff and workers in each region. The real GDP is derived from nominal GDP deflated by a price index with base year 1985. Wu (2004) made several observations regarding the price index. Due to the price control policy in China, prices changed very little during the pre-reform period. Consequently, the price movement has become more volatile since economic reform began as the economy has been transformed towards a market economy. The following approach similar to equation (2.6) is adopted for computing the price index:

$$P_{it} = \frac{Y_{it}^{cur}}{Y_{it}^{con}} \tag{6.2}$$

  where $P_{it}$, $Y_{it}^{cur}$ and $Y_{it}^{con}$ represent the price index, GDP in current price, and GDP in constant price for the *i*th region at period *t*, respectively.

- *The intensity of FDI* is defined as the ratio of actually used foreign direct investment over fixed asset investment at the provincial level. Wu (2004) found that the regional growth rates of FDI vary substantially over time; therefore, to reflect this variation, the proportion of FDI over the total fixed asset investment is used. FDI, initially measured in US dollars, is converted to Chinese currency yuan using the official exchange rate.
- *Capital stock intensity* is defined as the ratio of capital stock per worker. The value of capital stock in each year is derived using the perpetual inventory approach, which was employed in Wu (2004). The estimation was based on the gross investment value deflated by a price index expressed in 1953 prices.
- *Trade intensity* is defined as the ratio of the total value of trade over GDP at the provincial level. It is expected that trade intensity is positively related to labour productivity.

It is posited in previous research that foreign firms train local employees who later join local firms or establish their own companies, resulting in the transfer of technological, marketing and managerial knowledge from MNEs to domestic firms. In light of this, the number of *workers employed by foreign-funded enterprises* (FFEs) over the total number of staff and workers is used to test for spillover effects on labour productivity.

The descriptive statistics for all variables used in the study are presented in Table 6.3. The skewness of all the variables is close to zero. Furthermore, the Jarque–Bera test statistics imply that most series *PRO*, *FDI*, *K*, *TRADE*, and *LF* are normally distributed.

Figure 6.1 reports labour productivity for the three municipal cities (Beijing, Shanghai, and Tianjin) and provinces in the coastal, central and western regions of China from 1993 to 2002. It can be seen that labour productivity for the four regions experienced positive growth in the last decade. In addition, the magnitude of labour productivity in the coastal region is almost twice as great as that in the western region.

## 6.4  Empirical results and interpretation of the results

### 6.4.1  Tests for stationarity

The empirical work begins by testing the stationarity of variables to be used in equation (6.1). Two panel data unit-root tests, that is the LLC test developed by Levin et al. (2002) and the IPS test by Im et al. (2003), are conducted to see if all the variables are stationary (refer to the appendix to this chapter for more details about the two tests). The results of the LLC

*Table 6.3*   Descriptive statistics of the variables

|  | *ln(PRO)* | *ln(FDI)* | *ln(K)* | *ln(TRADE)* | *ln(LF)* |
|---|---|---|---|---|---|
| Mean | 9.694 | −3.920 | 10.453 | −1.835 | 10.740 |
| Median | 9.685 | −3.800 | 10.433 | −2.210 | 10.597 |
| Maximum | 11.116 | −1.517 | 12.045 | 2.550 | 13.201 |
| Minimum | 8.751 | −7.428 | 9.400 | −3.453 | 6.908 |
| Std. dev. | 0.506 | 1.167 | 0.545 | 1.043 | 1.296 |
| Skewness | 0.301 | −0.449 | 0.370 | 0.992 | 0.129 |
| Kurtosis | 2.523 | 2.904 | 2.695 | 3.472 | 2.074 |
| Jarque–Bera | 6.869 | 9.527 | 7.475 | 48.542 | 10.774 |
| Probability | 0.032 | 0.009 | 0.024 | 0.000 | 0.005 |
| Sum sq. dev. | 71.351 | 379.976 | 82.764 | 303.435 | 468.4442 |
| Sample size | 280 | 280 | 280 | 280 | 280 |

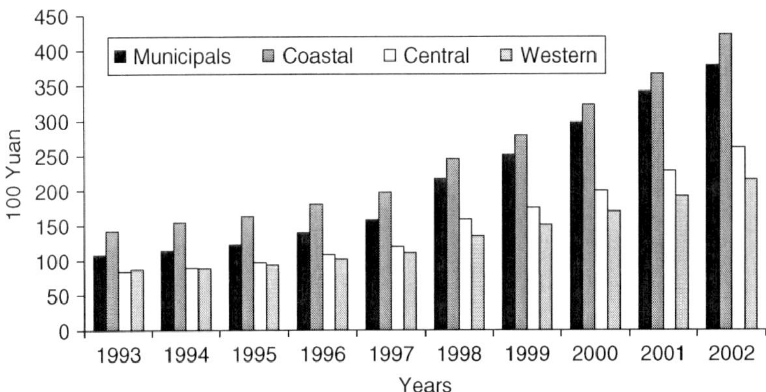


*Figure 6.1*   Annual average of labour productivity in China, 1993–2002
*Source*: *China Statistical Yearbook* 1994–2003.

test are shown in Table 6.4, and indicate that variables like *PRO* and *K* are non-stationary when a time trend is excluded. However, these variables become stationary when a time trend is included. Other variables such as *FDI*, *TRADE* and *LF* are stationary. Conversely, the results of the IPS test are listed in Table 6.5, and these results differ from the findings of the LLC test. This casts a shadow of ambiguity on the results. The IPS test shows that most variables are non-stationary either with or without the inclusion of a time trend. However, the LLC test gives a clear-cut result that all variables are stationary when a time trend is included. Thus, the results of the LLC test are preferred in the study. For the purpose of

*Table 6.4*   LLC unit-root test results

| No. of lags | ln(PRO) | ln(FDI) | ln(K) | ln(TRADE) | ln(LF) |
|---|---|---|---|---|---|
| *No trend* | | | | | |
| 0 | 6.450 | −3.462 | 3.675 | −7.217 | −16.436 |
| | (1.000) | (0.000) | (1.000) | (0.000) | (0.000) |
| 1 | 4.695 | −6.854 | 2.556 | −11.273 | −4.394 |
| | (1.000) | (0.000) | (0.995) | (0.000) | (0.000) |
| 2 | 0.347 | −14.105 | 1.937 | −7.506 | −0.697 |
| | (0.636) | (0.000) | (0.974) | (0.000) | (0.757) |
| *Trend* | | | | | |
| 0 | −7.330 | −8.050 | −4.556 | −9.470 | −28.043 |
| | (0.000) | (0.000) | (0.000) | (0.000) | (0.000) |
| 1 | −6.076 | −5.895 | −7.978 | −2.490 | −10.493 |
| | (0.000) | (0.000) | (0.000) | (0.006) | (0.000) |
| 2 | −3.704 | −20.482 | −10.667 | 2.003 | −44.261 |
| | (0.000) | (0.000) | (0.000) | (0.977) | (0.000) |
| | $\Delta ln(LP)$ | $\Delta ln(FDI)$ | $\Delta ln(K)$ | $\Delta ln(TRADE)$ | $\Delta ln(LF)$ |
| *No trend* | | | | | |
| 0 | −9.750 | −15.105 | −9.972 | −17.524 | −22.076 |
| | (0.000) | (0.000) | (0.000) | (0.000) | (0.000) |
| 1 | −3.633 | −8.166 | −6.010 | −10.264 | −11.822 |
| | (0.000) | (0.000) | (0.000) | (0.000) | (0.000) |
| 2 | −2.319 | −14.327 | −6.879 | 1.667 | −46.835 |
| | (0.010) | (0.000) | (0.000) | (0.952) | (0.000) |
| *Trend* | | | | | |
| 0 | −10.420 | −17.114 | −10.318 | −20.821 | −14.528 |
| | (0.000) | (0.000) | (0.000) | (0.000) | (0.000) |
| 1 | 0.423 | −27.632 | −4.403 | −18.748 | −8.098 |
| | (0.664) | (0.000) | (0.000) | (0.000) | (0.000) |
| 2 | 3.168 | −5.882 | 0.012 | −3.623 | −32.826 |
| | (0.999) | (0.000) | (0.505) | (0.000) | (0.000) |

*Notes*: The null hypothesis is $H_0$: non-stationary (unit-root). *p*-values are in parentheses. Significant values are in bold type.

comparison, panel data estimations both with and without a time trend will be carried out. The panel data estimation results without a time trend are listed in Table 6.6. The estimation results with a time trend are listed in Table 6.7.

## 6.4.2   Tests for heteroscedasticity

After identifying the stationarity of the variables to be used in this chapter the issue of heteroscedasticity in the regression models is now

*Table 6.5*   IPS unit-root test results

| No. of lags | ln(LP) | ln(INV) | ln(FDI) | ln(K) | ln(TRADE) | ln(LF) |
|---|---|---|---|---|---|---|
| **No trend** | | | | | | |
| 0 | 10.517 | 5.326 | 0.623 | 9.058 | **−2.650** | **−10.487** |
| | (1.000) | (1.000) | (0.733) | (1.000) | **(0.004)** | **(0.000)** |
| 1 | 7.533 | 1.422 | −0.675 | 6.971 | **−3.423** | **−2.489** |
| | (1.000) | (0.923) | (0.250) | (1.000) | **(0.000)** | **(0.006)** |
| 2 | 4.525 | 1.776 | −0.743 | 5.639 | −1.643 | 0.749 |
| | (1.000) | (0.962) | (0.229) | (1.000) | (0.050) | (0.773) |
| **Trend** | | | | | | |
| 0 | −0.749 | **−1.760** | −0.476 | 1.236 | −1.281 | **−5.990** |
| | (0.227) | **(0.039)** | (0.317) | (0.892) | (0.100) | **(0.000)** |
| 1 | −0.132 | 0.951 | 0.395 | 0.376 | −0.176 | **−1.868** |
| | (0.448) | (0.829) | (0.654) | (0.647) | (0.430) | **(0.031)** |
| 2 | 0.344 | **−2.645** | −0.468 | 0.076 | 1.026 | −1.497 |
| | (0.634) | **(0.004)** | (0.320) | (0.530) | (0.848) | (0.067) |

| No. of lags | $\Delta$ln(LP) | $\Delta$ln(INV) | $\Delta$ln(FDI) | $\Delta$ln(K) | $\Delta$ln(TRADE) | $\Delta$ln(LF) |
|---|---|---|---|---|---|---|
| **No trend** | | | | | | |
| 0 | **−4.629** | **−4.705** | **−7.509** | **−3.406** | **−8.635** | **−9.280** |
| | **(0.000)** | **(0.000)** | **(0.000)** | **(0.000)** | **(0.000)** | **(0.000)** |
| 1 | −1.166 | −0.107 | **−3.039** | −0.660 | **−4.423** | **−5.312** |
| | (0.122) | (0.457) | **(0.001)** | (0.255) | **(0.000)** | **(0.000)** |
| 2 | 0.132 | **−2.977** | −1.359 | 0.083 | 0.468 | **−4.687** |
| | (0.552) | **(0.002)** | (0.087) | (0.533) | (0.680) | **(0.000)** |
| **Trend** | | | | | | |
| 0 | −0.714 | 0.616 | **−2.845** | −0.484 | **−3.688** | **−1.905** |
| | (0.238) | (0.731) | **(0.002)** | (0.314) | **(0.000)** | **(0.028)** |
| 1 | 1.945 | 2.042 | −1.508 | 1.222 | **−2.180** | −0.078 |
| | (0.974) | (0.979) | (0.066) | (0.889) | **(0.015)** | (0.469) |
| 2 | 2.628 | −6.595 | 0.037 | 2.196 | 0.466 | **−6.407** |
| | (0.996) | (0.000) | (0.515) | (0.986) | (0.679) | **(0.000)** |

*Notes*: The null hypothesis is $H_0$: non-stationary (unit-root). *p*-values are in parentheses. The normalized IPS *t*-bar statistic is distributed as $N$ (0,1).

investigated. The results of White's test for heteroscedasticity using OLS estimates are shown at the bottom of Tables 6.6 and 6.7. White's test shows highly significant results, that is, the *p*-values of the test statistics are almost zero in both cases. The results indicate the presence of heteroscedasticity and hence the *t*-statistics are corrected using White's heteroscedasticity corrected estimators. Estimation by GLS is also applied to allow for heteroscedasticity across regions.

*Table 6.6* Regression results without a time trend

| | Standard | | | | | Fixed effects | | | | | Random effects | | |
|---|---|---|---|---|---|---|---|---|---|---|---|---|---|
| | OLS | OLS $(t-1)$ | 2SLS | GLS | GLS $(t-1)$ | OLS | OLS $(t-1)$ | 2SLS | GLS | GLS $(t-1)$ | 2SLS | GLS | GLS $(t-1)$ |
| Constant | −0.878 | −0.540 | −1.486 | −0.797 | −0.255 | 0.656 | **1.368** | −0.381 | **0.513** | **1.203** | −0.923 | 0.170 | 0.826 |
| | (−2.047) | (−1.415) | (−4.087) | (−2.766) | (−0.853) | (1.564) | (2.982) | (−1.373) | (2.112) | (3.649) | (−2.173) | (0.316) | (1.675) |
| ln($FDI_{it}$) | 0.081 | 0.080 | 0.088 | 0.068 | 0.067 | 0.037 | 0.034 | 0.077 | 0.029 | 0.027 | 0.083 | 0.042 | 0.039 |
| | (4.827) | (4.117) | (4.062) | (5.182) | (4.145) | (3.005) | (1.944) | (2.743) | (3.257) | (2.061) | (2.749) | (2.857) | (1.930) |
| ln($K_{it}$) | 0.893 | 0.849 | 0.938 | 0.878 | 0.825 | 0.876 | 0.774 | 0.940 | 0.867 | 0.774 | 0.950 | 0.872 | 0.778 |
| | (38.232) | (24.579) | (36.185) | (59.732) | (28.717) | (30.110) | (15.589) | (35.533) | (44.284) | (22.325) | (28.870) | (31.928) | (16.875) |
| ln($TRADE_{it}$) | −0.145 | −0.147 | −0.181 | −0.125 | −0.129 | 0.003 | 0.007 | −0.009 | −0.021 | −0.009 | −0.054 | −0.015 | −0.012 |
| | (−10.848) | (−9.218) | (−10.356) | (−12.105) | (−9.567) | (0.197) | (0.379) | (−0.310) | (−1.307) | (−0.594) | (−1.453) | (−1.090) | (−0.631) |
| ln($LF_{it}$) | 0.093 | 0.111 | 0.105 | 0.096 | 0.107 | 0.001 | 0.037 | 0.047 | 0.016 | 0.049 | 0.047 | 0.017 | 0.051 |
| | (5.899) | (7.020) | (7.678) | (7.463) | (8.513) | (0.059) | (1.750) | (1.630) | (1.968) | (2.988) | (1.476) | (0.762) | (2.108) |
| Coastal | 0.276 | 0.266 | 0.235 | 0.316 | 0.266 | – | – | – | – | – | 0.356 | 0.370 | 0.362 |
| | (14.461) | (12.076) | (14.921) | (20.105) | (16.251) | | | | | | (5.385) | (5.522) | (5.702) |
| Central | 0.326 | 0.319 | 0.298 | 0.376 | 0.320 | – | – | – | – | – | 0.511 | 0.433 | 0.428 |
| | (11.025) | (11.404) | (8.338) | (15.140) | (12.261) | | | | | | (8.845) | (4.397) | (5.761) |
| Western | 0.333 | 0.331 | 0.316 | 0.364 | 0.302 | – | – | – | – | – | 0.456 | 0.323 | 0.339 |
| | (11.960) | (11.250) | (9.625) | (14.428) | (14.139) | | | | | | (4.292) | (3.198) | (5.749) |
| Post-1997 | 0.017 | 0.090 | −0.002 | 0.024 | 0.108 | 0.044 | **0.159** | 0.025 | **0.038** | 0.146 | 0.014 | 0.044 | 0.152 |
| | (0.646) | (2.426) | (−0.095) | (1.289) | (3.506) | (1.971) | (4.338) | (1.286) | (2.203) | (4.870) | (0.545) | (1.913) | (4.345) |
| Adjusted $R^2$ | 0.937 | 0.928 | 0.939 | 0.977 | 0.977 | 0.984 | 0.982 | 0.986 | 0.994 | 0.992 | 0.972 | 0.969 | 0.964 |
| Durbin–Watson | 0.236 | 0.411 | 0.287 | 0.341 | 0.698 | 0.512 | 0.998 | 0.597 | 0.595 | 1.281 | 0.551 | 0.440 | 0.859 |
| Log likelihood | 185.354 | 154.892 | – | – | – | 386.523 | 342.832 | – | – | – | – | – | – |
| White's test ($nR^2$) | **77.183** (0.000) | | | | | | | | | | | | |

*Notes*: $t$-statistics are in parentheses with the exception of White's test statistic ($nR^2$) for which the $p$-value is reported. Significant values at the level of 5% are in bold type.

*Table 6.7*  Regression results with a time trend

| | Standard | | | | | Fixed effects | | | | | Random effects | | |
|---|---|---|---|---|---|---|---|---|---|---|---|---|---|
| | OLS | OLS (t−1) | 2SLS | GLS | GLS (t − 1) | OLS | OLS (t − 1) | 2SLS | GLS | GLS (t − 1) | 2SLS | GLS | GLS (t − 1) |
| Constant | −1.004 | −0.698 | −1.420 | −0.945 | −0.451 | 1.776 | 3.620 | 1.561 | 2.658 | 3.975 | 0.330 | 0.877 | 2.426 |
| | (−2.924) | (−1.990) | (−4.679) | (−4.767) | (−1.974) | (3.451) | (4.049) | (1.696) | (10.496) | (6.790) | (0.276) | (1.032) | (2.501) |
| ln($FDI_{it}$) | 0.080 | 0.079 | 0.089 | 0.066 | 0.063 | 0.041 | 0.040 | 0.085 | 0.037 | 0.036 | 0.090 | 0.045 | 0.044 |
| | (4.916) | (4.043) | (4.230) | (5.603) | (4.521) | (2.908) | (2.092) | (2.362) | (3.745) | (3.170) | (2.513) | (2.745) | (2.062) |
| ln($K_{it}$) | 0.905 | 0.865 | 0.931 | 0.891 | 0.841 | 0.773 | 0.568 | 0.772 | 0.676 | 0.524 | 0.842 | 0.810 | 0.637 |
| | (65.835) | (33.033) | (37.044) | (148.580) | (32.515) | (20.849) | (6.372) | (13.809) | (32.740) | (8.622) | (11.147) | (15.665) | (7.784) |
| ln($TRADE_{it}$) | −0.146 | −0.148 | −0.181 | −0.125 | −0.130 | 0.006 | 0.010 | 0.005 | −0.013 | −0.010 | −0.046 | −0.012 | −0.008 |
| | −(11.196) | (−9.220) | (−10.190) | (−12.040) | (−9.616) | (0.442) | (0.540) | (0.209) | (−0.862) | (−0.676) | (−1.281) | (−0.950) | (−0.556) |
| ln($LF_{it}$) | 0.094 | 0.111 | 0.105 | 0.098 | 0.109 | −0.010 | 0.014 | 0.023 | −0.009 | 0.015 | 0.035 | 0.012 | 0.037 |
| | (6.124) | (7.188) | (7.562) | (8.224) | (9.156) | (−0.535) | (0.704) | (0.558) | (−1.489) | (1.190) | (0.831) | (0.446) | (1.376) |
| Trend | −0.004 | −0.005 | 0.002 | −0.003 | −0.005 | 0.016 | 0.037 | 0.026 | 0.030 | 0.044 | 0.017 | 0.010 | 0.026 |
| | (−0.607) | (−0.693) | (0.314) | (−0.736) | (−0.693) | (2.631) | (3.083) | (2.374) | (8.612) | (5.202) | (1.376) | (1.370) | (2.233) |
| Coastal | 0.277 | 0.268 | 0.235 | 0.318 | 0.273 | – | – | – | – | – | 0.337 | 0.357 | 0.331 |
| | (13.296) | (11.871) | (14.039) | (20.017) | (15.708) | | | | | | (4.650) | (5.315) | (4.794) |
| Central | 0.332 | 0.327 | 0.295 | 0.385 | 0.336 | – | – | – | – | – | 0.434 | 0.384 | 0.308 |
| | (10.475) | (10.259) | (8.429) | (15.595) | (10.516) | | | | | | (4.641) | (3.279) | (3.227) |
| Western | 0.338 | 0.336 | 0.314 | 0.369 | 0.314 | – | – | – | – | – | 0.382 | 0.276 | 0.222 |
| | (10.394) | (10.054) | (9.042) | (13.713) | (10.637) | | | | | | (2.999) | (2.654) | (3.285) |
| Post-1997 | 0.027 | 0.104 | −0.007 | 0.026 | 0.115 | 0.046 | 0.131 | 0.033 | 0.044 | 0.114 | 0.017 | 0.044 | 0.130 |
| | (0.645) | (2.025) | (−0.200) | (1.059) | (2.882) | (2.350) | (4.749) | (2.237) | (3.589) | (4.632) | (0.782) | (2.040) | (4.465) |
| Adjusted $R^2$ | 0.937 | 0.928 | 0.938 | 0.977 | 0.977 | 0.984 | 0.983 | 0.987 | 0.995 | 0.993 | 0.972 | 0.969 | 0.966 |
| Durbin–Watson | 0.238 | 0.404 | 0.287 | 0.338 | 0.695 | 0.510 | 0.882 | 0.618 | 0.665 | 1.224 | 0.557 | 0.437 | 0.795 |
| Log likelihood | 185.521 | 155.096 | – | – | – | 389.063 | 352.638 | – | – | – | – | – | – |
| White's test ($nR^2$) | 96.841 (0.000) | | | | | | | | | | | | |

Notes: *t*-statistics are in parentheses with the exception of White's test statistic ($nR^2$) for which the *p*-value is reported. Significant values at the level of 5% are in bold type.

### 6.4.3  Endogeneity issue

From a theoretical point of view, the relationship between FDI and labour productivity in a sector may be bidirectional. Inward FDI is also expected to have a positive effect on productivity. Similarly, the level of labour productivity in a sector may also be an important factor influencing the level of FDI (Sun et al., 2002; Liu and Wang, 2003). If there exists a two-way relationship between FDI and productivity, there is an endogeneity problem. In addition, the problem might exist for other regressors as well. The problem of endogeneity arises when, in addition to a line of causation from an independent variable to the dependent variable, there is also a line of causation running from the dependent variable to the independent variable (Wooldridge, 2002). To avoid the consequences of biased and inefficient estimation results as well as wrong hypothesis tests due to endogeneity, equation (6.1) is also estimated by a two-stage least square (2SLS) method.

### 6.4.4  Estimation results

The model is estimated in the standard, fixed and random effect form and by OLS, 2SLS and GLS methods. However, the random effect model only reports the results of 2SLS and GLS. All estimations are carried out using current and lagged regressors separately except for 2SLS. The purpose of running OLS, 2SLS and GLS estimations is to compare the results before and after potential endogeneity and heteroscedasticity are addressed. The OLS is used without addressing any possible endogeneity and heteroscedasticity issues. The 2SLS estimations address possible endogeneity issues, and the GLS estimations address possible heteroscedasticity issues.

In Table 6.6, the results show that all OLS estimated coefficients without a time trend are statistically significant. The coefficient of *TRADE* shows a negative coefficient, though a positive coefficient is expected. Similar results are revealed in Table 6.7 when a time trend is included in the estimation. The estimation using OLS based on lagged regressors is performed in order to find whether lagged explanatory variables affect *PRO* and address the possibility of an endogeneity problem. All estimated coefficients using the standard model are statistically significant, and *TRADE* again has a negative coefficient either with or without a time trend included.

The results of the 2SLS estimation are now examined. The use of the 2SLS estimation addresses possible endogeneity problems. The results of the 2SLS estimation shown in Tables 6.6 and 6.7 are similar to those obtained in previous estimations, that is, all estimated coefficients are statistically significant and the coefficient of *TRADE* is negative. This suggests that the significant negative coefficient for *TRADE* cannot be attributed to a potential endogeneity problem and that perhaps the relationships would be more appropriately estimated by other types of models.

The GLS estimation is run to address the possibility of cross-sectional heteroscedasticity in the model. The results of the GLS and GLS $(t-1)$ estimations with a time trend included or excluded reveal that there is not much difference between the two estimations. All other variables are statistically significant.

For panel data, it is necessary to consider the fixed and random effect models. The same estimation procedures as used for the standard model are followed for both fixed effect and random effect models. When a time trend is excluded in the fixed effect model, the variable $K$ is the only significant variable in all estimations. The coefficient of *TRADE* is insignificant in all estimations. The coefficient of *FDI* is insignificant in the OLS $(t-1)$ estimation but significant in all other estimations. The *LF* variable is statistically significant in the GLS $(t-1)$ estimation, but insignificant in all other estimations. An examination of the results of the fixed effect model with a time trend reveals that *FDI* and $K$ are statistically significant in all estimations and that *TRADE* and *LF* are insignificant in all estimations. All statistically significant estimated coefficients have the expected sign. The results of the fixed effect model without a time trend indicate that $K$ is statistically significant in all estimations. Conversely, *FDI* and *TRADE* are statistically insignificant in all estimations. The *LF* variable is statistically significant only in OLS, OLS $(t-1)$ and GLS with negative sign. The results are similar when a time trend is included.

In the random effect model without a time trend, again, the coefficient of $K$ is statistically significant and *TRADE* is insignificant in all estimations. The coefficient of *FDI* is insignificant in the GLS $(t-1)$ estimation, but statistically significant for all other estimations. LF is statistically significant in the GLS $(t-1)$ estimation, but insignificant for all other estimations. The results of the random effect model with a time trend reveal that only two estimated coefficients of *FDI* and $K$ are statistically significant in all estimations with the expected sign.

### 6.4.5  Choice of models

In the final stage, two tests, that is the fixed effect and Hausman tests, are conducted to see whether the standard, fixed or random effect model is appropriate. The fixed effect test is conducted first to find whether the standard model or the fixed effect model is appropriate. The fixed effect test evaluates the statistical significance of the estimated fixed effect

*Table 6.8*   Fixed effect test results

|  | Degrees of freedom | Statistic | p-value |
|---|---|---|---|
| *Without a time trend* | | | |
| *Current regressors:* | | | |
| Cross-section F | (27, 248) | 40.421 | 0.000 |
| Cross-section chi-square | 27 | 472.226 | 0.000 |
| *Lagged regressors:* | | | |
| Cross-section F | (27, 220) | 25.112 | 0.000 |
| Cross-section chi-square | 27 | 354.457 | 0.000 |
| *With a time trend* | | | |
| *Current regressors:* | | | |
| Cross-section F | (27, 247) | 40.933 | 0.000 |
| Cross-section chi-square | 27 | 476.025 | 0.000 |
| *Lagged regressors:* | | | |
| Cross-section F | (27, 219) | 31.319 | 0.000 |
| Cross-section chi-square | 27 | 398.485 | 0.000 |

model under the OLS estimation. The null hypothesis is that the fixed effects are redundant. Table 6.8 shows the test statistics and *p*-values with and without a time trend. The results of the tests suggest that the corresponding tests are statistically significant. It therefore strongly rejects the null hypothesis that the fixed effect models are redundant. The results of the fixed effect model cannot be rejected.

The Hausman test is conducted to determine whether the fixed or random effect models are appropriate for the study. A fixed effect model is preferred if the null hypothesis is rejected. The test results with and without a time trend are shown in Table 6.9. The results suggest that the fixed effect model is preferred over the random effect model.

With the acceptance of the results based on the fixed effect model, the precise estimations for spillover effects of FDI on productivity in the Chinese economy can be observed. When there is no time trend included, the results of the fixed effect model based on lagged regressors after adjustment for heteroscedasticity show that FDI does generate spillovers on productivity. In addition, $K$ and $LF$ have positive effects on productivity. The results suggest that a 1 per cent increase in $FDI$, $K$ or $LF$ will lead to percentage increases of 0.027, 0.774 and 0.049 in productivity at the provincial level, respectively, other things being equal. When a time trend is included, the results suggest that only $FDI$ and $K$ have positive effects on productivity. It suggests that a 1 per cent increase in $FDI$ and $K$ will lead to an increase of 0.036 and 0.524 per cent in productivity

*Table 6.9*   Hausman test results

|  | Degrees of freedom | Statistic | p-value |
|---|---|---|---|
| *Without a time trend* | | | |
| *Current regressors:* | | | |
| Cross-section chi-square | 4 | 38.348 | 0.000 |
| *Lagged regressors:* | | | |
| Cross-section chi-square | 4 | 32.187 | 0.000 |
| *With a time trend* | | | |
| *Current regressors:* | | | |
| Cross-section chi-square | 5 | 35.555 | 0.000 |
| *Lagged regressors:* | | | |
| Cross-section chi-square | 5 | 29.001 | 0.000 |

at the provincial level, respectively, other things being equal. Overall, it can be concluded that inward FDI does generate spillover effects on labour productivity in China.

### 6.4.6   Regional and periodic variations

It is expected that the spillover effect of FDI in China exhibits regional differences with regard to the distribution of FDI flows over the past decades. The existing literature such as Cheung and Lin (2004) defined regions in China as the coastal, central and western regions. This chapter extends the literature by excluding the three municipal cities, that is, Beijing, Shanghai and Tianjing, from the coastal region to form a new classification structure, that is, the municipal cities, coastal, central and western regions. In addition to concerns regarding regional variation, this chapter is also interested in testing the periodic variation of FDI inflows into China before and after the 1997 Asian financial crisis.

To examine the extent of such regional and periodic differences, equation (6.1) is estimated with slope dummy variables for regions and periods. The municipal cities are treated as the base category for the regional slope dummy variables, while the pre-1997 period is treated as the base category for the periodic slope dummy variables. As the fixed effect model is the most appropriate one for this study, the estimation with the slope dummy variables is based on the fixed model. The estimation results are shown in Table 6.10.

The results show that the variable FDI is insignificant with regional slope dummy variables introduced. However, FDI is significant when the periodic slope dummy variable is introduced. The slope dummy variable of the coastal region has a positive and significant coefficient, suggesting

*Table 6.10*   Regional and periodic variations of the spillover effects

|  | Coefficients (t-ratios) | |
| --- | --- | --- |
| Constant | 0.194 | 0.346 |
|  | (0.665) | (0.831) |
| $\ln(FDI_{it})$ | −0.042 | **0.040** |
|  | (−0.853) | **(2.932)** |
| $\ln(K_{it})$ | **0.921** | **0.910** |
|  | **(53.232)** | **(30.604)** |
| $\ln(TRADE_{it})$ | −0.012 | −0.003 |
|  | (−1.204) | (−0.280) |
| $\ln(LF_{it})$ | −0.004 | −0.002 |
|  | (−0.239) | (−0.119) |
| $\ln(FDI_{it})$(coastal) | **0.118** | – |
|  | **(2.668)** |  |
| $\ln(FDI_{it})$(central) | 0.023 | – |
|  | (0.468) |  |
| $\ln(FDI_{it})$(western) | **0.095** | – |
|  | **(1.793)** |  |
| $\ln(FDI_{it})$(post-1997) | – | −0.004 |
|  |  | (−0.869) |
| Adjusted $R^2$ | 0.984 | 0.983 |
| Durbin–Watson | 0.578 | 0.486 |
| Log likelihood | 394.798 | 383.781 |

*Notes*: *t*-statistics are in parentheses. Significant values at the level of 5% are in bold type.

that the magnitude of spillover effects of FDI on productivity is greater in the coastal region than in the municipal cities. The result for the slope dummy variable in the western region is at the marginally significant level. This suggests that the spillover effects of FDI on productivity in the western region are slightly greater than in the municipal cities. In addition, the slope dummy variable for periods post-1997 show no significant changes in spillover effects of FDI on productivity in comparison to the periods prior to 1997. The overall estimation results reveal that the coastal and western regions both have greater magnitude of spillover effects of FDI than the municipal cities.

## 6.5   Conclusion

This chapter tested empirically the spillover effects of FDI on productivity at the provincial level. It employed data from three municipal cities and 25 provinces for the period from 1993 to 2002. The results demonstrate that inward FDI and the presence of FFE activities generate spillover effects on productivity in China. With respect to regional variation in FDI spillover effects, it was concluded that the coastal and western regions both experienced a greater amount of spillover effects from FDI than the municipal cities. Interestingly, the spillover effects of FDI appear to be no different between pre- and post-1997 Asian financial crisis. Overall, this study shows that foreign affiliations do play an important role in fostering growth of the Chinese economy.

## Appendix

### Tests for stationarity

It is important to check whether all variables are stationary in levels, that is, all the variables in levels are I(0). A review by Maddala and Wu (1999) has listed key unit root tests proposed in the literature. They argued that different panel data unit root tests have different limitations and hence may yield different results. To compare the test results under different unit root tests, two procedures are chosen and they have been widely used in the literature. These are the LLC test which is named after its developers, Levin, Lin and Chu (2002) and the IPS test which is named after its developers, Im, Pesaran and Shin (2003).

### The LLC test

Since the seminal works of Quah (1992, 1994), Breitung and Meyer (1994) and Levin and Lin (1992), the use of panel data unit root tests has been widely recognized. Quah (1992) proposed a panel data version of the Dickey–Fuller test (DF test) without fixed effects. These do not accommodate heterogeneity across groups such as individual specific effects and different patterns of serial correlations. The tests proposed by Breitung and Meyer (1994) allow the analysis of panel data with time-specific effects and higher-order serial correlation, but they cannot be extended to allow for heterogeneous residual distributions. Levin and Lin (1993) later extended these tests to allow for individual specific intercepts and deterministic trends. It also allows the error variance and the pattern of serial correlation to vary across individuals. However, for the LLC test, it was found that the asymptotic mean and variance of the unit root test statistic varied under different specifications of the regression model. To overcome this problem, Levin et al. (2002) proposed a new test based on augmented Dickey–Fuller (ADF) regressions to generate orthogonalized residuals and a correction by the ratio of the long-run to the short-run variance of a variable.

The LLC test is based on an analysis of the following model:

$$\Delta y_{it} = \delta y_{it-1} + \sum_{L=1}^{P_i} \theta_{iL} \Delta y_{it-L} + \sum_{m=1}^{M} \alpha_{mi} d_{mt} + \varepsilon_{it} \qquad (6A.1)$$

$$(i = 1, 2, \ldots, N \text{ and } t = 1, 2, \ldots, T)$$

where $d_{mt}$ represents deterministic variables and $\alpha_{mi}$ their coefficients. $\delta$ is the crucial parameter for stationarity testing. Note that all coefficients are allowed to be different for individuals, but $\delta$ is constrained to be constant. This panel-based unit root test allows for time trends and individual specific intercepts. Moreover, the error variance and the pattern of higher-order serial correlation are also permitted to vary across individuals, so the error term, $\varepsilon_{it}$, is distributed independently across individuals. The null hypothesis of the LLC test shows the existence of a unit root when $\delta = 0$, against the alternative hypothesis of no unit root when $\delta < 0$. This can be written as

$$H_0 : \delta = 0 \qquad (6A.2)$$

$$H_1 : \delta < 0 \qquad (6A.3)$$

**The IPS test**

The IPS test was also conducted to further confirm that the variables are I(0), in levels. Im et al. (2003) proposed a unit root test which allows for heterogeneity of the coefficients on lagged dependent variables and is based on the following regression:

$$\Delta y_{it} = \alpha_i + \rho_i y_{it-1} + \sum_{j=1}^{P_i} \theta_{ij} \Delta y_{it-j} + \varepsilon_{it} \qquad (6A.4)$$

$$(i = 1, 2, \ldots, N \text{ and } t = 1, 2, \ldots, T)$$

Like the LLC test, the IPS test allows for serial correlation as well as heterogeneity of the dynamics and error variances. The test was developed based on the average of the ADF $t$-statistics for individual cross-section units. The null hypothesis is that $\rho_i = 0$ for all $i$. The alternative hypothesis is that $\rho_i < 0$ for $i = 1, 2, \ldots N_1$, $\rho_i = 0$ for $i = N_1 + 1, N_1 + 2, \ldots, N$. This can be written as

$$H_0 : \rho_i = 0, \quad \text{for } \forall i \qquad (6A.5)$$

$$H_1: \begin{cases} \rho_i < 0 & i = 1, 2, \ldots, N_1 (N_1 \geq 0) \\ \rho_i = 0 & i = N_1 + 1, N_1 + 2, \ldots, N \end{cases} \qquad \text{(6A.6)}$$

For both the LLC and IPS unit root tests, the null hypothesis is the existence of a unit root for each series in the panel, that is, non-stationarity. The verification of the alternative hypotheses of the two tests is different. The alternative hypothesis in the LLC test is that all individual cross-sections in the panel are stationary; it should be recalled that $\delta$ is constrained to be equal for all individual cross-sections. However, the IPS test allows for some (but not all) of the individual series to have unit roots under the alternative hypothesis.

# 7
# Efficiency of Foreign-Funded and Domestic Enterprises

Since the inception of economic reform in 1978, China has experienced almost three decades of rapid growth of foreign direct investment (FDI). The importance of FDI inflows for the growth of the Chinese economy is well recognized (Wu, 2004). However, one may ask how efficient foreign affiliates are in the Chinese economy. This chapter presents an analysis of this issue. In particular, it focuses on comparing foreign-funded enterprises (FFEs) with stated-owned enterprises (SOEs) among the Chinese regions. The performance of FFEs in the Chinese economy provides an indicator of the efficiency of FDI in the country.

To evaluate the performance of enterprises over time, the data envelopment analysis (DEA) technique combined with the Malmquist productivity index is used. Few studies have used DEA to compare productive efficiency between FFEs and SOEs in the Chinese economy. This chapter aims to make a contribution to the literature. The rest of the chapter begins with a review of the concepts of efficiency in Section 7.1. Section 7.2 presents a brief survey of the existing literature that is relevant in this field. Section 7.3 describes the methods used, and Section 7.4 discusses data issues and preliminary results. Finally, Section 7.5 concludes the chapter.

## 7.1  Concepts of efficiency

In general, efficiency relates to how well a firm allocates scarce resources to meet production targets. The efficiency of a production unit is defined by the relationship between the observed and optimal values of its inputs and outputs. Farrell (1957) proposed and outlined two types of efficiency, that is, technical efficiency and allocative efficiency.

Technical efficiency is a measure of how well an individual firm transforms inputs into a set of outputs based on a given level of technology. The ratio of the actual to the potential (or frontier) outputs defines the level of technical efficiency of a firm. If production sits below a frontier output then the firm is technically inefficient. Allocative efficiency refers to the ability of a firm to combine available inputs and outputs in optimal proportions, given the actual prices of the inputs and outputs. These two kinds of efficiency are then combined to provide a measure of the firm's total economic or productive efficiency.

An input-oriented efficiency measure for firms is illustrated in Figure 7.1. It is assumed that a firm uses two inputs ($X_1$ and $X_2$) to produce a single output ($Y$). Note that the illustrated case assumes constant-returns-to-scale (CRS) conditions. The FF′ curve represents the unit *isoquant* of fully efficient firms.[1] If a given firm uses a combination of inputs per unit of output, defined by the point P, the technical *inefficiency* could be represented by the distance GP. A technically efficient firm can produce each unit of output using fewer inputs at point G. The technical inefficiency, defined by the distance GP, may occur due to the redundancy of some inputs – it can be proportionally reduced without a reduction in output to become more technically efficient. The distance GP is used to ascertain how much input consumption may be reduced per unit of output. This is given by the ratio

$$Technical\ Inefficiency = \frac{GP}{OP} \qquad (7.1)$$

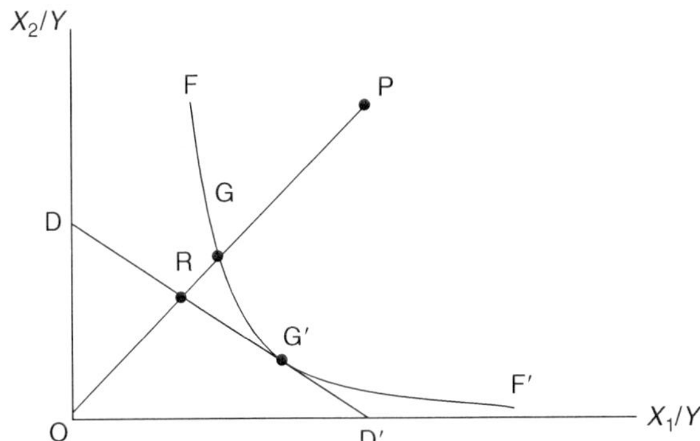


*Figure 7.1*   Input-oriented efficiency measures

Once technical *inefficiency* is known, technical efficiency (*TE*) of the firm can be derived. The input-oriented measure of technical efficiency can be expressed

$$\text{Technical Efficiency } (TE_i) = 1 - \frac{GP}{OP} = \frac{OG}{OP} \tag{7.2}$$

The above technical efficiency measure results in a value between zero and one. The higher the value, the higher the technical efficiency of the firm.

To calculate the allocative efficiency of a firm, the input-price ratio of a given firm must be ascertained. Assume that a given firm is operating at P and the input-price ratio is represented by the slope DD′ in Figure 7.1. DD′ is also called the *isocost* curve which corresponds to the quantities of each input factor that could be purchased for the same cost (per unit of *Y*) as at G′.

The production cost of each input for a technically efficient firm is denoted by point R; the distance RG represents the reduction in production costs that would occur if allocative and technical efficiency were achieved. Note that if the input-price ratio (production cost) is taken into consideration for the input-oriented efficiency measure, the efficiency point of the firm is no longer operating at point G. The firm at point G is operating with allocative inefficiency. This is because the firm can potentially produce more output for the given production costs. The point of tangency between the isocost line (DD′) and the isoquant (FF′) shows the minimum cost required to produce a given output. Therefore, the efficient point of the firm operating with both technical and allocative efficiency is at point G′. The allocative efficiency (*AE*) of the firm is defined as a ratio:

$$\text{Allocative Efficiency } (AE_i) = \frac{OR}{OG} \tag{7.3}$$

Given both *TE* and *AE*, the total economic efficiency of the firms can be calculated as

$$\text{Economic Efficiency } (EE_i) = TE_i \times AE_i = \frac{OG}{OP} \times \frac{OR}{OG} = \frac{OR}{OP} \tag{7.4}$$

The above input-oriented measure of economic efficiency addresses the degree to which firms can minimize the cost of inputs per unit of output. This measurement is appropriate only if the condition of constant returns to scale is assumed. However, another type of measurement, scale efficiency, has also been widely applied in the literature to measure efficiency when the assumption of constant returns to scale is relaxed (see the appendix to this chapter for more details).

To briefly explain how to define scale efficiency, a simple example where a given firm uses one input to produce one output is considered. The two types of technology, constant return to scale (CRS) and variable return to scale (VRS), are shown in Figure 7.2. The envelopment lines shown may be either linear, as in the CRS case, or convex as with VRS. The VRS convex line shown indicates increasing returns to scale from point B to G', and decreasing returns to scale from G' to C. The assumption of VRS implies that in any circumstance a rise in inputs is expected to result in a disproportionately larger rise in outputs. The point G', the point of tangency between CRS and VRS, indicates production by a firm that is technically and scale efficient. According to the CRS efficiency measurement, the distance $PG_C$ represents the input-oriented technical inefficiency when a given firm is operating at the point P. Similarly, when employing VRS, the technical inefficiency is the distance $PG_V$. Therefore, the scale inefficiency of a given firm reflects the difference between the technical inefficiency under CRS and VRS. This can be represented as the distance $G_CG_V$. This relationship can be expressed in ratio form:

$$\text{Technical Efficiency } (TE_{CRS}) = \frac{AG_C}{AP} \tag{7.5}$$

$$\text{Technical Efficiency } (TE_{VRS}) = \frac{AG_V}{AP} \tag{7.6}$$

$$\text{Scale Efficiency}(SE) = \frac{TE_{CRS}}{TE_{VRS}} = \frac{AG_C}{AG_V} \tag{7.7}$$

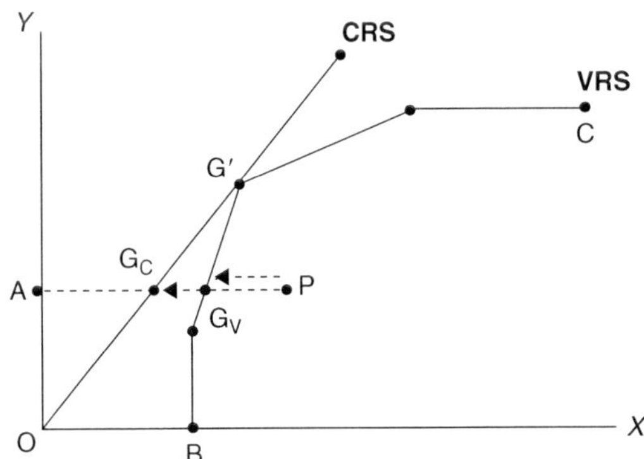


*Figure 7.2*   Scale efficiency

If there is a difference in the efficiency scores between CRS and VRS for a firm, this implies that the firm is experiencing scale inefficiency. The degree of scale inefficiency is the difference between VRS and CRS technical efficiency scores (Coelli et al., 1998). Again, the above efficiency measure results in a value between zero and one.

The above discussion of efficiency measurement only demonstrates how different types of efficiency are defined. Such a theoretical explanation differs in several respects from reality. First, in reality, although a firm's input–output combinations are observable, their efficiency frontiers are not and there are no benchmark firms for efficiency comparison. The above theoretical explanation does not provide any technique to compute the efficiency frontier from the actual data, so firms' actual efficiency performance cannot be estimated. The second limitation is that the concepts of efficiency measurements presented do not address the fact that multiple inputs and outputs are used and produced. These limitations require the adoption of a more realistic analysis by either using parametric or non-parametric methods. The difference between these two methods will be discussed in Section 7.2.

## 7.2   Literature reviews

Most studies of the relative efficiency of firms or entities are based on two methods. One is the stochastic frontier approach (a parametric approach); the other is DEA (a non-parametric approach).[2] The non-parametric approach is also known as the mathematical programming approach.

The parametric approach is based on the estimation of production functions using regression methods. The approach requires the imposition of a specific functional form relating the independent variables to the dependent variables. Furthermore, the functional form selected also requires specific assumptions about the distribution of the error terms. These are also the main arguments against the parametric method.

Production frontiers are also estimated using non-parametric methods. DEA was originally introduced by Charnes et al. (1978) and is a non-parametric linear programming approach. The method involves the use of linear programming methods to construct a non-parametric piecewise linear surface (or frontier) over the data, against which efficiency is measured. It obviates the need to specify a functional form for the production frontier and is capable of handling multiple inputs as well as multiple outputs (refer to the appendix to this chapter for more details about the DEA method).

In the past decade, DEA has often been used as a tool for evaluating efficiency of a decision-making unit (DMU) relative to its peers. Research applications using DEA to evaluate productivity performance can be found in areas including the public and private sectors of many countries and in specific industries (Asmild et al., 2004; Chandra et al., 1998).

The study by Asmild et al. (2004) used DEA and the Malmquist index as tools to examine the Canadian banking industry's productivity performance over the period from 1981 to 2000. Their results show that the Canadian banking industry experienced varied productivity performance and that all Canadian banking institutes underwent similar productivity changes during that period. The paper by Chandra et al. (1998) evaluated the performance of 29 Canadian textile companies in 1994. They used the Charnes et al. (1978) model to obtain efficiency scores. The paper concluded that most Canadian textile companies did not perform well.

There are also an increasing number of studies applying DEA to Chinese data. For example, DEA has been adopted to address productivity and efficiency issues in several industries in China. These include agriculture (Mao and Koo, 1997), the electrical power industry (Lam and Shiu, 2004), the manufacturing industry (Sun et al., 1999), education (Ng and Li, 2000) and mixed industries (Chen, 2003; Zheng et al., 1998). Some authors, such as Charnes and Cooper (1989), used DEA to evaluate the performance of Chinese cities.

The econometric approach has been widely used to compare the efficiency of SOEs and FFEs in China (Murray et al., 2005; Ai and Wen, 2005; Frazier, 2006). However, the use of DEA has been limited to Shiu (2002) and Zhu (1996). The paper by Shiu (2002) applied the DEA techniques to provincial data. It decomposes technical efficiency into across-group and within-group components to compare efficiency across firm ownership types in China. It is found that SOEs in China performed less efficiently than non-SOEs (that is, FFEs, township-owned enterprises and collectively owned enterprises). The paper by Zhu (1996) employed DEA to evaluate the efficiency of 35 textile factories and found that collectively owned units performed better than state-owned units in the two years analysed. Both papers provided some evidence that SOEs operate less efficiently than non-SOEs in China.

The approach combining DEA with the Malmquist index is rarely employed to compare efficiency performance between SOEs and FFEs in the Chinese economy. For example, Shiu (2002) did not address efficiency changes of SOEs and non-SOEs over time and the Malmquist productivity index was absent from her paper. This chapter hence distinguishes itself from the existing literature by:

- Comparing efficiency performance between SOEs and FFEs in China through combining DEA with the Malmquist productivity index.
- Applying both gross output value and value-added measures to address the debate in the literature that the two measures may generate different results. The efficiency scores based on these measures are then compared.
- Examining efficiency changes at the provincial level for both SOEs and FFEs.

## 7.3   DEA and Malmquist productivity index

DEA involves the evaluation of DMUs that use inputs to produce outputs. It attempts to identify which of the DMUs can determine an envelopment surface. This envelopment surface is called the *empirical production function* or the *efficient frontier*. So by comparing each DMU to the envelopment surface, the relative efficiency scores are calculated. The outputs of DEA (that is, the efficiency scores) represent the distance to the production frontier. Charnes et al. (1994) pointed out three features of the DEA method:

- Each DMU is characterized by a single summary relative-efficiency score.
- DMU-specific projections for improvements are based on observable reference revealed, best-practice DMUs.
- DEA obviates the alternative and indirect approach of specifying abstract statistical models and making inferences based on residuals and parameter coefficient analysis.

In addition to the above arguments, the Steering Committee for the Reviews of Commonwealth/State Service Provision (1997) also specified the main advantages of DEA as follows:

- DEA can readily incorporate multiple inputs and outputs. It only requires information on output and input quantities to calculate technical efficiency.
- Possible sources of inefficiency as well as efficiency levels can be determined.
- DEA provides a set of potential role models by which an inefficient organization can improve its operations.

However, a limitation of the outputs of DEA is that they do not show improvement or deterioration of efficiency over time. DEA only shows the efficiency level of individual years. The production frontier is constructed differently for each sample year because of different input per unit of output used for each sample year by each firm. In order to determine changes in total factor productivity, technological progress, technical and scale efficiency, the Malmquist index method is used in conjunction with DEA methods.

### 7.3.1  Malmquist productivity index (MPI)

The DEA approach constructs a production frontier, and measures the distance functions relative to the frontier for firms' given inputs and outputs for each sample year (so-called efficiency scores). The distance functions derived by DEA for each sample year are used to construct the Malmquist indexes. Given these distance functions, the Malmquist index calculates the change of efficiency for a given firm for a certain sample year relative to the year before.

The concept of the index was inspired by Malmquist (1953) who introduced a commodity price index representing the ratios of distance functions. Caves, Christensen and Diewert (1982a, b) or CCD extended Malmquist's idea to a productivity index based on Shephard's (1970) distance functions (input and output based). Shephard's functions also provided the theoretical framework for the measurement of productivity. This forms the basis for what has become known as the Malmquist productivity index (MPI). The MPI is based on distance functions that allow the description of a multi-input, multi-output production framework. An input distance function characterizes the production technology by observing a minimal proportional contraction of the input vector, given an output vector. An output distance function considers a maximal proportional expansion of the output vector, given an input vector. However, both input distance functions and output distance functions can be defined and used in a similar manner.

The MPI has several characteristics that make it suitable for the study of productivity. No data regarding input or output prices or shares are required to estimate the index. This makes it ideal for applications where the cost or revenue of production units is not available. Färe et al. (1985, 1994a) have shown Shephard's (1970) distance functions are reciprocals to Farrell's (1957) technical efficiency measures, so the estimation of the MPI is obtainable using results derived from DEA methods. MPI scores are then decomposed into efficiency change and technological change, that is

$$MPI = TC^*PECH^*SC \qquad (7.8)$$

where TC, PECH and SC represent technological change, pure efficiency change and scale efficiency, respectively (for more details, see the appendix to this chapter).

## 7.4  Data issues and preliminary analysis

The data used in the empirical analysis were collected separately for SOEs and FFEs for a sample of 30 provinces in China over the period 1999–2002. The data were sourced from the official *China Statistical Yearbook*.[3] Three sets (A, B and C) were constructed based on different inputs and outputs of the SOEs and FFEs obtained at the provincial level. These are defined as follows:

- *Set (A):*
  Output:   Value added of industry
  Inputs:   Annual average of the net value of fixed assets (*capital*)
          Average number of staff and workers (*labour*)
- *Set (B):*
  Output:   Gross industrial output value
  Inputs:   Annual average of the net value of fixed assets (*capital*)
          Average number of staff and workers (*labour*)
- *Set (C):*
  Output:   Gross industrial output value
  Inputs:   Annual average of the net value of fixed assets (*capital*)
          Average number of staff and workers (*labour*)
          Annual average balance of circulating funds (*intermediate input*)

These sets are differentiated by two basic measures of output; that is, the value-added and gross-value output. According to the official *China Statistical Yearbook*, the *gross industrial output value* refers to the total volume of final industrial products produced and industrial services provided during a given period. It reflects the total achievements and overall scale of industrial production during a given period. H. Wu (1993) in his research on China's productivity argues that using the gross industrial output value in examining productivity may generate biased results. This is because it includes all intermediate inputs resulting in double counting in the final value. Gullickson (1995) stated that two possible problems might arise as a result of this form of double counting. First, double counting tends to obscure the evidence of technological change or changes in efficiency actually occurring in industries and sectors as a whole. Second, the degree of integration in the data used might change over time, and this might introduce a bias into productivity growth trends.

The other measure of output is *value-added of industry*. It is, however, argued that value-added productivity measures, by excluding intermediate inputs, may fail to capture the full impact of inputs on productivity (Sudit and Finger, 1981). As both output measures (that is gross output value and value-added) are criticized in the literature and they capture differing aspects of productivity, both measures of output are applied to compare the results of efficiency performance of SOEs and FFEs. Inputs and outputs that are in value terms are deflated by a price index with base year 2000.

Table 7.1 compares the average annual output–labour (that is, labour productivity) and capital–labour ratios between SOEs and FFEs for data set (A). Both output–labour and capital–labour ratios of FFEs are significantly higher than those of SOEs over the entire 1999–2002 sample period. Shanghai and Guangdong province have high output–labour ratios in their SOEs compared to other provinces. However, Qinghai province has the highest capital–labour ratio for SOEs. For FFEs, Jilin province has the highest output–labour ratio, and Qinghai has the highest capital–labour ratio.

## 7.5   Interpretation of the results

The annual average technical efficiency scores for SOEs and FFEs are reported in Table 7.2. Efficiency scores by region (that is, the municipal cities, coastal, central and western regions) are reported in Table 7.3 (refer to Table 7A.1 in the appendix to this chapter for details of the efficiency scores of individual provinces). Table 7.2 shows that FFEs are more efficient than SOEs for all data sets during the sample period. The average efficiency scores range from 0.4 to 0.6, while the scores for FFEs range from approximately 0.6 to 0.8. It is argued in the literature that the inefficiency of SOEs is due to the misaligned and improperly defined control of property rights and soft-budget constraints. In SOEs, many people have control of the firm and access to the firm's resources, while no individuals clearly bear any responsibility. In the meantime, most SOEs in China are operating under conditions of overemployment of

*Table 7.1*  Average output–labour and capital–labour ratios for set A

| Province | Output–labour | | Capital–labour | |
| --- | --- | --- | --- | --- |
| | *SOEs* | *FFEs* | *SOEs* | *FFEs* |
| Beijing | 63.981 | 118.410 | 171.352 | 129.946 |
| Tianjin | 50.278 | 90.818 | 194.386 | 135.737 |
| Hebei | 42.868 | 61.752 | 118.357 | 149.274 |
| Shanxi | 26.394 | 64.716 | 102.808 | 186.346 |
| Inner Mongolia | 35.846 | 60.666 | 135.242 | 90.304 |
| Liaoning | 45.449 | 77.480 | 165.445 | 182.301 |
| Jilin | 43.205 | 151.369 | 120.702 | 216.208 |
| Heilongjiang | 66.797 | 73.188 | 112.268 | 165.262 |
| Shanghai | 109.308 | 111.893 | 240.021 | 171.456 |
| Jiangsu | 53.444 | 85.246 | 117.384 | 144.306 |
| Zhejiang | 83.595 | 55.120 | 206.578 | 88.991 |
| Anhui | 39.832 | 77.417 | 101.903 | 164.801 |
| Fujian | 79.042 | 58.354 | 182.444 | 90.134 |
| Jiangxi | 29.085 | 44.481 | 86.268 | 94.019 |
| Shandong | 55.628 | 59.153 | 115.621 | 82.350 |
| Henan | 33.198 | 85.593 | 86.566 | 164.402 |
| Hubei | 46.785 | 107.056 | 118.754 | 205.973 |
| Hunan | 37.441 | 67.812 | 100.496 | 124.155 |
| Guangdong | 105.940 | 60.391 | 251.546 | 85.802 |
| Guangxi | 36.012 | 64.844 | 116.137 | 169.156 |
| Hainan | 47.305 | 66.954 | 157.870 | 178.453 |
| Chongqing | 35.543 | 98.368 | 114.304 | 256.049 |
| Sichuan | 38.806 | 81.818 | 126.016 | 151.002 |
| Guizhou | 34.334 | 28.626 | 103.870 | 71.822 |
| Yunnan | 90.560 | 90.887 | 150.537 | 238.563 |
| Shaanxi | 34.795 | 147.713 | 110.121 | 248.561 |
| Gansu | 34.394 | 56.661 | 116.019 | 131.140 |
| Qinghai | 48.218 | 148.656 | 280.061 | 304.237 |
| Ningxia | 32.683 | 59.803 | 125.022 | 103.694 |
| Xinjiang | 81.764 | 67.187 | 234.825 | 185.011 |
| Mean | 52.084 | 80.748 | 145.431 | 156.982 |

labour, overproduction of products and misallocation of resources, and are hence inefficient (Wu, 1996).

### 7.5.1  Technical efficiency across the regions

Since economic reform began, the Chinese central government has mainly focused on the development of the coastal provinces to attract more investment from overseas. Thus, the conventional wisdom holds

*Table 7.2*  Annual average of efficiency scores (1999–2002)

| | Set A | | Set B | | Set C | |
| --- | --- | --- | --- | --- | --- | --- |
| | *SOEs* | *FFEs* | *SOEs* | *FFEs* | *SOEs* | *FFEs* |
| 1999 | 0.448 | 0.689 | 0.359 | 0.682 | 0.531 | 0.806 |
| 2000 | 0.360 | 0.572 | 0.297 | 0.589 | 0.474 | 0.695 |
| 2001 | 0.443 | 0.647 | 0.310 | 0.557 | 0.463 | 0.683 |
| 2002 | 0.447 | 0.663 | 0.313 | 0.577 | 0.551 | 0.745 |
| Mean | 0.435 | 0.643 | 0.320 | 0.601 | 0.505 | 0.732 |

*Table 7.3*  Average technical efficiency in the regions

| | Set A | | Set B | | Set C | |
| --- | --- | --- | --- | --- | --- | --- |
| | *SOEs* | *FFEs* | *SOEs* | *FFEs* | *SOEs* | *FFEs* |
| *Municipal cities* | | | | | | |
| 1999 | 0.541 | 0.875 | 0.480 | 0.995 | 0.561 | 1.000 |
| 2000 | 0.374 | 0.804 | 0.433 | 0.889 | 0.496 | 0.943 |
| 2001 | 0.519 | 0.870 | 0.479 | 0.850 | 0.528 | 0.906 |
| 2002 | 0.481 | 0.876 | 0.447 | 0.880 | 0.558 | 0.910 |
| *Mean* | *0.479* | *0.856* | *0.460* | *0.904* | *0.536* | *0.940* |
| *Coastal* | | | | | | |
| 1999 | 0.484 | 0.640 | 0.417 | 0.676 | 0.606 | 0.875 |
| 2000 | 0.386 | 0.531 | 0.344 | 0.543 | 0.541 | 0.734 |
| 2001 | 0.475 | 0.627 | 0.362 | 0.546 | 0.521 | 0.759 |
| 2002 | 0.490 | 0.714 | 0.362 | 0.620 | 0.624 | 0.853 |
| *Mean* | *0.459* | *0.628* | *0.371* | *0.596* | *0.573* | *0.805* |
| *Central* | | | | | | |
| 1999 | 0.433 | 0.703 | 0.329 | 0.639 | 0.518 | 0.776 |
| 2000 | 0.363 | 0.557 | 0.256 | 0.538 | 0.468 | 0.648 |
| 2001 | 0.415 | 0.626 | 0.257 | 0.506 | 0.457 | 0.635 |
| 2002 | 0.433 | 0.637 | 0.275 | 0.523 | 0.556 | 0.728 |
| *Mean* | *0.411* | *0.630* | *0.279* | *0.552* | *0.500* | *0.697* |
| *Western* | | | | | | |
| 1999 | 0.397 | 0.661 | 0.290 | 0.625 | 0.460 | 0.701 |
| 2000 | 0.327 | 0.551 | 0.246 | 0.585 | 0.406 | 0.621 |
| 2001 | 0.413 | 0.614 | 0.257 | 0.522 | 0.389 | 0.582 |
| 2002 | 0.405 | 0.566 | 0.257 | 0.488 | 0.469 | 0.597 |
| *Mean* | *0.386* | *0.598* | *0.263* | *0.555* | *0.431* | *0.625* |

*Notes:  Municipal cities:* Beijing, Tianjin, and Shanghai; *Coastal regions:* Hebei, Liaoning, Jiangsu, Zhejiang, Fujian, Shandong, Guangdong, Guangxi, and Hainan; *Central regions:* Shanxi, Mongolia, Jilin, Heilongjiang, Anhui, Jiangxi, Henan, Hubei, and Hunan; *Western regions:* Chongqing, Sichuan, Guizhou, Yunnan, Shaanxi, Gansu, Ningxia, and Xingjiang.

that firms (either SOEs or FFEs) in coastal provinces are more efficient than firms in central or western regions. This leads to the following hypothesized ranking of technical efficiency of the regions, that is, Municipal Cities > Coastal Provinces > Central Provinces > Western Provinces. However, efficiency scores at the provincial level in Table 7.3 contradict (albeit slightly) the conventional wisdom. The technical efficiency scores for SOEs and FFEs at the provincial level for each data are ranked as:

- *Set (A)*:
  SOEs:   Municipals (0.479) > Coastal (0.459) > Central (0.411) > Western (0.389)
  FFEs:   Municipals (0.856) > *Central (0.630)* > *Coastal (0.628)* > Western (0.598)
- *Set (B)*:
  SOEs:   Municipals (0.460) > Coastal (0.371) > Central (0.279) > Western (0.263)
  FFEs:   Municipals (0.904) > Coastal (0.596) > *Western (0.555)* > *Central (0.552)*
- *Set (C)*:
  SOEs:   *Coastal (0.573)* > *Municipals (0.536)* > Central (0.500) > Western (0.431)
  FFEs:   Municipals (0.940) > Coastal (0.805) > Central (0.697) > Western (0.625)

In the above rankings, regions in italic indicate unexpected positions. The results suggest that FFEs in central provinces were slightly more efficient than in coastal provinces (data set A); FFEs in western provinces were slightly more efficient than those in central provinces (data set B); and SOEs in coastal provinces were more efficient than in municipal cities (data set C). Overall, the results indicate that during the period 1999–2002, the municipal cities and the coastal regions had better performing SOEs and FFEs than the central and western regions. Furthermore, it is clear that the average efficiency scores using data set A are greater than those using data set B.

### 7.5.2  MPI of SOEs and FFEs across the regions

Table 7.4 reports the average MPI calculated using the data of 30 provinces in China over the period 1999–2002. If a score is greater than 1, it implies productivity growth from period $t$ to $t+1$. However, if a score is

*Table 7.4* Malmquist productivity index: average during 2000–2

| Regions | Set A | | Set B | | Set C | |
|---|---|---|---|---|---|---|
| | *SOEs* | *FFEs* | *SOEs* | *FFEs* | *SOEs* | *FFEs* |
| Municipal cities | 1.105 | 1.098 | 1.188 | 1.103 | 1.114 | 1.092 |
| Coastal | 1.098 | 1.118 | 1.116 | 1.100 | 1.071 | 1.062 |
| Central | 1.047 | 1.066 | 1.047 | 1.078 | 1.057 | 1.056 |
| Western | 1.079 | 1.057 | 1.098 | 1.076 | 1.045 | 1.061 |
| *Mean* | *1.082* | *1.085* | *1.112* | *1.089* | *1.072* | *1.068* |

less than 1, it means a decline in productivity over the period. A result of 1 indicates no productivity change. The three components, that is, technological change, pure technical efficiency change and scale efficiency change, are calculated and presented in Table 7.5.

On average, the productivity of SOEs and FFEs in all regions increased slightly during the period 1999–2002 (Table 7.4). In the case of data set (A), overall productivity of FFEs has increased more than that of SOEs. However, in the case of data sets (B) and (C), the overall productivity gains of SOEs are higher than that of FFEs (refer to Table 7A.2 in the appendix to this chapter for details of the efficiency scores of individual provinces).

At the regional level, in the case of data set (A) for SOEs, the municipal cities have the highest average annual productivity gains. However, FFEs in the coastal region experienced higher productivity improvement than those in other regions. The results for SOEs using data set (B) are quite similar to those using data set (A). The results using data set (C) differ slightly. FFEs in the western region have attained higher productivity improvement than those in the central region. Overall, the results show that SOEs and FFEs in municipal cities have experienced more productivity growth than those in the other three regions.

Table 7.5 shows the average of annual changes of MPI components for all data sets. On average, in terms of data set (A), SOEs have improved their performance in innovation (TC) and efficiency (PECH). However, the index numbers show that the productivity growth of FFEs over the period 1999–2002 was mainly due to innovation (TC) rather than improvements in efficiency (PECH). For data set (B), productivity growth in SOEs and FFEs was due to innovation rather than improvements in efficiency. Results for data set (C) are similar to those for data

*Table 7.5*  Average of annual changes of MPI components

| Regions | SOEs | | | FFEs | | |
|---|---|---|---|---|---|---|
| | *TC* | *PECH* | *SC* | *TC* | *PECH* | *SC* |
| *Data set (A)* | | | | | | |
| Municipal cities | 1.151 | 1.014 | 0.946 | 1.093 | 1.043 | 0.964 |
| Coastal | 1.096 | 1.031 | 0.974 | 1.086 | 1.032 | 1.000 |
| Central | 1.036 | 1.015 | 0.996 | 1.103 | 0.961 | 1.007 |
| Western | 1.066 | 1.029 | 0.985 | 1.121 | 0.968 | 0.972 |
| *Mean* | *1.087* | *1.022* | *0.975* | *1.101* | *1.001* | *0.986* |
| *Data set (B)* | | | | | | |
| Municipal cities | 1.216 | 1.060 | 0.922 | 1.151 | 0.994 | 0.965 |
| Coastal | 1.170 | 0.990 | 0.964 | 1.135 | 0.984 | 0.986 |
| Central | 1.119 | 0.941 | 1.003 | 1.165 | 0.925 | 1.000 |
| Western | 1.142 | 0.972 | 0.989 | 1.165 | 0.963 | 0.961 |
| *Mean* | *1.162* | *0.991* | *0.969* | *1.154* | *0.966* | *0.978* |
| *Data set (C)* | | | | | | |
| Municipal cities | 1.113 | 1.050 | 0.954 | 1.129 | 1.000 | 0.968 |
| Coastal | 1.061 | 1.029 | 0.982 | 1.067 | 1.009 | 0.986 |
| Central | 1.032 | 1.039 | 0.986 | 1.083 | 0.976 | 0.999 |
| Western | 1.041 | 1.014 | 0.990 | 1.115 | 0.982 | 0.970 |
| *Mean* | *1.062* | *1.033* | *0.978* | *1.099* | *0.992* | *0.981* |

*Note*:   TC = Technical change. PECH = Pure Technical Efficiency change. SC = Scale Efficiency change.

set (A) (refer to Table 7A.3 in the appendix to this chapter for details of the annual average changes in MPI components of individual provinces).

## 7.6  Conclusion

This chapter examines the performance of foreign-funded enterprises (FFEs) and state-owned enterprises (SOEs) in China using provincial data. The DEA approach combined with the Malmquist productivity index analysis was employed in the chapter to investigate the technical efficiency and its changes over the period 1999–2002. The chapter has considered three sets of data for comparison, which is complementary to the existing literature regarding enterprise efficiency in the Chinese economy.

First, the overall efficiency scores show that FFEs in China are more efficient than SOEs. This supports the results of other authors (Shiu, 2002;

Zhu, 1996). The efficiency scores of SOEs and FFEs among the regions, that is the municipal cities, coastal, central and western regions, are slightly different. But a general trend is observed, that is, SOEs and FFEs in the municipal cities and coastal region experienced greater productivity gains than those in the central and western regions during the sample period.

Second, the results from the three constructed data sets indicate that the average efficiency scores based on value-added output are greater than those based on gross output value. The results support the argument in previous literature that productivity growth measured by the value-added method will systematically exceed the measure based on the gross output.

Finally, by using MPI, the chapter also concludes that both SOEs and FFEs in the municipal cities have experienced more productivity growth than those in other regions, with SOEs in the central region and FFEs in the western region experiencing the least productivity growth. The increase in performance among SOEs was due to both innovation and the improvement in efficiency, whereas the improved performance among FFEs was due to innovation only.

## Appendix

To formalize the DEA model, it is assumed that there are $n$ decision-making units ($DMU_1$, $DMU_2$,..., and $DMU_n$) to be evaluated and observed in $T$ periods ($t = 1$,...,$T$), and each DMU uses $m$ inputs to produce $s$ outputs. The sample thus has $n \times T$ observations and an observation $i$ in period $t$, $DMU_t^i$ has an $m$-dimensional input vector

$$x^t = (x_{1t}, x_{2t}, \ldots, x_{mt})' \tag{7A.1}$$

It also has an $s$-dimensional output vector

$$y^t = (y_{1t}, y_{2t}, \ldots, y_{st})' \tag{7A.2}$$

Specifically, $DMU_t^i$ consumes amount $x_{ij}$ of input $i$ and produces amount $y_{rj}$ of output $r$. It is assumed that $0 \leq x_{ij}$ and $0 \leq y_{ij}$ and that each DMU has at least one positive input and one positive output value. The input-oriented DEA model introduced by Charnes, Cooper and Rhodes (the CCR input model) evaluates the efficiency score of each DMU: $DMU_o$

$(o = 1, 2, \ldots, n)$ relative to other DMUs under a constant-returns-to-scale (CRS) assumption. The model can be described as

$$\min \theta - \sum_{i=1}^{m} s_i^- - \sum_{r=1}^{m} s_r^+ \tag{7A.3}$$

subject to

$$\sum_{j=1}^{n} x_{ij}\lambda_j + s_i^- = \theta x_{io} \qquad i = 1, 2, \ldots, m; \tag{7A.4}$$

$$\sum_{j=1}^{s} y_{rj}\lambda_j - s_r^+ = y_{ro} \qquad r = 1, 2, \ldots, s; \tag{7A.5}$$

$$\theta, s_i^-, s_r^+, \lambda_j \geq 0 \qquad \forall i, r, j \tag{7A.6}$$

where $\theta$ is an efficiency ratio, $x_{ij}$ represents the amount of input $i$ $(i = 1, \ldots, m)$, and $y_{rj}$ represents the amount of output $r$ $(r = 1, \ldots, s)$ used by $DMU_j$ $(j = 1, \ldots, n)$. The $x_{io}$ and $y_{ro}$ are the amount of input $i$ and output $r$ obtained from $DMU_o$ respectively.

The objective function of this model is to minimize the efficiency score, $\theta$, and to maximize input and output slacks. The symbols $s_i^-$ and $s_r^+$ represent slack variables (also called input surplus and output slacks). The slack variables used in the model are to avoid efficiency dilemma results. The efficiency dilemma arises because sections of the piecewise linear form of the non-parametric frontier run parallel to the axes (see Cooper et al., 2000; Coelli et al., 1998). Constraint (7A.4) specifies that the optimal input of $i$ for $DMU_o$ should be equal to the linear combination of the inputs of a set of efficient DMUs plus an input surplus of $i$ consumed by $DMU_o$. Similarly, constraint (7A.5) states that the optimal output $r$ of $DMU_o$ should be equal to the linear combination of the outputs of the same set of efficient DMUs minus an output slack of $DMU_o$.

To introduce MPI, consider the production technology $S^t$ which is capable of transforming inputs into outputs

$$S^t = \{(x^t, y^t) : x^t \text{ can produce } y^t\} \tag{7A.7}$$

The input distance function at time $t$ is defined as

$$D_i^t(x^t, y^t) = \max\left[ \lambda : \left(\frac{x_i^t}{\lambda}, y_i^t\right) \in S^t \right] \tag{7A.8}$$

where $\lambda$ is a positive scalar. The distance function $D_i^t(x^t, y^t)$ is non-decreasing, positively linearly homogeneous and concave in $x$, and non-increasing and quasi-concave in $y$. The value of the distance will be equal to one or greater than one if the input vector $x$ is an element of the feasible input set, $S^t$, that is $D_i^t(x^t, y^t) \geq 1$ if $x \in S^t$. Construction of the Malmquist index requires calculating two mixed-distance functions, which are computed by comparing observations in one time period with the best practice frontier of another time period. To define the Malmquist index, a distance function is characterized with respect to two different time periods:

$$D_i^t\left(x^{t+1}, y^{t+1}\right) = \max \left[ \lambda : \left( \frac{x_i^{t+1}}{\lambda}, y_i^{t+1} \right) \in S^t \right] \qquad (7A.9)$$

This function measures the minimal proportional change in inputs required to make $(x^{t+1}, y^{t+1})$ feasible in relation to reference or benchmark technology at time $t$. Similarly, a distance function that measures the minimal proportional change in input required to make $(x^t, y^t)$ feasible in relation to the technology at time $t + 1$, denoted $D_i^{t+1}(x^t, y^t)$, may be defined. The value of the distance function for each sample period can be measured using DEA. The Malmquist productivity index subsequently uses these distance functions to calculate the growth change of efficiency for a given firm for a certain sample year relative to the year before. The Malmquist index modifies the distance function from DEA to incorporate time and define these distance functions with respect to two different time periods. Following Färe et al. (1994b), the MPI (input oriented) between period $t$ and period $t + 1$ is given by

$$M\left(x^t, x^{t+1}, y^t, y^{t+1}\right) = \left[ \frac{D_c^t\left(x^t, y^t\right)}{D_c^t\left(x^{t+1}, y^{t+1}\right)} \cdot \frac{D_c^{t+1}\left(x^t, y^t\right)}{D_c^{t+1}\left(x^{t+1}, y^{t+1}\right)} \right]^{1/2} \qquad (7A.10)$$

The subscript $c$ denotes measurement with reference to CRS technology. It represents the productivity change of the production point $(x^{t+1}, y^{t+1})$ relative to the production point $(x^t, y^t)$. In order to avoid choosing an arbitrary benchmark between periods $t$ and $t + 1$, the input-based Malmquist productivity index is specified as the geometric mean of two Malmquist productivity indexes, one with technology at period $t$ and the other at period $t + 1$ as benchmarks. An equivalent way of writing this index is

$$M\left(x^t, x^{t+1}, y^t, y^{t+1}\right) = \frac{D_c^t\left(x^t, y^t\right)}{D_c^{t+1}\left(x^{t+1}, y^{t+1}\right)} \cdot$$

$$\left[\frac{D_c^{t+1}\left(x^{t+1}, y^{t+1}\right)}{D_c^t\left(x^{t+1}, y^{t+1}\right)} \cdot \frac{D_c^{t+1}\left(x^t, y^t\right)}{D_c^t\left(x^t, y^t\right)}\right]^{1/2} \quad (7A.11)$$

The Malmquist productivity index above can be decomposed in terms of a technical efficiency change (*TEC*) and a technological change (*TC*). The technological change is the comparison of technologies at periods 0 and 1. The index from equation (7A.11) can be expressed as

$$M\left(x^t, x^{t+1}, y^t, y^{t+1}\right) = TEC.TC \quad (7A.12)$$

where

$$TEC = \frac{D_c^t\left(x^t, y^t\right)}{D_c^{t+1}\left(x^{t+1}, y^{t+1}\right)} \quad (7A.13)$$

$$TC = \left[\frac{D_c^{t+1}\left(x^t, y^t\right)}{D_c^t\left(x^t, y^t\right)} \cdot \frac{D_c^{t+1}\left(x^{t+1}, y^{t+1}\right)}{D_c^t\left(x^{t+1}, y^{t+1}\right)}\right]^{1/2} \quad (7A.14)$$

Specifically, technical efficiency change is derived from inputs and outputs observed in period $t$ relative to inputs and outputs observed in period $t+1$. Technological change is based on the geometric means of the change of inputs and outputs observed in period $t$ to the technology of periods $t$ and $t+1$ with the change of inputs and outputs observed in the period $t+1$ to the technology of periods $t$ and $t+1$.

The initial idea of Färe et al. (1994b) was to measure the MPI for a reference technology exhibiting constant returns to scale. However, Ray and Desli (1997) argued that the decomposition of technical efficiency change could be further factored into pure technical efficiency change (PECH) and scale efficiency change (SC). Therefore, if the VRS assumption is correct, the original technical change component of Färe et al. (1994b) will distort the results. Due to this limitation, Ray and Desli (1997) proposed an extended decomposition of the MPI:[4]

$$M\left(x^t, x^{t+1}, y^t, y^{t+1}\right) = TC.PECH.SC \quad (7A.15)$$

where

$$TC = \left[ \frac{D^{t+1}\left(x^t, y^t\right)}{D^t\left(x^t, y^t\right)} \cdot \frac{D^{t+1}\left(x^{t+1}, y^{t+1}\right)}{D^t\left(x^{t+1}, y^{t+1}\right)} \right]^{1/2} \tag{7A.16}$$

$$PECH = \frac{D^t\left(x^t, y^t\right)}{D^{t+1}\left(x^{t+1}, y^{t+1}\right)} \tag{7A.17}$$

and

$$SC = \left[ \frac{D_c^{t+1}\left(x^t, y^t\right)}{D^{t+1}\left(x^t, y^t\right)} \cdot \frac{D^{t+1}\left(x^{t+1}, y^{t+1}\right)}{D_c^{t+1}\left(x^{t+1}, y^{t+1}\right)} \cdot \right.$$

$$\left. \frac{D_c^t\left(x^t, y^t\right)}{D^t\left(x^t, y^t\right)} \cdot \frac{D^t\left(x^{t+1}, y^{t+1}\right)}{D_c^t\left(x^{t+1}, y^{t+1}\right)} \right]^{1/2} \tag{7A.18}$$

Scale efficiency change (SC) in each time period is constructed as a ratio of the distance function under variable returns to scale, while the pure technical efficiency change (PECH) is defined as a ratio of the own-period distance functions in each period under variable returns to scale. Note that if the technology exhibits CRS, the scale change components equal 1 and the extended decomposition by Ray and Desli (1997) is the same as Färe et al. (1994b).

*Table 7A.1*   Efficiency scores of individual provinces

| Regions | SOEs | | | | FFEs | | | |
|---|---|---|---|---|---|---|---|---|
| | *1999* | *2000* | *2001* | *2002* | *1999* | *2000* | *2001* | *2002* |
| *Data set (A)* | | | | | | | | |
| Beijing | 0.513 | 0.397 | 0.448 | 0.417 | 1.000 | 1.000 | 1.000 | 1.000 |
| Tianjin | 0.353 | 0.262 | 0.343 | 0.320 | 0.665 | 0.76 | 0.77 | 0.871 |
| Hebei | 0.436 | 0.377 | 0.388 | 0.403 | 0.564 | 0.459 | 0.449 | 0.489 |
| Shanxi | 0.294 | 0.238 | 0.294 | 0.302 | 0.606 | 0.57 | 0.462 | 0.423 |
| Inner Mongolia | 0.298 | 0.258 | 0.292 | 0.321 | 0.76 | 0.704 | 0.747 | 0.750 |
| Liaoning | 0.329 | 0.297 | 0.339 | 0.306 | 0.571 | 0.506 | 0.540 | 0.544 |
| Jilin | 0.345 | 0.358 | 0.405 | 0.442 | 0.959 | 0.616 | 1.000 | 1.000 |
| Heilongjiang | 0.813 | 0.623 | 0.645 | 0.612 | 0.665 | 0.446 | 0.496 | 0.543 |
| Shanghai | 0.756 | 0.462 | 0.766 | 0.707 | 0.961 | 0.653 | 0.840 | 0.757 |
| Jiangsu | 0.529 | 0.431 | 0.514 | 0.530 | 0.733 | 0.6 | 0.673 | 0.730 |
| Zhejiang | 0.539 | 0.407 | 0.549 | 0.593 | 0.6 | 0.592 | 0.740 | 0.833 |
| Anhui | 0.491 | 0.352 | 0.414 | 0.475 | 0.572 | 0.441 | 0.532 | 0.621 |
| Fujian | 0.565 | 0.424 | 0.538 | 0.553 | 0.735 | 0.616 | 0.655 | 0.862 |

*(Continued)*

136

*Table 7A.1   (Continued)*

| Regions | SOEs | | | | FFEs | | | |
|---|---|---|---|---|---|---|---|---|
| | 1999 | 2000 | 2001 | 2002 | 1999 | 2000 | 2001 | 2002 |
| Jiangxi | 0.361 | 0.315 | 0.376 | 0.416 | 0.537 | 0.385 | 0.576 | 0.612 |
| Shandong | 0.518 | 0.472 | 0.543 | 0.57 | 0.708 | 0.685 | 0.865 | 0.919 |
| Henan | 0.453 | 0.367 | 0.419 | 0.451 | 0.740 | 0.647 | 0.554 | 0.562 |
| Hubei | 0.434 | 0.397 | 0.452 | 0.447 | 0.886 | 0.521 | 0.681 | 0.661 |
| Hunan | 0.405 | 0.355 | 0.440 | 0.429 | 0.603 | 0.683 | 0.583 | 0.565 |
| Guangdong | 0.674 | 0.469 | 0.726 | 0.673 | 0.701 | 0.695 | 0.818 | 0.904 |
| Guangxi | 0.361 | 0.311 | 0.334 | 0.361 | 0.539 | 0.297 | 0.432 | 0.591 |
| Hainan | 0.407 | 0.286 | 0.340 | 0.418 | 0.608 | 0.332 | 0.471 | 0.552 |
| Chongqing | 0.295 | 0.311 | 0.354 | 0.389 | 0.633 | 0.409 | 0.667 | 0.521 |
| Sichuan | 0.347 | 0.261 | 0.350 | 0.387 | 0.702 | 0.547 | 0.613 | 0.677 |
| Guizhou | 0.431 | 0.319 | 0.345 | 0.379 | 0.515 | 0.503 | 0.542 | 0.234 |
| Yunnan | 0.768 | 0.576 | 0.703 | 0.699 | 0.702 | 0.395 | 0.548 | 0.509 |
| Shaanxi | 0.350 | 0.323 | 0.350 | 0.363 | 1.000 | 0.626 | 0.863 | 0.931 |
| Gansu | 0.331 | 0.271 | 0.350 | 0.348 | 0.446 | 0.370 | 0.535 | 0.578 |
| Qinghai | 0.291 | 0.185 | 0.342 | 0.308 | 0.614 | 1.000 | 0.585 | 0.723 |
| Ningxia | 0.289 | 0.272 | 0.311 | 0.277 | 0.639 | 0.771 | 0.701 | 0.515 |
| Xinjiang | 0.469 | 0.429 | 0.612 | 0.499 | 0.695 | 0.340 | 0.471 | 0.407 |
| *Mean* | *0.4482* | *0.360* | *0.443* | *0.447* | *0.689* | *0.572* | *0.647* | *0.663* |
| *Data set (B)* | | | | | | | | |
| Beijing | 0.482 | 0.425 | 0.453 | 0.429 | 1.000 | 1.000 | 1.000 | 1.000 |
| Tianjin | 0.312 | 0.282 | 0.303 | 0.298 | 0.986 | 0.851 | 0.727 | 0.848 |
| Hebei | 0.339 | 0.252 | 0.237 | 0.252 | 0.553 | 0.430 | 0.350 | 0.416 |
| Shanxi | 0.219 | 0.162 | 0.175 | 0.175 | 0.559 | 0.461 | 0.368 | 0.324 |
| Inner Mongolia | 0.221 | 0.170 | 0.177 | 0.207 | 0.651 | 0.629 | 0.549 | 0.476 |
| Liaoning | 0.315 | 0.272 | 0.306 | 0.293 | 0.627 | 0.537 | 0.546 | 0.507 |
| Jilin | 0.327 | 0.313 | 0.300 | 0.349 | 0.823 | 0.876 | 0.934 | 1.000 |
| Heilongjiang | 0.415 | 0.291 | 0.260 | 0.261 | 0.575 | 0.401 | 0.409 | 0.396 |
| Shanghai | 0.645 | 0.591 | 0.681 | 0.614 | 1.000 | 0.816 | 0.823 | 0.793 |
| Jiangsu | 0.518 | 0.390 | 0.411 | 0.431 | 0.814 | 0.647 | 0.614 | 0.674 |
| Zhejiang | 0.458 | 0.422 | 0.454 | 0.439 | 0.702 | 0.648 | 0.697 | 0.763 |
| Anhui | 0.397 | 0.269 | 0.275 | 0.301 | 0.586 | 0.443 | 0.450 | 0.521 |
| Fujian | 0.425 | 0.368 | 0.386 | 0.387 | 0.750 | 0.532 | 0.545 | 0.645 |
| Jiangxi | 0.340 | 0.269 | 0.272 | 0.300 | 0.645 | 0.406 | 0.469 | 0.533 |
| Shandong | 0.408 | 0.324 | 0.330 | 0.376 | 0.742 | 0.615 | 0.655 | 0.700 |
| Henan | 0.370 | 0.289 | 0.274 | 0.287 | 0.614 | 0.469 | 0.420 | 0.455 |
| Hubei | 0.354 | 0.290 | 0.299 | 0.331 | 0.717 | 0.617 | 0.511 | 0.537 |
| Hunan | 0.318 | 0.254 | 0.269 | 0.262 | 0.58 | 0.539 | 0.447 | 0.463 |
| Guangdong | 0.603 | 0.563 | 0.611 | 0.523 | 0.786 | 0.673 | 0.724 | 0.804 |
| Guangxi | 0.316 | 0.227 | 0.224 | 0.255 | 0.505 | 0.36 | 0.36 | 0.509 |
| Hainan | 0.371 | 0.279 | 0.301 | 0.305 | 0.609 | 0.443 | 0.424 | 0.565 |
| Chongqing | 0.285 | 0.253 | 0.253 | 0.279 | 0.646 | 0.622 | 0.585 | 0.481 |

*(Continued)*

*Table 7A.1   (Continued)*

| Regions | SOEs | | | | FFEs | | | |
|---|---|---|---|---|---|---|---|---|
| | *1999* | *2000* | *2001* | *2002* | *1999* | *2000* | *2001* | *2002* |
| Sichuan | 0.272 | 0.200 | 0.210 | 0.246 | 0.602 | 0.473 | 0.468 | 0.473 |
| Guizhou | 0.332 | 0.225 | 0.220 | 0.230 | 0.516 | 0.462 | 0.398 | 0.438 |
| Yunnan | 0.389 | 0.274 | 0.304 | 0.329 | 0.570 | 0.504 | 0.470 | 0.443 |
| Shaanxi | 0.284 | 0.227 | 0.228 | 0.234 | 1.000 | 0.814 | 0.706 | 0.678 |
| Gansu | 0.276 | 0.223 | 0.248 | 0.242 | 0.461 | 0.435 | 0.420 | 0.473 |
| Qinghai | 0.216 | 0.231 | 0.242 | 0.215 | 0.704 | 1.000 | 0.768 | 0.648 |
| Ningxia | 0.257 | 0.221 | 0.222 | 0.212 | 0.532 | 0.506 | 0.470 | 0.389 |
| Xinjiang | 0.299 | 0.361 | 0.382 | 0.322 | 0.592 | 0.453 | 0.410 | 0.372 |
| *Mean* | *0.360* | *0.300* | *0.310* | *0.310* | *0.680* | *0.590* | *0.560* | *0.580* |
| *Data set (C)* | | | | | | | | |
| Beijing | 0.577 | 0.508 | 0.510 | 0.577 | 1.000 | 1.000 | 1.000 | 1.000 |
| Tianjin | 0.440 | 0.381 | 0.391 | 0.483 | 1.000 | 1.000 | 0.881 | 0.93 |
| Hebei | 0.548 | 0.500 | 0.470 | 0.568 | 0.827 | 0.706 | 0.637 | 0.721 |
| Shanxi | 0.385 | 0.334 | 0.332 | 0.427 | 0.697 | 0.600 | 0.585 | 0.742 |
| Inner Mongolia | 0.478 | 0.455 | 0.460 | 0.530 | 0.651 | 0.629 | 0.549 | 0.496 |
| Liaoning | 0.490 | 0.487 | 0.426 | 0.509 | 0.864 | 0.778 | 0.703 | 0.782 |
| Jilin | 0.508 | 0.494 | 0.492 | 0.650 | 0.966 | 0.944 | 1.000 | 1.000 |
| Heilongjiang | 0.576 | 0.614 | 0.521 | 0.591 | 0.596 | 0.487 | 0.438 | 0.535 |
| Shanghai | 0.665 | 0.598 | 0.683 | 0.614 | 1.000 | 0.830 | 0.837 | 0.800 |
| Jiangsu | 0.677 | 0.540 | 0.579 | 0.624 | 1.000 | 0.821 | 0.828 | 0.900 |
| Zhejiang | 0.585 | 0.527 | 0.483 | 0.602 | 0.901 | 0.777 | 0.903 | 0.902 |
| Anhui | 0.609 | 0.464 | 0.495 | 0.612 | 0.851 | 0.630 | 0.629 | 0.820 |
| Fujian | 0.71 | 0.642 | 0.588 | 0.759 | 0.983 | 0.801 | 0.785 | 0.888 |
| Jiangxi | 0.511 | 0.443 | 0.423 | 0.543 | 0.792 | 0.553 | 0.647 | 0.752 |
| Shandong | 0.625 | 0.608 | 0.567 | 0.730 | 1.000 | 0.857 | 0.909 | 0.937 |
| Henan | 0.509 | 0.468 | 0.452 | 0.537 | 0.729 | 0.561 | 0.503 | 0.592 |
| Hubei | 0.542 | 0.468 | 0.483 | 0.559 | 0.874 | 0.735 | 0.701 | 0.804 |
| Hunan | 0.543 | 0.475 | 0.451 | 0.559 | 0.829 | 0.693 | 0.664 | 0.813 |
| Guangdong | 0.708 | 0.591 | 0.628 | 0.603 | 0.977 | 0.787 | 0.93 | 0.957 |
| Guangxi | 0.564 | 0.498 | 0.459 | 0.592 | 0.711 | 0.587 | 0.565 | 0.835 |
| Hainan | 0.545 | 0.478 | 0.488 | 0.628 | 0.609 | 0.488 | 0.569 | 0.758 |
| Chongqing | 0.431 | 0.377 | 0.360 | 0.441 | 0.731 | 0.628 | 0.619 | 0.702 |
| Sichuan | 0.410 | 0.369 | 0.378 | 0.439 | 0.694 | 0.586 | 0.591 | 0.584 |
| Guizhou | 0.425 | 0.328 | 0.326 | 0.413 | 0.539 | 0.495 | 0.437 | 0.502 |
| Yunnan | 0.574 | 0.482 | 0.417 | 0.481 | 0.692 | 0.530 | 0.498 | 0.548 |
| Shaanxi | 0.455 | 0.400 | 0.391 | 0.497 | 1.000 | 0.814 | 0.721 | 0.689 |
| Gansu | 0.455 | 0.408 | 0.440 | 0.524 | 0.540 | 0.487 | 0.551 | 0.620 |
| Qinghai | 0.414 | 0.244 | 0.275 | 0.323 | 0.824 | 1.000 | 0.809 | 0.648 |
| Ningxia | 0.457 | 0.420 | 0.384 | 0.440 | 0.597 | 0.551 | 0.577 | 0.642 |
| Xinjiang | 0.523 | 0.624 | 0.527 | 0.667 | 0.692 | 0.500 | 0.438 | 0.442 |
| *Mean* | *0.531* | *0.474* | *0.463* | *0.551* | *0.806* | *0.695* | *0.683* | *0.745* |

138

*Table 7A.2*  Malmquist productivity index: annual average, 2000–2

| Regions | Set A | | Set B | | Set C | |
|---|---|---|---|---|---|---|
| | *SOEs* | *FFEs* | *SOEs* | *FFEs* | *SOEs* | *FFEs* |
| Beijing | 1.052 | 1.059 | 1.165 | 1.137 | 1.091 | 1.133 |
| Tianjin | 1.136 | 1.180 | 1.205 | 1.077 | 1.090 | 1.062 |
| Hebei | 1.006 | 1.064 | 0.998 | 1.050 | 1.043 | 1.002 |
| Shanxi | 1.040 | 0.962 | 1.027 | 1.011 | 1.067 | 1.075 |
| Inner Mongolia | 1.094 | 1.026 | 1.116 | 0.992 | 1.067 | 1.008 |
| Liaoning | 1.109 | 1.142 | 1.207 | 1.093 | 1.056 | 1.024 |
| Jilin | 1.120 | 1.210 | 1.125 | 1.272 | 1.123 | 1.171 |
| Heilongjiang | 0.941 | 1.056 | 0.946 | 1.059 | 1.040 | 1.054 |
| Shanghai | 1.126 | 1.056 | 1.193 | 1.096 | 1.160 | 1.082 |
| Jiangsu | 1.038 | 1.099 | 1.040 | 1.094 | 1.027 | 1.037 |
| Zhejiang | 1.192 | 1.150 | 1.236 | 1.138 | 1.110 | 1.080 |
| Anhui | 1.019 | 1.149 | 1.009 | 1.180 | 1.032 | 1.033 |
| Fujian | 1.150 | 1.087 | 1.202 | 1.052 | 1.066 | 1.027 |
| Jiangxi | 1.080 | 1.077 | 1.061 | 1.039 | 1.052 | 1.061 |
| Shandong | 1.068 | 1.124 | 1.076 | 1.085 | 1.087 | 1.032 |
| Henan | 1.029 | 1.028 | 1.017 | 1.055 | 1.049 | 1.030 |
| Hubei | 1.047 | 1.070 | 1.083 | 1.061 | 1.046 | 1.049 |
| Hunan | 1.051 | 1.015 | 1.036 | 1.030 | 1.041 | 1.027 |
| Guangdong | 1.148 | 1.122 | 1.152 | 1.115 | 1.105 | 1.083 |
| Guangxi | 1.037 | 1.155 | 1.032 | 1.177 | 1.048 | 1.106 |
| Hainan | 1.131 | 1.123 | 1.100 | 1.092 | 1.098 | 1.169 |
| Chongqing | 1.130 | 1.142 | 1.096 | 1.087 | 1.048 | 1.083 |
| Sichuan | 1.088 | 1.091 | 1.082 | 1.081 | 1.058 | 1.038 |
| Guizhou | 0.987 | 0.792 | 0.979 | 1.047 | 1.037 | 1.064 |
| Yunnan | 1.065 | 1.078 | 1.124 | 1.103 | 0.986 | 1.047 |
| Shaanxi | 1.043 | 1.129 | 1.032 | 1.046 | 1.062 | 1.033 |
| Gansu | 1.051 | 1.159 | 1.055 | 1.143 | 1.082 | 1.149 |
| Qinghai | 1.154 | 1.183 | 1.205 | 1.191 | 0.979 | 1.068 |
| Ningxia | 1.030 | 0.961 | 1.045 | 0.993 | 1.021 | 1.088 |
| Xinjiang | 1.167 | 0.975 | 1.262 | 0.989 | 1.131 | 0.976 |
| *Mean* | *1.078* | *1.082* | *1.097* | *1.086* | *1.063* | *1.063* |

*Table 7A.3* Annual average of decomposition of MPI

| Regions | SOEs | | | FFEs | | |
|---|---|---|---|---|---|---|
| | TC | PECH | SC | TC | PECH | SC |
| *Data set (A)* | | | | | | |
| Beijing | 1.128 | 0.988 | 0.944 | 1.059 | 1.000 | 1.000 |
| Tianjin | 1.174 | 1.055 | 0.917 | 1.078 | 1.130 | 0.969 |
| Hebei | 1.033 | 0.970 | 1.005 | 1.116 | 0.949 | 1.004 |
| Shanxi | 1.03 | 1.021 | 0.989 | 1.084 | 0.872 | 1.018 |
| Inner Mongolia | 1.067 | 1.053 | 0.974 | 1.030 | 0.994 | 1.002 |
| Liaoning | 1.136 | 1.054 | 0.927 | 1.161 | 0.993 | 0.991 |
| Jilin | 1.032 | 1.100 | 0.987 | 1.193 | 1.000 | 1.014 |
| Heilongjiang | 1.035 | 0.918 | 0.991 | 1.129 | 0.941 | 0.994 |
| Shanghai | 1.151 | 1.000 | 0.978 | 1.143 | 1.000 | 0.924 |
| Jiangsu | 1.038 | 0.992 | 1.008 | 1.101 | 1.046 | 0.954 |
| Zhejiang | 1.155 | 1.131 | 0.913 | 1.030 | 1.133 | 0.984 |
| Anhui | 1.030 | 0.988 | 1.001 | 1.118 | 1.027 | 1.001 |
| Fujian | 1.158 | 1.095 | 0.906 | 1.030 | 1.036 | 1.018 |
| Jiangxi | 1.030 | 1.048 | 1.000 | 1.030 | 1.049 | 0.996 |
| Shandong | 1.035 | 1.027 | 1.006 | 1.030 | 1.094 | 0.997 |
| Henan | 1.030 | 0.981 | 1.018 | 1.127 | 0.916 | 0.997 |
| Hubei | 1.037 | 1.003 | 1.008 | 1.180 | 0.873 | 1.039 |
| Hunan | 1.030 | 1.026 | 0.994 | 1.037 | 0.980 | 0.999 |
| Guangdong | 1.149 | 0.989 | 1.010 | 1.030 | 1.000 | 1.089 |
| Guangxi | 1.037 | 1.000 | 1.000 | 1.120 | 1.033 | 0.998 |
| Hainan | 1.120 | 1.017 | 0.992 | 1.160 | 1.006 | 0.963 |
| Chongqing | 1.030 | 1.096 | 1.000 | 1.219 | 0.938 | 1.000 |
| Sichuan | 1.049 | 1.043 | 0.994 | 1.104 | 0.991 | 0.996 |
| Guizhou | 1.030 | 0.957 | 1.000 | 1.030 | 0.872 | 0.881 |
| Yunnan | 1.099 | 1.006 | 0.964 | 1.200 | 0.897 | 1.002 |
| Shaanxi | 1.030 | 1.028 | 0.984 | 1.156 | 0.986 | 0.991 |
| Gansu | 1.034 | 1.028 | 0.989 | 1.063 | 1.129 | 0.966 |
| Qinghai | 1.132 | 1.017 | 1.003 | 1.121 | 1.000 | 1.056 |
| Ningxia | 1.045 | 0.991 | 0.995 | 1.033 | 0.961 | 0.968 |
| Xinjiang | 1.143 | 1.095 | 0.932 | 1.164 | 0.940 | 0.891 |
| *Mean* | *1.074* | *1.024* | *0.981* | *1.103* | *0.993* | *0.990* |
| *Data set (B)* | | | | | | |
| Beijing | 1.211 | 1.021 | 0.942 | 1.137 | 1.000 | 1.000 |
| Tianjin | 1.224 | 1.065 | 0.925 | 1.132 | 0.981 | 0.970 |
| Hebei | 1.101 | 0.904 | 1.002 | 1.154 | 0.909 | 1.000 |
| Shanxi | 1.107 | 0.928 | 1.000 | 1.213 | 0.823 | 1.013 |
| Inner Mongolia | 1.140 | 0.979 | 1.000 | 1.101 | 0.908 | 0.992 |
| Liaoning | 1.237 | 1.049 | 0.930 | 1.173 | 0.945 | 0.987 |
| Jilin | 1.101 | 1.026 | 0.996 | 1.192 | 1.062 | 1.005 |

(Continued)

*Table 7A.3   (Continued)*

| Regions | SOEs | | | FFEs | | |
|---|---|---|---|---|---|---|
| | *TC* | *PECH* | *SC* | *TC* | *PECH* | *SC* |
| Heilongjiang | 1.104 | 0.857 | 1.000 | 1.200 | 0.889 | 0.993 |
| Shanghai | 1.213 | 1.094 | 0.899 | 1.184 | 1.000 | 0.926 |
| Jiangsu | 1.105 | 0.951 | 0.989 | 1.165 | 1.006 | 0.934 |
| Zhejiang | 1.254 | 1.076 | 0.916 | 1.107 | 1.047 | 0.982 |
| Anhui | 1.107 | 0.899 | 1.015 | 1.227 | 0.961 | 1.000 |
| Fujian | 1.240 | 1.042 | 0.931 | 1.107 | 0.953 | 0.998 |
| Jiangxi | 1.107 | 0.960 | 0.999 | 1.107 | 0.955 | 0.982 |
| Shandong | 1.105 | 0.998 | 0.975 | 1.107 | 0.989 | 0.991 |
| Henan | 1.107 | 0.915 | 1.004 | 1.165 | 0.908 | 0.997 |
| Hubei | 1.107 | 0.979 | 0.998 | 1.169 | 0.892 | 1.018 |
| Hunan | 1.106 | 0.927 | 1.011 | 1.111 | 0.930 | 0.997 |
| Guangdong | 1.208 | 1.014 | 0.941 | 1.107 | 1.000 | 1.008 |
| Guangxi | 1.108 | 0.932 | 0.999 | 1.175 | 1.004 | 0.998 |
| Hainan | 1.174 | 0.945 | 0.992 | 1.120 | 1.002 | 0.973 |
| Chongqing | 1.104 | 0.994 | 0.999 | 1.199 | 0.908 | 0.998 |
| Sichuan | 1.119 | 0.965 | 1.002 | 1.171 | 0.927 | 0.995 |
| Guizhou | 1.107 | 0.887 | 0.997 | 1.107 | 1.021 | 0.927 |
| Yunnan | 1.189 | 0.983 | 0.962 | 1.199 | 0.920 | 1.000 |
| Shaanxi | 1.102 | 0.940 | 0.997 | 1.191 | 0.890 | 0.988 |
| Gansu | 1.102 | 0.958 | 1.000 | 1.133 | 1.069 | 0.943 |
| Qinghai | 1.206 | 1.001 | 0.998 | 1.225 | 1.000 | 0.973 |
| Ningxia | 1.115 | 0.943 | 0.994 | 1.102 | 0.959 | 0.939 |
| Xinjiang | 1.230 | 1.081 | 0.949 | 1.155 | 0.971 | 0.882 |
| *Mean* | *1.148* | *0.977* | *0.979* | *1.155* | *0.961* | *0.980* |
| *Data set (c)* | | | | | | |
| Beijing | 1.091 | 1.044 | 0.958 | 1.133 | 1.000 | 1.000 |
| Tianjin | 1.057 | 1.053 | 0.979 | 1.088 | 1.000 | 0.976 |
| Hebei | 1.031 | 1.020 | 0.992 | 1.049 | 0.956 | 0.999 |
| Shanxi | 1.031 | 1.052 | 0.984 | 1.053 | 1.021 | 1.000 |
| Inner Mongolia | 1.031 | 1.045 | 0.991 | 1.104 | 0.916 | 0.997 |
| Liaoning | 1.042 | 1.032 | 0.981 | 1.058 | 0.987 | 0.980 |
| Jilin | 1.035 | 1.107 | 0.981 | 1.157 | 1.011 | 1.000 |
| Heilongjiang | 1.031 | 1.018 | 0.991 | 1.093 | 0.967 | 0.997 |
| Shanghai | 1.191 | 1.054 | 0.924 | 1.166 | 1.000 | 0.928 |
| Jiangsu | 1.055 | 0.991 | 0.982 | 1.074 | 1.000 | 0.965 |
| Zhejiang | 1.100 | 1.052 | 0.959 | 1.080 | 1.011 | 0.990 |
| Anhui | 1.031 | 1.020 | 0.982 | 1.046 | 0.987 | 1.001 |
| Fujian | 1.042 | 1.040 | 0.983 | 1.063 | 0.991 | 0.975 |
| Jiangxi | 1.031 | 1.033 | 0.987 | 1.080 | 0.985 | 0.998 |
| Shandong | 1.032 | 1.054 | 0.999 | 1.054 | 1.000 | 0.979 |

*(Continued)*

*Table 7A.3   (Continued)*

| Regions | SOEs | | | FFEs | | |
|---|---|---|---|---|---|---|
| | *TC* | *PECH* | *SC* | *TC* | *PECH* | *SC* |
| Henan | 1.031 | 1.027 | 0.991 | 1.105 | 0.934 | 0.999 |
| Hubei | 1.036 | 1.022 | 0.988 | 1.079 | 0.971 | 1.001 |
| Hunan | 1.031 | 1.029 | 0.982 | 1.034 | 0.994 | 0.999 |
| Guangdong | 1.166 | 0.998 | 0.950 | 1.091 | 1.000 | 0.993 |
| Guangxi | 1.031 | 1.026 | 0.991 | 1.048 | 1.054 | 1.001 |
| Hainan | 1.047 | 1.051 | 0.998 | 1.087 | 1.083 | 0.994 |
| Chongqing | 1.039 | 1.018 | 0.991 | 1.097 | 0.990 | 0.997 |
| Sichuan | 1.035 | 1.040 | 0.984 | 1.099 | 0.945 | 0.999 |
| Guizhou | 1.046 | 0.995 | 0.996 | 1.090 | 1.021 | 0.956 |
| Yunnan | 1.046 | 0.962 | 0.980 | 1.132 | 0.932 | 0.992 |
| Shaanxi | 1.031 | 1.048 | 0.983 | 1.170 | 0.895 | 0.987 |
| Gansu | 1.033 | 1.059 | 0.990 | 1.097 | 1.069 | 0.980 |
| Qinghai | 1.063 | 0.923 | 0.997 | 1.157 | 1.000 | 0.923 |
| Ningxia | 1.034 | 0.989 | 0.998 | 1.062 | 1.043 | 0.982 |
| Xinjiang | 1.043 | 1.096 | 0.989 | 1.133 | 0.947 | 0.910 |
| *Mean* | *1.051* | *1.030* | *0.983* | *1.093* | *0.990* | *0.983* |

*Notes*:   TC = Technical change. PECH = Pure Technical Efficiency change. SC = Scale Efficiency change.

# 8
# Conclusion

The interrelationship between productivity, efficiency and economic growth is complicated and controversial, and hence the focus of the core chapters of this volume using the Chinese economy as the case studies. The objectives of this concluding chapter are twofold. It first presents a summary of the main findings in this book (Section 8.1). It then sheds some light on the outlook for sustainable growth in China (Section 8.2).

## 8.1 Summary of the main findings

Broadly the six core chapters in this book, that is Chapters 2–7, can be divided into three parts, with Chapters 2 and 3 addressing the role of capital formation and productivity in economic growth, Chapters 4 and 5 looking into the impact of the new economy on growth and productivity performance, and Chapters 6 and 7 exploring the influence of foreign capital on productivity and efficiency at the firm level. The main findings of the chapters are summarized in Table 8.1.

Chapter 2 lays the foundation for empirical analysis in Chapter 3. This chapter introduced a novel approach to derive China's regional capital stock series which is made available to the public (presented in the appendix to Chapter 2). A preliminary examination reveals the close association between capital formation and economic growth which is to be further investigated in Chapter 3. This chapter also shows that regional disparity in capital endowment worsened after the mid 1980s, but this trend has been reversed to some extent due to the 'go-west' programme initiated by the Chinese government in 1999. Chapter 3 formally examines the contribution of total factor productivity to economic growth. As speculated in Chapter 2, capital stock is found to be the largest contributor to economic growth, followed by TFP growth.

*Table 8.1*  Summary of the main findings

| Chapters | Issues | Findings |
| --- | --- | --- |
| 2 | Capital stock estimates | Close movement between capital stock increase and economic growth; disparity in capital endowment; positive effect of 'go-west' programme |
| 3 | Productivity and economic growth | Main growth drivers: capital and total factor productivity (TFP); scope for catch-up with the world's best practice |
| 4 | ICT and its contribution to economic growth | Though still small in intensity, ICT capital made a relatively large contribution to economic growth |
| 5 | ICT and its impact on regional efficiency | Regional variation exists; ICT investment affects efficiency positively |
| 6 | FDI's spillover effects on productivity | Positive effect on labour productivity at the industry level; more benefits for the coastal and western regions |
| 7 | Performance of foreign-funded and domestic enterprises | FFEs more efficient than SOEs; regional differences; sensitive to data used |

While the positive role of TFP in economic growth indicates the sustainability of growth in the near future, there is still scope for China to catch up with the world's best practice, which implies that economic growth is dominantly driven by productivity expansion.

While Chapters 2 and 3 dealt with a classical issue, Chapters 4 and 5 addressed a relatively new topic, that is, the impact of the new economy on productivity and efficiency and hence economic growth in China. In Chapter 4, it is found that, though still small in shares over total capital stock, ICT capital stock has made a relatively large contribution to China's economic growth. This contribution is anticipated to expand in the future as ICT investment increases rapidly. There is, however, regional variation as shown in Chapter 5. The coastal regions have invested more in ICT than other regions. In general ICT investment has a positive impact on regional technical efficiency.

Chapters 6 and 7 extend the preceding chapters to probe the effects of foreign investment on productivity, efficiency and economic growth in China. Chapter 6 focused on labour productivity. It is found that foreign direct investment (FDI) did generate positive spillover effects on labour productivity at the sector level. It is also found that the coastal and western regions tend to benefit more from FDI than the central regions. This, however, needs more detailed investigation. Chapter 7 compared efficiency performance of foreign-funded (FFEs) and domestic state-owned enterprises (SOEs). It shows that enterprises in the coastal areas are in general more efficient than those in other regions and that FFEs are more efficient than SOEs. However, the results are sensitive to whether value-added or gross value of output is employed in the modelling exercises.

## 8.2   Is China's economic growth sustainable? An outlook

According to the findings in this book and other studies (see Table 1.1), productivity has played a significant role in China's economic growth over recent decades, which implies the prospect of sustainable growth in the future. However, this prospect is affected by several factors.

Productivity growth can appear in two forms, that is efficiency improvement and technological advancement. The former represents gains in output by utilizing existing resources more efficiently through institutional changes, improvement in resource allocation, micro-economic management, infrastructure and so on (Liu, 2002b). It is argued that, in past decades, especially at the early stage of economic reforms, China's productivity growth largely resulted from efficiency improvement associated with economic reforms which brought about reallocation of resources among the sectors, such as labour movement from the farming sector to the more productive manufacturing sector and diversion of capital from loss-making state-owned enterprises to the private sector. The contribution of such efficiency improvement can, however, be a one-off gain or a level effect. As a result, the second component of productivity growth, that is technological advancement, becomes more important. This component can have a long-lasting effect or a growth effect. In China, as economic reform deepens, the potential in efficiency improvement has gradually been exhausted or marginalized. Technological advancement is thus vital to long-term economic growth.

China's technological advancement has benefited from the country's embracement of foreign capital and technology as well as increasing investment in education and R&D in the past decades. Both governments

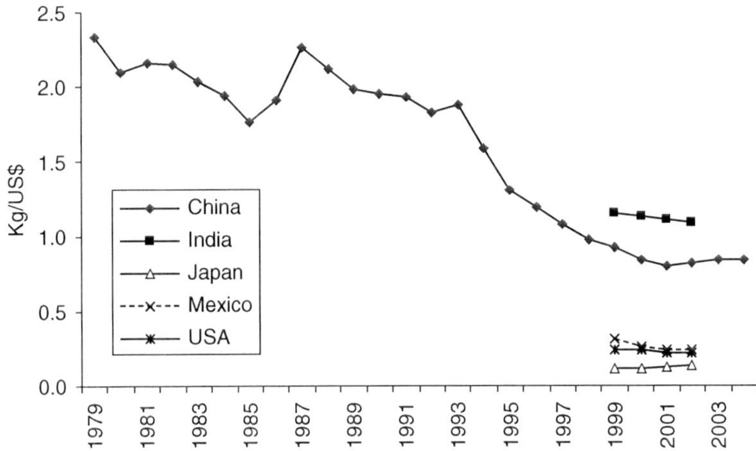

*Figure 8.1*   Energy intensity in selected economies
*Notes and sources*: Data are author's own estimates using statistics from the National Bureau
of Statistics (various issues), IMF (2005) and World Bank (2005).

and the private sector have been very active in investing in human capital and knowledge creation. For example, in 2003, about 34 per cent
of education expenditure and 76 per cent of R&D spending came from
non-government sources (National Bureau of Statistics, 2004).

Technological advancement also appears in the form of improved
energy efficiency. China's energy efficiency has improved substantially,
though it is still well behind the international standard. Figure 8.1 shows
the declining trend in terms of energy consumption per US dollar of GDP
during the period 1979–2004. It also demonstrates that China's energy
efficiency is well behind that of the more developed economies such as
the US, Japan and Mexico, though China has done better than India in
recent years.

Further improvement in energy efficiency is possible due to several
factors. Technological progress will lead to the invention and adoption
of energy-saving technologies. Over time, the less energy-intensive service sector will also expand at the expense of the more energy-intensive
manufacturing industry. Thus, energy efficiency improvement will also
stem from the structural transformation of the economy. Finally, the
rising cost of energy (due to the surge in oil prices, for instance)
and increasing competition will also force consumers and producers to
optimize the use of energy.

*Table 8.2*   Labour productivity (China/US, %)

| Sectors | 1980 | 1990 | 2002 |
|---|---|---|---|
| 1. Food products | 3.4 | 4.3 | 22.4 |
| 2. Textile mill products | 10.0 | 6.3 | 23.7 |
| 3. Wearing apparel | 4.7 | 4.6 | 8.1 |
| 4. Leather products and footwear | 11.5 | 9.3 | 30.4 |
| 5. Wood products | 5.9 | 2.3 | 25.9 |
| 6. Paper products, printing and publishing | 2.8 | 2.8 | 14.4 |
| 7. Petroleum and coal products | 29.2 | 6.3 | 3.3 |
| 8. Chemicals and allied products | 2.0 | 1.8 | 5.6 |
| 9. Rubber and plastic products | 7.1 | 4.7 | 12.6 |
| 10. Non-metallic mineral products | 9.0 | 7.4 | 23.7 |
| 11. Basic metal products | 6.0 | 5.6 | 13.2 |
| 12. Fabricated metal products | 6.5 | 5.9 | 24.2 |
| 13. Machinery and equipment | 5.2 | 6.4 | 35.3 |
| 14. Transport equipment | 4.7 | 6.4 | 40.0 |
| 15. Electrical machinery and equipment | 31.4 | 12.3 | 5.3 |
| 16. Instruments | 13.5 | 9.9 | 32.8 |
| 17. Furniture | 7.0 | 5.3 | 42.6 |
| 18. Miscellaneous | 4.6 | 3.3 | 9.2 |

*Source*: Szirmai et al. (2005).

However, in international perspectives, China still has to do a lot more to promote innovation and hence productivity growth so that the country can catch up with the world's best practice. In terms of labour productivity, though considerable progress has been made over the years, there is still a huge gap between China and the world's best practice (Table 8.2). In addition, there is disparity across the sectors. Catch-up in some sectors is much faster than that in others. The causes for the variation should be investigated and may have important policy implications. For instance, productivity in the electrical machinery and electronics sectors has been declining because of the astounding US productivity growth in these sectors.

Though China's investment in R&D and education has increased substantially, its share over GDP is well below those in the world's major economies. For example, most OECD countries spend twice as much as China does on R&D activities (Table 8.3). These countries also invest much more in education than China does. Overall, China's human development ranking is far behind that of the world's major economies (Table 8.3).

*Table 8.3*   R&D and education expenditure over GDP

| Countries | R&D expenditure over GDP (2000/1) | Education spending over GDP (1999/2000) | HDI (world ranking) (2003) |
| --- | --- | --- | --- |
| Australia | 1.5 | 4.7 | 0.955 (3) |
| Canada | 1.9 | 5.5 | 0.949 (5) |
| USA | 2.8 | 4.8 | 0.944 (10) |
| Japan | 3.1 | 3.5 | 0.943 (11) |
| UK | 1.9 | 4.5 | 0.939 (15) |
| France | 2.2 | 5.8 | 0.938 (16) |
| Italy | 1.1 | 4.5 | 0.934 (18) |
| Germany | 2.5 | 4.6 | 0.930 (20) |
| Singapore | 2.1 | 3.3 | 0.907 (25) |
| Korea | 3.0 | 3.8 | 0.901 (28) |
| Mexico | 0.4 | 4.4 | 0.814 (53) |
| Malaysia | 0.4 | 6.2 | 0.796 (61) |
| China | 1.1 | 2.9 | 0.755 (85) |

*Notes*: R&D expenditure as a proportion of GDP is based on 2000 or 2001 statistics and the education spending as a share of GDP is 1999 or 2000 figures. HDI (human development index) data are 2003 figures and world ranking is given in parentheses.
*Sources*: National Bureau of Statistics (2004) and United Nations (2005).

It can be anticipated that investment in R&D and education in China will keep growing in the future. This growth will come from both the public and private sectors. Potential policy initiatives would include the development of a venture investment market, establishment of the science and technology board market, introduction of R&D bonds and incentives for the promotion of indigenous R&D activities. The implementation of these initiatives would further boost spending on innovation and hence productivity growth in China.

# Notes

## 1  Introduction

1. See, for example, Färe et al. (1994b), Griliches (1994), Prescott (1998) and Hamilton and Monteagudo (1998).
2. This is the average growth rate calculated using data from the National Bureau of Statistics (2007).
3. The four East Asian Tigers refer to South Korea, Taiwan, Singapore and Hong Kong.
4. The developing Asia (23) includes Bangladesh, Bhutan, Cambodia, China, Fiji, India, Indonesia, Kiribati, Lao PDR, Malaysia, Maldives, Myanmar, Nepal, Pakistan, Papua New Guinea, the Philippines, Samoa, Solomon Islands, Sri Lanka, Thailand, Tonga, Vanuatu and Vietnam.
5. Reviews of earlier literature can be found in Y. Wu (1993), Wu and Yang (1999), and Zheng and Hu (2006).
6. See Chapter 7 of this book for more detailed discussion of the efficiency concepts.
7. Empirical studies include Fan (1991), Lin (1992), Wu (1995) and Mao and Koo 1997), to cite a few. Wu and Yang (1999) presented a review of the earlier literature.

## 2  Measuring China's Capital Stock

1. Examples include the World Bank (1997a), Maddison (1998), Woo (1998), Bramall (2000), Wang and Fan (2000), Young (2003), Wu (2004) and Garnaut and Song (2004, 2005).
2. Refer to Zhang and Zhang (2003) and Holz (2006a) for a brief review.
3. Zhang and Zhang (2003) also used the accumulation data. H. Wu (1993) presented some discussion comparing MPS with SNA (System of National Accounts).
4. This implies that, after 25 years, less than 1 per cent of the original value remains.
5. Chow (1993) did report estimates for five sectors (agriculture, industry, construction, transportation and commerce) and Wu (1995) considered three sectors (agriculture, urban state and rural industry).
6. Qian and Smyth (2006) also estimated regional capital stock with 1990 being treated as the initial year. They summed up 'fixed assets accumulation' for all years from 1949 to 1989 as the initial value of capital stock and then assumed a rate of depreciation of 5 per cent to estimate regional capital stock up to the year 2000.
7. Islam et al. (2006) also assumed the rate of depreciation to be 3 per cent during 1952–78, 4 per cent during 1979–92 and 5 per cent during 1993–2002.
8. Detailed descriptions are available in Zhang et al. (2007).

9. Several price indexes such as regional CPI are available from 1978 onwards while this study needs information from 1953 onwards.

10. It is noted that researchers have attempted to derive their own deflators for samples which are much smaller than the one used in this chapter and which involve either sectoral or nationwide statistics only (e.g. Chen et al., 1988 and Woo et al., 1994). Zhang et al. (2007) derived price deflators using implicit deflators of fixed capital formation. The latter, however, has many missing observations which have to be filled by using other price indexes as Zhang et al. did.

11. The searching process stops when the two sets of values converge. For example, in this study, the process stops when the difference of the two values is less than 0.001 per cent. It should be noted that the simulation process could introduce a time dimension allowing for time-varying rates of depreciation. This is more complicated and beyond the scope of this study.

12. See, for example, Jorgenson (1989) for a detailed survey of the literature.

13. The 'go-west' programme was initiated in 1999 and covers China's 12 administrative areas, that is, five autonomous regions (Guangxi, Inner Mongolia, Ningxia, Tibet and Xinjiang), six provinces (Gansu, Guizhou, Qinghai, Shaanxi, Sichuan and Yunnan) and one municipality (Chongqing).

# 3  Revisiting the Productivity Debate

1. See, for example, the World Bank (1993), Krugman (1994), Young (1994) and Kim and Lau (1994).

2. Examples include Ito and Krueger (1995), Young (1995), Fu et al. (1999) and Wu (2002), to cite a few.

3. See, for instance, Sachs and Woo (1997), the World Bank (1997a), Maddison (1998), Wang and Meng (2001) and Chow (2002).

4. Examples include Borensztein and Ostry (1996), Fleisher and Chen (1997), Woo (1998), Chow and Lin (2002), Wang and Yao (2003), Young (2003), Wu (2003) and Zheng and Hu (2004).

5. The Japanese and German figures are estimated by Dougherty and Jorgenson (1996).

6. For more detailed surveys of economic growth in China, see the World Bank (1997a), Bramall (2000), Chow (2002), Garnaut and Song (2003) and Wu (2004).

7. For surveys of the measurement of economic openness, see Harrison (1996).

8. China officially became a WTO member in November 2001.

9. In agriculture, the state sector is very small. However, private ownership of land has ceased to exist in China since 1949.

10. Reviews of stochastic frontier models are presented by Lovell (1996), Greene (1997), Coelli et al. (1998) and Kumbhakar and Lovell (2000), to cite a few.

11. See, for example, Färe et al. (1994b), Lovell (1996) and Coelli et al. (1998).

12. There are of course many other environmental factors affecting economic performance. For example, Sala-i-Martin (1997) identified more than 60 variables which may be related to economic growth. Due to data constraint (requirement of data for 29 regions and over 13 years), only three factors are considered in this study.

13. Examples of the one-step literature include Kumbhakar et al. (1991), Huang and Liu (1994) and Battese and Coelli (1995).
14. In total, there are 31 regions in mainland China. In this study, Tibet is excluded due to missing data. In 1997 Chongqing became a municipality supervised directly by the central government and is included in Sichuan province in this study.
15. See the appendix to this chapter for the classification of Chinese regions.
16. This rate of depreciation is chosen for consistency with the estimation of domestic capital stock (see Chapter 2). For most Chinese regions, the initial value of foreign capital stock in 1978 was assumed to be zero.
17. It is argued that this indicator of economic reform or marketization may be biased due to its ignorance of many other factors. The author is aware of other measures of marketization for the regions such as the one developed by the National Centre for Economic Research, Beijing (Wang, 2004). They may be investigated in further studies.
18. There are many different ways measuring economic openness. For a brief survey, see Harrison (1996) and Edwards (1998).
19. It is noted that the consistency and efficiency of the estimates from some of the models is an issue of controversy (Battese and Broca, 1997). All models in this study are estimated using Frontier 4.1 developed by Coelli (1996).

## 4   New Economy, Productivity and Growth

1. The terms ICT and IT (information technology), have been used interchangeably in the literature. In general, American scholars prefer to use IT (Brynjolfsson, 2003; Dedrick et al., 2003; and Jorgenson et al., 2005, for instance), whereas European (and OECD) scholars tend to use ICT (Becchetti et al., 2003; Fabiani et al., 2005; and Inklaar et al., 2003, for example).
2. *China Statistical Abstract 2006*, pp. 20–1.
3. For an overview of ICT development in China, see Wong (2007).
4. Discussion about the estimation of ICT capital stock is presented in the appendix to this chapter.
5. Other data such as the number of staff and workers, as well as labour compensation as proxies for labour input, did not work well in the regressions. Labour compensation, as defined in *China Statistical Yearbook*, includes 'wages, bonuses and allowances the labourers earn in monetary form and in kind, as well as the free medical services and expenses provided to the labourers, traffic subsidies, social insurance and housing fund paid by employers'.
6. In another study, the depreciation rate of China's capital stock for the period 1990–2000 is assumed to be 5 per cent (Qian and Smyth, 2006).
7. For instance, in a study of 69 countries over the world, 48 have an adjusted $R^2$ of 0.99 or higher (Dadkhah and Zahedi, 1990). Similarly, Diewert and Lawrence (2005) obtained an $R^2$ of 0.9986 for the Australian production function.
8. Data were obtained from World Information Technology and Services Alliance (WITSA) and International Data Corporation (IDC). However, data on hardware spending were reported to be biased upwards as they include household spending.

9. Adopted from Diewert and Lawrence (2005) who estimated productivity growth for Australia.

## 5 New Economy and Efficiency among the Regions

1. The other sectors include biotechnology and new medicines, new materials, manufacturing, resource development, environmental protection, aeronautics and astronautics, agriculture and transportation. See 'High-Tech Industries Gain State Priority', *China Daily* (North American edn), New York: 9 July 2004.
2. After two decades of pursuing coastal development, the western development strategy was proposed by former Chinese President Jiang Zemin during the Ninth National People's Congress (NPC) in March 1999 and the policy was officially endorsed in June the same year in which the phrase 'great western development' (*xibu da kaifa*) was used in Jiang's 'Xi'an speech' (Lai, 2002, p. 436).
3. Aimed at nurturing China for home-grown leading technologies, these ICT bases would focus on the development of mobile telecommunications, digital TV, software, as well as semiconductor technologies and products. See 'Launch of IT Bases Planned', *China Daily* (North American edn), New York: 16 August 2004.
4. Ibid.
5. The preferential policies are listed in the official publication *A Catalogue of Advantaged Industries for Foreign Investment in the Central and Western Region*, in which 'provinces in the central and western regions may upgrade an existing developmental zone in the capital cities into a national economic and technological development zone' (Lai, 2002, p. 457).
6. 'IT Industry to Maintain Fast Growth', *China Daily*, Beijing: 6 December 2004.
7. Regional division used in this chapter is based on *China Statistical Yearbook*. The municipal cities are Beijing, Tianjin and Shanghai. Eastern region consists of Hebei, Liaoning, Jiangsu, Zhejiang, Fujian, Shandong, Guangdong, Guangxi and Hainan provinces. The central region is made up of the provinces of Shanxi, Inner Mongolia, Jilin, Heilongjiang, Anhui, Jiangxi, Henan, Hubei and Hunan. The western region makes up the remaining provinces and autonomous regions of Sichuan (includes Chongqing municipality), Guizhou, Yunnan, Shaanxi, Gansu, Ningxia and Xinjiang. As data on ICT investment are not available for Tibet and Qinghai, these two autonomous regions are omitted from the analysis.
8. See Miyagawa et al. (2004) for Japanese IT investment figures. Note that the shares reported in this chapter are considerably lower than those in Chapter 4 as the latter looks at the share of ICT capital stock to GDP instead of investment.
9. DEA is an alternative method for modelling the relationship between inputs and output in the production process, and has become popular especially in the study of public sectors such as school and hospitals (Susiluoto, 2003).
10. The likelihood ratio (LR) test statistic is given by $\lambda = -2(LL_{Restricted} - LL_{Unrestricted})$.
11. The instructions for the programme can be found in Coelli (1996).

12. Headed by the Chinese Premier Wen Jiabao, the 'North-east revitalization' programme was initiated when an office in charge was formed in the State Council in October 2003. The programme provides preferential policies and financial support with the aim to revive the industrial bases and spur the economic growth of north-east China (Dong, 2006).
13. 'IT Giants to Assist in Northeast Revitalization', *China Daily* (New York: 23 July 2004).

## 6  Foreign Direct Investment and Productivity Growth

1. Todo and Miyamoto (2002) clarified the concept of 'knowledge diffusion', which is a concept similar to 'technology transfer'. However, the term 'technology transfer' is more likely to imply relocation of 'machinery' and its 'operation methods' rather than 'idea and skills'.
2. Three types of patents have been mentioned: *Invention*, which is a new technical solution relating to a product, process, or improvement. *Utility model*, which means a new technical solution relating to the shape or structure of a product that is not directly related to its aesthetic properties, and *External design*, which involves a new design of shape, pattern or combination (Cheung and Lin, 2004).
3. Due to the limitation of the Chinese statistics, the data for labour productivity cover both foreign and non-foreign firms.
4. Due to missing data, Chongqing, Tibet and Qinghai are excluded.

## 7  Efficiency of Foreign-Funded and Domestic Enterprises

1. Note that the horizontal and vertical axes in Figure 7.1 are labelled as input per unit of output. This is derived from the CRS property of the production function.

$$y = F(x_1, x_2) \text{ which, under CRS, } \alpha y = F(\alpha x_1, \alpha x_2)$$
$$\text{set } \alpha = \frac{1}{y} : 1 = F\left(\frac{x_1}{y}, \frac{x_2}{y}\right)$$

   Here the horizontal axis is $x_1/y$, and $x_2/y$ is the vertical axis.
2. An alternative technique of a non-parametric approach to measure efficiency is free disposal hull (FDH). FDH first appeared in Deprins et al. (1984) and is now gradually becoming popular. However, DEA has been widely used because it can be applied in a diverse variety of situations and it has also been the subject of a number of theoretical extensions that have increased its flexibility, ease of use, and applicability (Allen et al., 1997).
3. Tibet is excluded because of data unavailability.
4. For more details of the conceptual framework for this extended decomposition, refer to Ray and Desli (1997).

# References


Abramovitz, M. (1956) 'Resource and Output Trends in the U.S. since 1870', *American Economic Review (Papers and Proceedings)*, 46 (2), 5–23.

Abramovitz, M. (1986) 'Catching Up, Forging Ahead, and Falling Behind', *Journal of Economic History*, 46 (2), 385–406.

Ai, C. and M. Wen (2005) 'Ownership and Sector Performance in Present-Day China: a Regional Study', *Pacific Economic Review*, 10, 471–84.

Ali, M. and J.C. Flinn (1989) 'Profit Efficiency among Basmati Rice Producers in Pakistan Punjab', *American Journal of Agricultural Economics*, 71 (2), 303–10.

Allen, R., A. Athanassopoulos, R. G. Dyson and E. Thanassoulis (1997) 'Weights Restrictions and Value Judgements in Data Envelopment Analysis: Evolution, Development and Future Directions', *Annals of Operational Research*, 73, 13–34.

Asmild, M., C. J. Paradi, V. Aggarwall and C. Schaffnit (2004) 'Combining DEA Window Analysis with the Malmquist Index Approach in a Study of the Canadian Banking Industry', *Journal of Productivity Analysis*, 21 (1), 67–89.

Battese, G. E. and S. S. Broca (1997) 'Functional Forms of Stochastic Frontier Production Functions and Models for Technical Inefficiency Effects: a Comparative Study for Wheat Farmers in Pakistan', *Journal of Productivity Analysis*, 8 (4), 395–414.

Battese, G. E. and T. Coelli (1995) 'A Model for Technical Inefficiency Effects in a Stochastic Frontier Production Function for Panel Data', *Empirical Economics*, 20, 325–32.

Becchetti, L., D. A. L. Bedoya and L. Paganetto (2003) 'ICT Investment, Productivity and Efficiency: Evidence at Firm Level Using a Stochastic Frontier Approach', *Journal of Productivity Analysis*, 20, 143–67.

Bende-Nabende, A., J. L. Ford, B. Santoso and S. Sen (2003) 'The Interaction between FDI, Output and the Spillover Variables: Co-integration and VAR Analyses for APEC', *Applied Economics Letter*, 10 (3), 165–72.

Bhalla, A. S., S. Yao and Z. Zhang (2003) 'Causes of Inequalities in China, 1952 to 1999', *Journal of International Development*, 15 (8), 939–55.

Borensztein, E. and J. D. Ostry (1996) 'Accounting for China's Growth Performance', *American Economic Review (Papers and Proceedings)*, 86, 225–8.

Bosworth, B. and S. M. Collins (2003) 'The Empirics of Growth: an Update', unpublished, Brookings Institution, Washington, DC.

Bramall, C. (2000) *Sources of Chinese Economic Growth, 1978–1996* (Oxford and New York: Oxford University Press).

Breitung, J. and W. Meyer (1994) 'Testing for Unit Roots in Panel Data: Are Wages on Different Bargaining Levels Cointegrated', *Applied Economics*, 26, 353–61.

Brümmer, B., T. Glauben and W. Lu (2006) 'Policy Reform and Productivity Change in Chinese Agriculture: a Distance Function Approach', *Journal of Development Economics*, 81 (1), 61–79.

Brynjolfsson, E. (2003) 'The IT Productivity Gap', *Optimize*, July, accessed from ABI/INFORM Global.

Castellani, D. and A. Zanfei (2003) 'Technology Gaps, Absorptive Capacity and the Impact of Inward Investments on Productivity of European Firms', *Economic Innovation New Technology*, 12 (6), 555–76.

Caves, D. W., L. R. Christensen and W. E. Diewert (1982a) 'Multilateral Comparisons of Output, Input, and Productivity Using Superlative Index Numbers', *Economic Journal*, 92 (365), 73–86.

Caves, D. W., L. R. Christensen and W. E. Diewert (1982b) 'The Economic Theory of Index Numbers and the Measurement of Input, Output, and Productivity', *Econometrica*, 50 (6), 1393–414.

Chandra, P., W. W. Cooper, S. Li and A. Rahman (1998) 'Using DEA to Evaluate 29 Canadian Textile Companies – Considering Returns to Scale', *International Journal of Production Economics*, 54 (2), 129–41.

Charnes, A. and W. W. Cooper (1989) 'Using Data Envelopment Analysis to Evaluate Efficiency in the Economic Performance of Chinese Cities', *Socio-Economic Planning Sciences*, 23, 325–44.

Charnes, A., W. W. Cooper, A. Y. Lewin and L. M. Seiford (1994) *Data Envelopment Analysis: Theory, Methodology, and Application* (Boston: Kluwer Academic Publishers, USA).

Charnes, A., W. W. Cooper and E. Rhodes (1978) 'Measuring the Efficiency of Decision Making Units', *European Journal of Operational Research*, 2, 429–44.

Chen, K., H. C. Wang, Y. X. Zheng, G. H. Jefferson and T. G. Rawski (1988) 'Productivity Change in Chinese Industry, 1953–85', *Journal of Comparative Economics*, 12, 570–91.

Chen, Y. (2003) 'A Non-Radial Malmquist Productivity Index with an Illustrative Application to Chinese Major Industries', *International Journal of Production Economics*, 83, 27–35.

Cheung K. and P. Lin (2004) 'Spillover Effects of FDI on Innovation in China: Evidence from the Provincial Data', *China Economic Review*, 15 (1), 25–44.

Chow G. C. (1993) 'Capital Formation and Economic Growth in China', *Quarterly Journal of Economics*, 108, 809–42.

Chow, G. C. (2002) *China's Economic Transformation* (Malden, Mass.: Blackwell Publishers).

Chow, G. C. (2006) 'New Capital Estimates for China: Comments', *China Economic Review*, 17, 186–92.

Chow, G. C. and K.-W. Li (2002) 'China's Economic Growth: 1952–2010', *Economic Development and Cultural Change*, 51, 247–56.

Chow, G. C. and A. L. Lin (2002) 'Accounting for Economic Growth in Taiwan and Mainland China: a Comparative Analysis', *Journal of Comparative Economics*, 30 (3), 507–30.

Chung, W., W. Mitchell and B. Yeung (2003) 'Foreign Direct Investment and Host Country Productivity: the American Automotive Component Industry in the 1980s', *Journal of International Business Studies*, 34 (2), 199–218.

Coelli, T. (1996) 'A Guide to FRONTIER 4.1: a Computer Program for Stochastic Frontier Production Function and Cost Function Estimation', CEPA Working Paper 96/7, Department of Econometrics, University of New England, Armidale, Australia.

Coelli, T., D. S. P. Rao and G. E. Battese (1998) *An Introduction to Efficiency and Productivity Analysis* (Boston: Kluwer Academic Publishers).

Coelli, T., D. S. P. Rao, C. J. O'Donnell and G. E. Battese (2005) *An Introduction to Efficiency and Productivity Analysis*, 2nd edn (New York: Springer).

Cooper, W. W., L. M. Seiford and K. Tone (2000) *Data Envelopment Analysis: a Comprehensive Text with Models, Applications, References and DEA-Solver Software* (Boston; Dordrecht and London: Kluwer Academic).

Dadkhah, K. M. and F. Zahedi (1990) 'Estimation and Cross-Country Comparison of Capital Stocks', *Empirical Economics*, 15, 383–408.

Damijan, J. P., M. Knell, B. Majcen and M. Rojec (2003) 'The Role of FDI, R&D Accumulation and Trade in Transferring Technology to Transition Countries: Evidence from Firm Panel Data for Eight Transition Countries', *Economic Systems*, 27 (2), 189–204.

Dedrick, J., V. Gurbaxani and K. L. Kraemer (2003) 'Information Technology and Economic Performance: a Critical Review of the Empirical Evidence', *ACM Computing Surveys*, 35 (1), 1–28.

Deprins, D., L. Simar and H. Tulkens (1984) 'Measuring Labor-Efficiency in Post Office', in M. Marchand and H. Tulkens (eds), *The Performance of Public Enterprises: Concepts and Measurement* (Amsterdam: Elsevier).

Diewert, E. and D. Lawrence (2005) *Estimating Aggregate Productivity Growth for Australia: the Role of Information and Communications Technology*, Occasional Economic Paper (Canberra: Meyrick and Associates).

Dong, B. (2006) 'Northeast China Presents New Look', *China Daily* (New York: 16 August).

Dougherty, C. and D. W. Jorgenson (1996) 'International Comparisons of the Sources of Economic Growth', *American Economic Review (Papers and Proceedings)*, 86 (2), 25–9.

Edwards, S. (1998) 'Openness, Productivity, Growth: What Do We Really Know', *Economic Journal*, 108, 383–98.

Fabiani, S., F. Schivardi and S. Trento (2005) 'ICT Adoption in Italian Manufacturing: Firm-Level Evidence', *Industrial and Corporate Change*, 14 (2), 225–49.

Fan, S. (1991) 'Effects of Technological Change and Institutional Reform on Production Growth in Chinese Agriculture', *American Journal of Agricultural Economics*, 73 (2), 266–75.

Färe, R., S. Grosskopf and C. A. K. Lovell (1985) *The Measurement of Efficiency of Production* (Boston: Kluwer-Nijho Publishing).

Färe, R., S. Grosskopf and C. A. K. Lovell (1994a) *Production Frontiers* (Cambridge: Cambridge University Press).

Färe, R., S. Grosskopf, M. Norris and Z. Zhang (1994b) 'Productivity Growth, Technical Progress, and Efficiency Change in Industrialised Countries', *American Economic Review*, 84 (1), 66–83.

Färe, R., S. Grosskopf, Y. He and J. Horvath (1996) 'Industrial Productivity Growth in China: 1980–1984 vs. 1984–1985', in R. Färe and S. Grosskopf, *Intertemporal Production Frontiers: With Dynamic DEA* (Boston: Kluwer Academic).

Farrell, M. J. (1957) 'The Measurement of Productivity Efficiency', *Journal of the Royal Statistical Society*, 120, 253–81.

Feinberg, S. E. and S. K. Majumdar (2001) 'Technology Spillovers from Foreign Direct Investment in the Indian Pharmaceutical Industry', *Journal of International Business Studies*, 32 (3), 421–37.

Fleisher, B. M. and J. Chen (1997) 'The Coast–Noncoast Income Gap, Productivity and Regional Economic Policy in China', *Journal of Comparative Economics*, 25, 220–36.

Fosfuri, A., M. Motta and T. Ronde (2001) 'Foreign Direct Investment and Spillovers through Workers' Mobility', *Journal of International Economics*, 53 (1), 205–22.

Fraumeni, B. M. (1997) 'The Measurement of Depreciation in the U.S. National Income and Product Accounts', *Survey of Current Business*, 77 (7), 7–23.

Frazier, M. W. (2006) 'State-Sector Shrinkage and Workforce Reduction in China', *European Journal of Political Economy*, 22, 435–51.

Fu, T. T., C. J. Huang and C. A. K. Lovell (eds) (1999) *Economic Efficiency and Productivity Growth in the Asia-Pacific Region* (Cheltenham: Edward Elgar).

Garnaut, R. and L. Song (eds) (2003) *China: New Engine of World Growth* (Canberra: Asia Pacific Press, Australian National University).

Garnaut, R. and L. Song (eds) (2004) *China: Is Rapid Growth Sustainable?* (Canberra: Asia Pacific Press).

Garnaut, R. and L. Song (eds) (2005) *The China Boom and Its Discontents* (Canberra: ANU E Press and Asia Pacific Press).

Greene, W. H. (1993) 'The Econometric Approach to Efficiency Analysis', in H. O. Fried et al. (eds), *The Measurement of Productive Efficiency* (Oxford: Oxford University Press), pp. 68–119.

Greene, W. H. (1997) 'Frontier Production Functions', in M. H. Pesaran and P. Schmidt (eds) *Handbook of Applied Econometrics II: Microeconomics* (Oxford: Blackwell), pp. 81–166.

Griliches, Z. (1994) 'Productivity, R&D, and the Data Constraint', *American Economic Review*, 84 (1), 1–23.

Guillaumont Jeanneney, S., P. Hua and Z. Liang (2006) 'Financial Development, Economic Efficiency, and Productivity Growth: Evidence from China', *Developing Economies*, 44 (1), 27–52.

Gullickson, W. (1995) 'Measurement of Productivity Growth in U.S. Manufacturing', *Monthly Labor Review*, July, 13–28.

Hamilton, J. D. and J. Monteagudo (1998) 'The Augmented Solow Model and the Productivity Slowdown', *Journal of Monetary Economics*, 42 (3), 495–509.

Harberger, A. C. (1978) 'Perspectives on Capital and Technology in Less Developed Countries', in M. J. Artis and A. R. Nobay (eds) *Contemporary Economic Analysis* (London: Croom Helm).

Harrison, A. (1996) 'Openness and Growth: a Time-Series, Cross-Country Analysis for Developing Countries', *Journal of Development Economics*, 48, 419–47.

He, J. (1992) 'Estimates of Our Country's Capital' (Shuliang Jingji yu Jishu Jingji Yanjiu), *Quantitative and Technical Economics*, 8, 24–7.

Holz, C. A. (2006a) 'New Capital Estimates for China', *China Economic Review*, 17, 142–85.

Holz, C. A. (2006b) 'Response to Gregory C. Chow's "New Capital Estimates for China: Comments"', *China Economic Review*, 17, 193–7.

Hu, A. G. Z. and H. Jefferson (2002) 'FDI Impact and Spillover: Evidence from China's Electronic and Textile Industries', *World Economy*, 25 (8), 1063–76.

Hu, Z. F. and M. S. Khan (1997) 'Why Is China Growing So Fast?', IMF Staff Papers 44, 103–31.

Huang, C. J. and J. T. Liu (1994) 'Estimation of a Non-Neutral Stochastic Frontier Production Function', *Journal of Productivity Analysis*, 5, 171–80.

Im, K. S., M. H. Pesaran and Y. Shin (2003) 'Testing for Unit Root in Heterogeneous Panels', *Journal of Econometrics*, 115, 53–74.

Inklaar, R., M. O'Mahony and M. Timmer (2003) 'ICT and Europe's Productivity Performance Industry-Level Growth Account Comparisons with the United States', Paper presented at the Asia Pacific Productivity Conference, Brisbane, 14–16 July 2004.

International Monetary Fund (2005) *World Economic Outlook 2005*, Washington, DC, http://www.imf.org/external/pubs/ft/weo/2005/02/index.htm.

International Monetary Fund (2007) *World Economic Outlook 2007*, Washington, DC, http://www.imf.org/external/pubs/ft/weo/2007/02/pdf/text.pdf.

Islam, N. and E. Dai (2005) 'Alternative Estimates of TFP Growth in Mainland China: an Investigation Using the Dual Approach', paper presented at the 17th Annual Conference of the ACESA, University of Western Australia, Perth, 7–8 July 2005.

Islam, N., E. Dai and H. Sakamoto (2006) 'Sources of Growth' in Y. Wu (ed.) *Economic Growth, Transition and Globalization in China* (Cheltenham and Northampton: Edward Elgar Publishing).

Ito, T. and A. O. Krueger (eds) (1995) *Growth Theories in Light of the East Asian Experience* (Chicago: University of Chicago Press).

Jia, L. Q. (1998) 'Regional Catching Up and Productivity Growth in Chinese Reform Period', *International Journal of Social Economics*, 25 (6/7/8), 1160.

Jorgenson, D. W. (1989) 'Capital as a Factor of Production', in D. W. Jorgenson and R. Landau (eds) *Technology and Capital Formation* (Cambridge and London: The MIT Press).

Jorgenson, D. W. and K. Vu (2005) 'Information Technology and the World Economy', *Scandinavian Journal of Economics*, 107 (4), 631–50.

Jorgenson, D. W., M. S. Ho and K. J. Stiroh (2003) 'Lessons from the US Growth Resurgence', *Journal of Policy Modeling*, 25, 453–70.

Jorgenson, D. W., M. S. Ho and K. J. Stiroh (2005) *Productivity. Vol. 3: Information Technology and the American Growth Resurgence* (Cambridge, Mass.: The MIT Press).

Kalirajan, K. P. (1990) 'On Measuring Economic Efficiency', *Journal of Applied Econometrics*, 5, 75–85.

Kalirajan, K. P. and R. T. Shand (1988) 'Testing Causality between Technical and Allocative Efficiencies', Working Paper No. 88/6, Research School of Pacific Studies, Australian National University, Canberra, Australia.

Kalirajan, K. P. and S. J. Zhao (1997) 'Did the Technical Efficiency of State Enterprises Improve with the Same Speed in all Provinces in China?', *Applied Economics*, 29, 269–77.

Kendrick, J. W. (1956) *Productivity Trends: Capital and Labor* (New York: National Bureau of Economic Research).

Kim, J. I. and L. Lau (1994) 'The Sources of Economic Growth in the East Asian Newly Industrialised Countries', *Journal of the Japanese and International Economies*, 8, 235–71.

Kim, S.-J. (2002) 'Development of Information Technology Industry and Sources of Economic Growth and Productivity in Korea', *Journal of Economic Research*, 7, 177–213.

Kong, X., R. E. Marks and G. H. Wan (1998) 'Technical Efficiency, Technological Change and Total Factor Productivity Growth in Chinese State-Owned Enterprises during the Early 1990s', Working Paper 98-016, November, University of New South Wales, Sydney.

Kong, X., R. E. Marks and G. H. Wan (1999) 'Technical Efficiency, Technological Change and Total Factor Productivity Growth in Chinese State-Owned Enterprises in the Early 1990s', *Asian Economic Journal*, 13 (3), 267–81.

Koopmans, T. C. (1951) 'An Analysis of Production as an Efficient Combination of Activities', in T. C. Koopmans (ed.), *Activity Analysis of Production and Allocation*, Cowles Commission for Research in Economics, Monograph No. 13 (New York: John Wiley & Sons, Inc.).

Kraemer, K. L. and J. Dedrick (2002) 'Information Technology in Southeast Asia: Engine of Growth or Digital Divide', in S. Y. Chia and J. J. Lim (eds) *Information Technology in Asia: New Development Paradigms* (Singapore: Institute of Southeast Asian Studies).

Krugman, P. (1994) 'The Myth of Asia's Miracle', *Foreign Affairs*, 73 (6), November/December, 62–78.

Kumbhakar, S. C. and C. A. K. Lovell (2000) *Stochastic Frontier Analysis* (Cambridge University Press).

Kumbhakar, S. C. and H. J. Wang (2005) 'Estimation of Growth Convergence Using a Stochastic Production Frontier Approach', *Economics Letters*, 88, 300–5.

Kumbhakar, S. C., S. Ghosh and J. McGuckin (1991) 'A Generalised Production Frontier Approach for Estimating Determinants of Inefficiency in US Dairy Farms', *Journal of Business and Economic Statistics*, 9 (3), 279–86.

Lai, H. Y. (2002) 'China's Western Development Program', *Modern China*, 28 (4), 432–66.

Lam, P. L. and A. Shiu (2004) 'Efficiency and Productivity of China's Thermal Power Generation', *Review of Industrial Organization*, 24, 73–93.

Lan, X. and P. Sheehan (2002) 'China's Development Strategy', in G. Grewal et al. (eds) *China's Future in the Knowledge Economy* (Melbourne: Victoria University of Technology), pp. 1–24.

Lee, I. H. and Y. Khatri (2003) 'Information Technology and Productivity Growth in Asia', IMF Working Paper, January 2003.

Lenger, A. and E. Taymaz (2006) 'To Innovate or to Transfer: a Study on Spillovers and Foreign Firms in Turkey', *Journal of Evolutionary Economics*, 16 (1–2), 137–53.

Levin, A. and C. F. Lin (1992) 'Unit Root Tests in Panel Data: Asymptotic and Finite Sample Properties', Discussion Paper No. 92–93, Department of Economics, University of California at San Diego.

Levin, A., and C. F. Lin (1993) 'Unit Root Tests in Panel Data: New Results', Discussion Paper No. 93–95, Department of Economics, University of California at San Diego.

Levin, A., C. F. Lin and C. Chu (2002) 'Unit Root Tests in Panel Data: Asymptotic and Finite Sample Properties', *Journal of Econometrics*, 108, 1–24.

Li, J., G. Feihong and Z. Yisheng (1995) 'Productivity and China's Economic Growth, 1953–1990', in K. Y. Tsui, T. T. Hsueh and T. G. Rawski (eds) *Productivity, Efficiency and Reform in China's Economy* (Hong Kong: Chinese University of Hong Kong).

Lin, J. Y. (1992) 'Rural Reforms and Agricultural Growth in China', *American Economic Review*, 82 (1), 34–51.

Liu, X. and C. Wang (2003) 'Does Foreign Direct Investment Facilitate Technological Progress: Evidence for Chinese Industries', *Research Policy*, 32, 945–53.

Liu, X., P. Siler, C. Wang and Y. Wei (2000) 'Productivity Spillovers from Foreign Direct Investment: Evidence from UK Industry Level Panel Data', *Journal of International Business Studies*, 31 (3), 407–23.

Liu, Z. (2002a) 'Foreign Direct Investment and Technology Spillover: Evidence from China', *Journal of Comparative Economics*, 30 (3), 579–602.

Liu, Z. (2002b) 'The Nature and Sources of Economic Growth in China: Is There TFP Growth?', in John Wong and Lu Ding (eds),*China's Economy into the New Century: Structural Issues and Problems* (Singapore: Singapore University Press and World Scientific).

Lorentzen, J., P. Mollgaard and M. Rojec (2003) 'Host-Country Absorption of Technology: Evidence from Automotive Supply Networks in Eastern Europe', *Industry and Innovation*, 10 (4), 415–32.

Lovell, C. A. K. (1993) 'Production Frontiers and Productive Efficiency', in H. O. Fried et al. (eds), *The Measurement of Productive Efficiency* (Oxford: Oxford University Press), pp. 3–67.

Lovell, C. A. K. (1996) 'Applying Efficiency Measurement Techniques to the Measurement of Productivity Change', *Journal of Productivity Analysis*, 7, 329–40.

Mcvicar, D. (2002) 'Spillover and Foreign Direct Investment in UK Manufacturing', *Applied Economics Letters*, 9 (5), 297–300.

Maddala, G. S. and S. Wu (1999) 'A Comparative Study of Unit Root Tests with Panel Data and a New Simple Test', *Oxford Bulletin of Economics and Statistics* (Special Issue), 61, 631–52.

Maddison, A. (1998) *Chinese Economic Performance in the Long Run* (Paris: OECD Development Centre).

Malmquist, S. (1953) 'Index Numbers and Indifference Curves', *Trabajos de Estatistica*, 4, 209–42.

Mao, W. and W. W. Koo (1997) 'Productivity Growth, Technology Progress, and Efficiency Change in Chinese Agriculture after Rural Economic Reforms: a DEA Approach', *China Economic Review*, 8, 157–74.

Meng, L. and X. Wang (2000) 'Assessment of the Reliability of China's Economic Growth Statistics', Monograph, National Economic Research Institute, Beijing.

Mester, L. J. (1993) 'Efficiency in the Savings and Loan Industry', *Journal of Banking and Finance*, 17 (2/3), 267–86.

Mester, L. J. (1997) 'Measuring Efficiency at US Banks: Accounting for Heterogeneity Is Important', *European Journal of Operational Research*, 98 (2), 230–42.

Ministry of Information Industry (various years), *Yearbook of China Electronics Industry* (Beijing: Publishing House of Electronics Industry).

Miyagawa, T., Y. Ito and N. Harada (2004) 'The IT Revolution and Productivity Growth in Japan', *Journal of the Japanese and International Economies*, 18, 362–89.

Movshuk, O. (2004) 'Restructuring, Productivity and Technical Efficiency in China's Iron and Steel Industry, 1988–2000', *Journal of Asian Economics*, 15, 135–51.

Murray, J. Y., M. Kotabe and J. N. Zhou (2005) 'Strategic Alliance-Based Sourcing and Market Performance: Evidence from Foreign Firms Operating in China', *Journal of International Business Studies*, 36, 187–208.

Musgrave, J. C. (1992) 'Fixed Reproducible Tangible Wealth in the United States, Revised Estimates', *Survey of Current Business*, January, 106–19.

Nadiri, M. I. and I. R. Prucha (1996) 'Estimation of the Depreciation Rate of Physical and R&D Capital in the U.S. Total Manufacturing Sector', *Economic Inquiry*, 34, 43–56.

National Bureau of Statistics (2004) *China Statistical Yearbook 2004* (Beijing: Statistical Publishing House of China).

National Bureau of Statistics (various issues) *China Statistical Yearbook* (Beijing: Statistical Publishing House of China).

Nehru, V. and A. M. Dhareshwar (1993) 'A New Database on Physical Capital Stock: Sources, Methodology and Results', *Revista de Analisis Economico*, 8, 37–59.

Ng, Y. C. and S. K. Li (2000) 'Measuring the Research Performance of Chinese Higher Education Institutions: an Application of Data Envelopment Analysis', *Education Economics*, 8, 139–56.

Nishimizu, M. and J. M. Page (1982) 'Total Factor Productivity Growth, Technological Progress and Technical Efficiency Change', *Economic Journal*, 92, 920–36.

O'Donnell, C. J., D. S. P. Rao and G. E. Battese (2005) 'Metafrontier Frameworks for the Study of Firm-Level Efficiencies and Technology Ratios', paper presented at Economics Program Seminar, School of Economics and Commerce, University of Western Australia.

OECD (2001) *OECD Science, Technology and Industry Scoreboard 2001: Towards a Knowledge-Based Economy*, http://www1.oecd.org/publications/e-book/92-2001-04-1-2987/, date accessed 1 September 2003.

Perkins, D. (1988) 'Reforming China's Economic System', *Journal of Economic Literature*, 26, 601–45.

Pohjola, M. (2002) 'The New Economy: Facts, Impacts and Policies', *Information Economics and Policy*, 14, 133–44.

Prescott, E. C. (1998) 'Needed: a Theory of Total Factor Productivity', *International Economic Review*, 39 (3), 525–51.

Qian, X. and R. Smyth (2006) 'Growth Accounting for the Chinese Provinces 1990–2000: Incorporating Human Capital Accumulation', *Journal of Chinese Economic and Business Studies*, 4 (1), 21–38.

Quah, D. (1992) 'International Patterns of Growth II: Persistence, Path Dependence, and Sustained Take-Off in Growth Transition', Working Paper, London School of Economics.

Quah, D. (1994) 'Exploiting Cross Section Variation for Unit Root Inference in Dynamic Data', *Economics Letters*, 44, 9–19.

Rawski, T. G. (2001) 'What Is Happening to China's GDP Statistics?' *China Economic Review*, 12 (4), 347–54.

Ray, S. C. and E. Desli (1997) 'Productivity Gross, Technical Progress, and Efficiency Change in Industrialised Countries: Comment', *American Economic Review*, 87, 1033–9.

Reinsdorf, M. and M. Cover (2005) *Measurement of Capital Stocks, Consumption of Fixed Capital, and Capital Services*, Report on a Presentation to the Central American Ad Hoc Group on National Accounts, 12 May 2005 in Santo Domingo, Dominican Republic.

Ruane, F. and A. Ugur (2004) 'Foreign Direct Investment and Productivity Spillovers in Irish Manufacturing Industry: Evidence from Plant Level Panel Data', *International Journal of the Economics of Business*, 11 (3), 53–66.

Sachs, J. D. and W. T. Woo (1997) 'Understanding China's Economic Performance', NBER Working Paper 5935, National Bureau for Economic Research.

Sadik, A. T. and A. A. Bolbol (2001) 'Capital Flows, FDI, and Technology Spillovers: Evidence from Arab Countries', *World Development*, 29 (12), 2111–25.

Sala-i-Martin, X. (1997) 'I Just Ran Two Million Regressions', *American Economic Review (Papers and Proceedings)*, 87, 178–83.

Sanna-Randaccio, F. (2002) 'The Impact of Foreign Direct Investment on Home and Host Countries with Endogenous R&D', *Review of International Economics*, 10 (2), 278–98.

Shao, B. B. M. and W. T. Lin (2001) 'Measuring the Value of Information Technology in Technical Efficiency with Stochastic Production Frontiers', *Information and Software Technology*, 43, 447–56.

Shao, B. B. M. and W. T. Lin (2002) 'Technical Efficiency Analysis of Information Technology Investments: a Two-Stage Empirical Investigation', *Information and Management*, 39, 391–401.

Shephard, R.W. (1970) *Theory of Cost and Production Functions* (Princeton: Princeton University Press).

Shinjo, K. and X. Zhang (2003) 'Productivity Analysis of IT Capital Stock: the USA–Japan Comparison', *Journal of the Japanese and International Economies*, 17, 81–100.

Shiu, A. (2002) 'Efficiency of Chinese Enterprises', *Journal of Productivity Analysis*, 18 (3), 255–67.

Sjoholm, F. (1999) 'Technology Gap, Competition and Spillovers from Direct Foreign Investment: Evidence from Establishment Data', *The Journal of Development Studies*, 36 (1), 53–73.

Solow, R. M. (1957) 'Technical Change and the Aggregate Production Function', *Review of Economics and Statistics*, 39 (3), 312–20.

State Statistical Bureau (various years) *China Statistical Yearbook* (Beijing: China Statistics Press).

Steering Committee for the Review of Commonwealth/State Service Provision (1997) *Data Envelopment Analysis: a Technique for Measuring the Efficiency of Government Service Delivery* (Canberra: AGPS).

Sudit, E. F. and N. Finger (1981) 'Methodological Issues in Aggregate Productivity Analysis', in A. Dogramaci and N. R. Adam (eds), *Studies in Productivity Analysis 2: Aggregate and Industry-Level Analyses* (Boston: Martinus Nijhoff Publishing).

Sun H., P. Hone and H. Doucouliagos (1999) 'Economic Openness and Technical Efficiency', *Economics of Transition*, 7, 615–36.

Sun, Q., W. Tong and Q. Yu (2002) 'Determinants of Foreign Direct Investment across China', *Journal of International Money and Finance*, 21, 79–113.

Susiluoto, I. (2003) 'Effects of ICT on Regional Economic Efficiency', Web Publications 2003, 16, MUTEIS Impact Study, Helsinki City Urban Facts Office.

Swamy, S. (2003) *Economic Reforms and Performance: China and India in Comparative Perspective* (New Delhi: Konark Publishers Pvt Ltd).

Szirmai, A., Ruoen Ren and Manyin Bai (2005) 'Chinese Manufacturing Performance in Comparative Perspective, 1980–2002', Discussion Papers 5(6), Yale Economic Growth Center.

Taymaz, E. and G. Saatci (1997) 'Technical Change and Efficiency in Turkish Manufacturing Industries', *Journal of Productivity Analysis*, 8, 461–75.

Timmer, M. P. and B. van Ark (2005) 'Does Information and Communication Technology Drive EU–US Productivity Growth Differentials?', *Oxford Economic Papers*, 57, 693–716.

Todo, Y. and K. Miyamoto (2002) 'Knowledge Diffusion from Multinational Enterprises: the Role of Domestic and Foreign Knowledge-Enhancing Activities', OECD Technical Papers (196).

Tong, C. S. P. and H. L. Chan (2003) 'Disparity in Production Efficiency of China's TVEs across Regions: a Stochastic Frontier Production Function Approach', *Asia Pacific Journal of Management*, 20 (1), 113–31.

United Nations (2005) *Human Development Report 2005*, United Nations Development Programme.

Wang, X. L. (2004) 'Marketisation in China', in R. Garnaut and L. Song (eds) *China: Is Rapid Growth Sustainable?* (Canberra: Asia Pacific Press).

Wang, X. L. and G. Fan (eds) (2000) *The Sustainability of China's Economic Growth* (Beijing: Economic Sciences Press).

Wang, X. L. and L. Meng (2001) 'A Reevaluation of China's Economic Growth', *China Economic Review*, 12 (4), 338–46.

Wang, Y. and Y. D. Yao (2003) 'Sources of China's Economic Growth 1952–1999: Incorporating Human Capital Accumulation', *China Economic Review*, 14, 32–52.

Witzell, O. W. and J. K. L. Smith (1989) *Closing the Gap: Computer Development in the People's Republic of China* (Boulder, Colo.: Westview Press).

Wong, C. K. (2007) 'Information and Communications Technology (ICT), Productivity and Economic Growth in China', unpublished PhD dissertation, UWA Business School, University of Western Australia, Perth.

Woo, W. T. (1998) 'Chinese Economic Growth: Sources and Prospects', in M. Fouquin and F. Lemoine (eds) *The Chinese Economy* (Paris: Economica Ltd).

Woo, W. T., W. Hai, Y. Jin and G. Fan (1994) 'How Successful Has Chinese Enterprise Reform Been? Pitfalls in Opposite Biases and Focus', *Journal of Comparative Economics*, 18, 410–37.

Wooldridge, J. M. (2002) *Econometric Analysis of Cross Section and Panel Data* (London: MIT Press).

World Bank (1993) *The East Asian Miracle*, a World Bank policy research report (Oxford University Press).

World Bank (1997a) *China 2020: Development Challenges in the New Century* (Washington, DC: The World Bank).

World Bank (1997b) *China 2020: Sharing Rising Incomes* (Washington, DC: The World Bank).

World Bank (2005) *World Development Indicator 2005 Database* (Washington, DC: The World Bank).

Wu, H. X., (1993) 'The "Real" Chinese Gross Domestic Product (GDP) for the Pre-Reform Period 1952–77', *Review of Income and Wealth*, 39, 63–86.

Wu, Y. R. (1993) 'Productive Efficiency in Chinese Industry: a Review', *Asian-Pacific Economic Literature*, 7 (2), 58–66.

Wu, Y. R. (1995) 'Productivity Growth, Technological Progress and Technical Efficiency Change in China: a Three-Sector Analysis', *Journal of Comparative Economics*, 21, 207–29.

Wu, Y. R. (1996) *Productivity Performance in Chinese Enterprises* (London: Macmillan Press).

Wu, Y. R. (1999) 'Productivity and Efficiency in China's Regional Economies', in T. T. Fu et al. (eds), *Economic Efficiency and Productivity Growth in the Asia-Pacific Region* (Cheltenham: Edward Elgar), pp. 171–90.

Wu, Y. R. (2000) 'Is China's Economic Growth Sustainable: a Productivity Analysis', *China Economic Review*, 11, 278–96.

Wu, Y. R. (2001) 'Productivity Growth at the Firm Level: With Application to the Chinese Steel Mills', *Journal of Entrepreneurship*, 10 (1), 1–16.

Wu, Y. R. (2002) *The Macroeconomics of East Asian Growth* (Cheltenham and Northampton: Edward Elgar Publishing).

Wu, Y. R. (2003) 'Has Productivity Contributed to China's Growth?', *Pacific Economic Review*, 8 (1), 15–30.

Wu, Y. R. (2004) *China's Economic Growth: a Miracle with Chinese Characteristics* (London and New York: RoutledgeCurzon Press Limited).

Wu, Y. R. and H. Yang (1999) 'Productivity and Growth: a Review', in K. P. Kalirajan and Y. R. Wu (eds), *Productivity and Growth in Chinese Agriculture* (London: Macmillan Press), pp. 29–51.

Yao, S. and Z. Zhang (2001) 'On Regional Inequality and Diverging Clubs: a Case Study of Contemporary', *Journal of Comparative Economics*, 29 (3), 466–84.

Young, A. (1994) 'Lessons from the East Asian NICs: a Contrarian View', *European Economic Review*, 110, 641–80.

Young, A. (1995) 'The Tyranny of Numbers: Confronting the Statistical Realities of the East Asian Growth Experience', *Quarterly Journal of Economics*, 110 (3), 641–80.

Young, A. (2003) 'Gold Into Base Metals: Productivity Growth in the People's Republic of China during the Reform Period', *Journal of Political Economy*, 111 (6), 1220–61.

Zhang, J. (1991) 'Systemic Analysis of Economic Efficiency during the 5th Five Year Plan' (Jingji Yanjiu), *Journal of Economic Research*, 4, 8–17.

Zhang, J. and Y. Zhang (2003) 'Reestimates of China's Capital Stock' (Jingji Yanjiu), *Journal of Economic Research*, 7, 35–43.

Zhang, J., G. Wu and J. Zhang (2007) 'Estimation of China's Provincial Capital Stock Series', paper presented at Productivity and Efficiency Workshop, Tsinghua University, 13–14 January.

Zhang, X. (1999) 'Foreign Investment Policy, Contribution, and Performance', in Y. R. Wu (ed.), *Foreign Direct Investment and Economic Growth in China* (Cheltenham: Edward Elgar Publishing).

Zhang, X. G. and S. Q. Zhang (2001) 'Technical Efficiency in China's Iron and Steel Industry: Evidence from the New Census Data', *International Review of Applied Economics*, 15 (2), 199–211.

Zheng, J. H. and A. G. Hu (2004) 'An Empirical Analysis of Provincial Productivity in China (1979–2001)', Working Papers in Economics No. 127, Department of Economics, Göteborg University.

Zheng, J. and A. Hu (2006) 'An Empirical Analysis of Provincial Productivity in China (1979–2001)', *Journal of Chinese Economic and Business Studies*, 4 (3), 221–39.

Zheng, J., X. Liu and A. Bigsten (1998) 'Ownership Structure and Determinants of Technical Efficiency', *Journal of Comparative Economics*, 26, 465–84.

Zheng, J., X. Liu and A. Bigsten (2003) 'Efficiency, Technical Progress, and Best Practice in Chinese State Enterprises (1980–1994)', *Journal of Comparative Economics*, 31 (1), 134–52.

Zhu, J. (1996) 'DEA/AR Analysis of the 1988–1989 Performance of the Nanjing Textiles Corporation', *Annals of Operations Research*, 66 (5), 311–35.